Chambers Crossword Manual

CHAMBERS CROSSWORD MANUAL

Second edition

A guide for the novice *and* the enthusiast

by

DON MANLEY

Chambers

Published by W & R Chambers Ltd
43–45 Annandale Street, Edinburgh EH7 4AZ

Second edition
© Don Manley 1992

First edition 1986
Reprinted 1993

British Library Cataloguing in Publication Data

A catalogue record for this book is available from the British Library.

ISBN 0-550-19034-1

Typeset by Buccleuch Printers Ltd, Hawick
Printed in Great Britain by Clays Ltd, St Ives, plc

In loving memory of my father
Chave Manley
1904–1978

and of my mother
Alma Manley
1906–1992

About the author
Don Manley has been setting crosswords since he was a teenager, and he now sets for a number of national newspapers under the pseudonyms Duck, Pasquale and Quixote. He has made a specialist study of cryptic clues and won several national clue-writing competitions. Between crosswords he finds time for his family in Oxford and manages a day job in educational publishing.

Contents

Introduction to First Edition

This book is dedicated to the memory of my father, who must take much of the blame for my obsession with crossword puzzles. Chave Manley solved six puzzles a day (two each in the *Daily Mail*, the *Daily Express* and the *Daily Telegraph*) and one a week—usually on a Sunday afternoon—in the *Radio Times*. Until, that is, his son (with elder sister Jean's help) began filling the odd word in the 'small puzzle' of the *Express* and the 'quick crossword' of the *Telegraph*. By my teens I was hooked and was pestering my father to explain how the cryptic puzzles worked. Soon the back page of the school common-room *Times* was being inked in, and not long after I left school I made my crossword setting debut with the *London Evening News*, followed within 18 months by *Radio Times*. Then a few years later a whole new world opened up with the discovery of the *Observer*'s Ximenes and *The Listener*.

Not everyone has a father—or even a close friend—to explain the mysteries of the cryptic crossword, but I know that there are many in the ranks of the would-be solvers. 'You need a twisted mind for crosswords,' they say wryly—or else they denounce crosswords as a 'waste of time' without sounding convincing about it. The fact is that you *do* need to twist your mind to solve any problem, but why not? 'Problem-solving' is very much the fashion at the moment in the school curriculum. And there are, I believe, some real benefits in struggling with a good crossword: mental discipline and an increased vocabulary are two. But the benefits must not be overstated. Crosswords are primarily for fun, but isn't the swimming pool more enjoyable once you can swim?

Curiously, there have been very few books actually *about* crosswords; those that I know of are listed in the bibliography at the back. There is of course an insatiable demand for actual puzzles, and those who want a good selection should not be disappointed by the offerings in this book. My priority, though, has been to tutor the reader in the basic essentials *and* the essentials at the more advanced level. *Chambers 20th Century Dictionary* has long been the basic 'word bible' for the advanced crossword solver, but there has been little written to explain the puzzles for which it is so necessary. I hope I am putting this right.

In this work I deal with the background to the crossword, followed by the basic cryptic puzzle (such as you would find in your daily newspaper), and finally the more advanced puzzle. The ways in which clues are constructed have been described in detail and so too has 'crossword language', but this is in no sense a complete 'crib' for the lazy solver. My method, with its small tutorial puzzles, is essentially heuristic, and I want to encourage solvers to learn for themselves.

Dr Johnson may not have 'read books through' but my intention is that the complete novice should treat this particular book as a sequential course. Try the tutorial puzzles, and if you cannot finish them look up the answers and learn from the notes before moving on. Then by the time you get to Chapter 12 you should be ready to enjoy a cryptic each day in your daily paper. Many readers may reach that stage and settle there quite happily. To them I say: 'Buy a Chambers and try to stretch yourself a little further. There are further joys for you in store!'

I must thank all those who have made this book possible. Many fellow-setters and their crossword editors have been most generous in allowing me to reproduce their puzzles, and a list appears on pp.ix-x. My family allowed me to escape to the study for hours when domestic duties beckoned. Jonathan Crowther, Les May, Michael Holroyd and Alec Robins have all lent me interesting material; the Bodleian Library enabled me to track down some crosswords of yesteryear. Richard Palmer and Derek Arthur spotted numerous errors in the original script and made many useful suggestions for improvements. Micro Initiatives used the wonders of modern technology to computerize the diagrams and to word-process the MS. Catherine Schwarz of Chambers has been an encouraging and supportive editor. Making crosswords look good is no easy task when so many things can go wrong; I am grateful for the patient expertise shown by Jack Osborne, Production Director of Chambers. I can only hope that our efforts are not in vain. Whatever your current level of attainment I hope you will find something of benefit within these pages.

Don Manley
Oxford 1986

Notes for Second Edition. Chambers Twentieth Century Dictionary became *Chambers English Dictionary* in 1988. The acknowledgement list is now on pp.xiii-xiv.

Introduction to Second Edition

A lot has happened to me and a lot has happened to crosswords since I wrote the first edition six years ago, so I am delighted to have the opportunity for an update. When I wrote before, I had many years of experience behind me but no regular work as a crossword setter. Since then I have written puzzles for *Today* (a brief spell writing clues only), *The Independent* (from there I moved to *The Independent on Sunday* every week), *The Times*, and *The Guardian* (where I have taken on the new pseudonym Pasquale). I also edit puzzles for the *Church Times* every week and continue with solving whenever possible. All this with a family and full-time job!

The advent of *The Independent* has increased the range of good daily puzzles and the Saturday Magazine puzzle has plugged a gap between the dailies and the so-called 'advanced' puzzles. Never has there been so much variety before. Solvers are spoilt for choice.

In the press and on radio and TV the profile of crosswords and crossworders has been raised quite distinctly. That great Ximenes and Azed clue-writer Colin Dexter named his two principal characters Inspector Morse and Sergeant Lewis after C. J. Morse and 'Mrs B. Lewis', two fellow clue-writers. The Inspector likes nothing better than listening to Wagner and solving a difficult crossword, so I wonder whether the successful TV series has led to as many people tackling crosswords as taking up an interest in classical music. In one episode, Morse clutched a *Listener* while visiting a lady of ill repute, and in that same episode one Edward Manley perpetrated two murders. *The Listener*, alas, is no more, but we can be thankful that *The Listener*'s crossword has been resurrected in *The Times* every Saturday.

With so many new puzzles appearing, I have sought to change several of the puzzles in the first edition. Of the original 80, I have removed some old ones and added several new ones, giving a net gain of four puzzles. As before, I have worked on the principle that I should contribute half of the puzzles.

In reading through the first edition, I quickly became aware of how some of my attitudes have changed over six years and how much I missed out last time. I am still firmly a 'Ximenean' (you will get to know what this means) but realize, more than ever, that some issues regarding fair play are not so cut and dried. The successor to Ximenes, Azed, is still pondering over certain aspects of clue-writing and still seeing some new aspects of grammar in clues after 20 distinguished years with *The Observer*. I have given us lesser mortals a chance to see how he now views clues, especially in a new Chapter 17 with its 'further thoughts on fair play'.

The other major additions arise from my own day-to-day experience of crossword setting. Many people continue to ask me about how I set a crossword, so I have followed the tradition of Ximenes and Alec Robins in their books of taking the reader through the process step by step. In my further experiences as a setter I have collected many extra resources, and these have been added to Appendix 2.

As before, I have many people to thank. In addition to those mentioned in my earlier Introduction I want to mention Mrs Chris McHugh, who patiently interpreted the scribbled amendments to this edition and typed them on my Amstrad, Mrs Alfreda Blanchard who read the script for errors at manuscript stage, and Richard Jeffery who checked the proofs – and, of course, all those who have contributed the new puzzles. My wife (Susan) and children (Richard and Gilly) continue to give me an easy time with regard to domestic duties while the study is occupied evening after evening.

I hope this new paperback will open up a fascinating pastime to even more folk than before.

Don Manley, Oxford 1992

Sources and Acknowledgements

The source of each puzzle is given below along with the copyright holder who gave permission (where appropriate). Every effort has been made to contact all copyright holders, but if there are any omissions we shall be glad to make amends at the earliest opportunity. Some puzzles have been slightly amended/corrected. My own puzzles are asterisked.

Crossword No.	Source	Permission given by
1	New York World	St. Louis Post-Dispatch
2	The Crossword Puzzle Book (First Series)	Simon & Schuster
3–6	London Evening News*	London Express News and Features
7	Crossword	Crossword Club/ Carroll Mayers
8	Daily Telegraph	The Daily Telegraph
9–15	Specially set for this book*	—
16	Games and Puzzles*	—
17	Hamlyn Book of Crosswords No. 1*	—
18	The Independent*	Newspaper Publishing plc
19	The Independent on Sunday*	Newspaper Publishing plc
20	Hamlyn Book of Crosswords No. 4*	—
21	Oxford Times*	Oxford & County Newspapers
22	Church Times Crosswords*	The Canterbury Press Norwich
23–27	Specially set for this book*	—
28–29	Games and Puzzles*	—
30	Specially set for this book*	—
31	The Spectator*	The Spectator
32	Crossword*	Crossword Club

Thanks are also due to *The Guardian* for permission to reproduce the puzzle* in Chapter 18, *The Observer* and Colin Dexter for the letter on p. 75, and those who supplied the photographs on p. 119.

1

The Crossword Emerges

The Victorian age is commonly portrayed in terms of unmitigated gloom; and yet it was also an age of fun and invention, and certainly it was the age of the word puzzle. In 1892 you might have bought *Everybody's Illustrated Book of Puzzles* (selected by a certain Don Lemon) for 6d. That Don of yesteryear offered you 794 puzzles complete with answers, and if we look at a few we shall see hints of what was to come when the crossword emerged in the twentieth century:

No. 6—Anagrams.

For the benefit of very young readers we will explain that making an anagram consists in forming a new word or words from the letters of other words. An illustration is: Cheer sick lands—the anagram for Charles Dickens. We now invite you, with the permission of Good Housekeeping, to an anagrammatical Dickens party, the guests of which are prominent characters in Dickens' writing: Blame Crumple; We debtor to toys; Clever fop I did pad; Pair my ages; His by a linen clock; Toy lily blows; Canny Skyes; Mere Walls; O, feel my corn bed; We kill red vics; Over it wilts; Bug ran by dear.

No. 200.—Double Acrostic.

Two words are here to be found out,
Both you have heard of, I've no doubt;
One is a thing that gives its aid
To ships engaged in peaceful trade.
The other thing is often found
To war's chief weapon closely bound.
These stars replace with letters true,
And both the things will look at you.
In the first letters, downwards read,
Is that by which the vessel's sped;
And in the last, if downwards, spelt,
That which adorns the soldier's belt.

1

1st line— What a bull does, if he can.
2d line— What is the most beauteous span.
3d line— Hog in armor is my third.
4th line—Boy in barracks often heard.
5th line—What the street boys often run.
6th line—What gives light, not like the sun.
7th line—What makes doctors oft despair.
8th line—What is black, with curly hair.
9th line—What is very hard to bear.

```
    *        *        *        *
  *   *   *   *   *   *   *
*   *   *   *   *   *   *   *   *
  *   *   *   *   *   *   *
    *   *   *   *   *   *
  *        *        *        *
* * * * * * * * * * *
  *      *      *      *      *
    *        *        *        *
```

The word square was such 'old hat' that it evidently didn't need a diagram to explain it, but just in case you don't know what one looks like, here is the puzzle followed by its answer:

No. 420.—Easy Squares.

(a) 1. Crippled. 2. Hot and dry. 3. A deposit of mineral. 4. Paradise.
(b) 1. An article of food that appears early on the bill of fare. 2. To glance sideways. 3. A Turkish soldier. 4. The plural of an article used in writing.

(a)					(b)			
L	A	M	E		S	O	U	P
A	R	I	D		O	G	L	E
M	I	N	E		U	L	A	N
E	D	E	N		P	E	N	S

Some of the puzzles are even given titles like the one below, but this is not yet the true crossword:

No. 541.—Cross Word Enigma.

My first is in cotton, but not in silk;
My second in coffee, but not in milk;
My third is in wet, but not in dry;
My fourth is in scream, but not in cry;

My fifth is in lark, but not in sparrow;
My sixth is in wide, but not in narrow;
My seventh in pain, but not in sting;
My whole is a flower that blooms in spring.

Anagrams, acrostics and word squares had in fact been going for donkeys' years—from the times of the Greeks, the Romans, the Hebrews and the medieval monks. You may like to know, for example, that Psalm 119 was an acrostic based on the Hebrew alphabet. But the most remarkable word square from ancient times is the 'reversible' one found on a Roman site at Cirencester:

```
R O T A S
O P E R A
T E N E T
A R E P O
S A T O R
```

which is Latin for 'The sower Arepo controls the wheels with force' and which can be rearranged in 'crossword' form as:

```
              A

              P
              A
              T
              E
              R
A  P A T E R N O S T E R  O
              O
              S
              T
              E
              R

              O
```

Could this be an early Christian crossword with A for alpha and O for omega? some have asked.

But enough of ancient history, fascinating though it is. The fact remains that the Victorians (for all their ingenuity) remained 'stuck' at a certain level, and so it was that the crossword *per se* took longer to emerge than Einstein's theory of relativity!

It was in 1913 that a certain Arthur Wynne produced the puzzle below for the *New York World*.

CROSSWORD No. 1

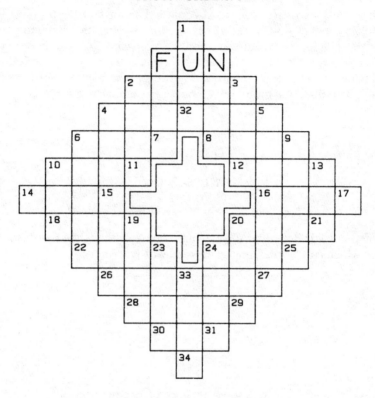

2-3	What bargain hunters enjoy
4-5	A written acknowledgment
6-7	Such and nothing more
10-11	A bird
14-15	Opposed to less
18-19	What this puzzle is
22-23	An animal of prey
26-27	The close of a day
28-29	To elude
30-31	The plural of is
8-9	To cultivate
12-13	A bar of wood or iron
16-17	What artists learn to do
20-21	Fastened
24-25	Found on the seashore
10-18	The fibre of the gomuti palm
6-22	What we all should be
4-26	A day dream
2-11	A talon
19-28	A pigeon
F-7	Part of your head
23-30	A river in Russia
1-32	To govern
33-34	An aromatic plant
N-8	A fist
24-31	To agree with
3-12	Part of a ship
20-29	One
5-27	Exchanging
9-25	To sink [Sunk?] in mud
13-21	A boy

Wynne, an immigrant from Liverpool, remained a leading crossword setter for about ten years, and then (sad to say) he faded into obscurity.

It was in the 1920s that crosswords took off. Messrs Simon and Schuster launched an amazingly successful publishing company in America and their *Cross Word Puzzle Book* was published in England by Hodder and Stoughton (a copy of which I purchased second-hand in the 1960s for 6d!). The book begins with a detailed account of how to do a crossword. For the benefit of my one reader who has *never* seen any crossword and the entertainment of the others here is how the book started:

THE CROSS WORD PUZZLE BOOK
FIRST SERIES

Cross word puzzles are a great deal simpler to explain than to solve. And as the quickest and clearest way to explain any game is by demonstration, let us do a typical, if rather easy, example together.

Here is the puzzle:

[CROSSWORD No. 2]

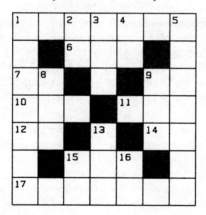

HORIZONTAL
  1 A pasty composition
  6 Prefix, meaning new
  7 Exist
  9 Sixth note of the musical scale
 10 A domestic animal
 11 Affirmative particle
 12 Indefinite article
 14 In
 15 Fuss
 17 Went into

VERTICAL
  1 Pacify
  2 Indefinite article
  3 Large body of water
  4 Toward
  5 Cooked before a fire
  8 Male human being
  9 Meadow
 13 Short poem
 15 Near
 16 Alternative

All the puzzles are not the same square shape as this, but all have one thing in common: the black squares among the white make a symmetrical pattern, so that the whole looks like a piece of cross-stitch needlework, as for instance an old-fashioned 'sampler'.

What have we to do?

Each white square represents a single letter. The puzzle is—to find out what letter belongs in each white square. And you determine this by working out the words from the definitions, which you will see beside the puzzle. When you have completed the puzzle correctly you will find that it consists of a number of words *which read both horizontally and vertically*, interlocking round the pattern made by the black squares.

You will notice numbers in many of the white squares, corresponding to numbers in the lists of 'horizontals' and 'verticals'. These show the starting-points of words, sometimes a horizontal word (*e.g.* 6), sometimes a vertical word (*e.g.* 2), sometimes both horizontal and vertical words (*e.g.* 1). Each word starts in the first space to the *right* of a black square if it is a horizontal, and in the first space *below* a black square if it is a vertical. Some words of both kinds of course start on the outside squares, *i.e.*, we imagine a ring of black squares all round the puzzle.

We now know where the words begin. How long are they to be? Each will consist of just as many letters, one letter to a square, as it will take to reach the next black square (or the edge of the puzzle where no black square intervenes) in whichever direction we are going. For example, '1 horizontal' will be 7 letters long, and so will '1 vertical'. But '6 horizontal' will have only 3 letters; '2 vertical' will have only 2 letters; '7 horizontal' will have only 2 letters; and '13 vertical' will have 3: and so on.

Sometimes a letter will come between two blacks in the pattern. In this case it will only be used in making one word, either a horizontal or a vertical one: for instance, the last letter of '3 vertical' or the first of '13 vertical'. But generally a letter has got to fit into two words—one horizontal and one vertical. For instance, the second letter of '6 horizontal' must also be right for the second letter of '3 vertical'.

And then the fun begins.

Now let us work out this puzzle. (It's a very simple one; you won't have such an easy time again, I warn you!). Start with '1 horizontal'.

'A pasty composition'. How many letters? Seven—since there is no black square right the way across the top line. 'A pasty composition' of seven letters? Let us try PLASTER. (Write it in lightly. You'll soon find you need india-rubber at this game.)

Now is this the right word? We can soon find out; for if it is the right word, it has given us some splendid clues for no less than five of our 'verticals' (1-5).

¹P	L	²A	³S	⁴T	E	⁵R
	■	⁶			■	
⁷	⁸	■		■	⁹	
¹⁰			■	¹¹		
¹²		■	¹³	■	¹⁴	
	■	¹⁵		¹⁶	■	
¹⁷						

What about 'vertical 1'? 'Pacify', seven letters beginning (apparently) with 'P'. How about PLACATE? Yes, it fits. Write it in lightly. One check is not enough. But we can soon get proof positive that we are on the right track. For it looks as if '2 vertical', which as you see has two letters only (and therefore ought to be easy to guess), ought to begin with 'A'.

What is '2 vertical'? 'Indefinite article'. Obviously AN. It fits, and it begins with 'A'. Write it in. But we can check again. For '3 vertical' presumably begins with 'S'. It has three letters. It is a 'large body of water'. Exultantly, we write in SEA.

And so it goes on. You may like to note incidentally that the practice of putting the number of letters in brackets after a clue had not yet been introduced.

Newspapers also latched on to crosswords in the 1920s, and by 1930 crosswords were commonplace. Indeed dictionaries were torn apart in libraries, worries were expressed about eyesight, and crosswords were increasingly regarded as an 'unsociable habit' (how little times have changed!). One of the developments in the twenties and thirties was the big-money puzzle with alternative answers. A clue might be offered as follows:

A yellow addition to your food (7)

with a corresponding answer in the diagram printed as

Solvers were invited to use their skill to choose between MUSTARD and CUSTARD and see if they could reach the same set of answers as the panel of experts. Lotteries like this thrived in *Titbits* and other magazines until well after the Second World War, but they have little appeal for the true aficionado, so we can forget them without further mention.

The rest of crossword history belongs largely to the cryptic crossword, but before we look ahead you may like to have a go at four definition-type puzzles below. Crosswords 3, 4, 5 and 6 are all fairly typical English puzzles with simple vocabulary. They are puzzles I made up for the *London Evening News*; and contributors were exhorted to avoid proper nouns, foreign words, abbreviations, two-letter words. Though I have called these definition-type puzzles there is a hint of the cryptic in the clues to 34 across of No. 3, 3 down of No. 4 and 10 across of No. 5. These are examples of the double definition clue which we shall be looking at in Chapter 3.

CROSSWORD No. 3

By D. F. Manley from the *London Evening News*

ACROSS

1 Wicket (5)
5 Fragrance (5)
9 Apartments (5)
10 Impel (4)
12 Fool (5)
13 Not total (7)
15 Quick look (4)
17 Retinue (4)
18 Den (4)
19 Machine (5)
22 Set (3)
23 Obliterate (5)
26 Love intensely (5)
28 Regulations (5)
31 Signify assent (3)
32 Mount (5)
34 Only a fish? (4)
35 Cask (4)
37 Warbled (4)
39 Settle (7)
41 Hair (5)
42 Detect (4)
43 Salute (5)
44 Music time? (5)
45 Tendency (5)

DOWN

1 Odd (8)
2 Fervidly hot (8)
3 Cringe (5)
4 Sharpener (4)
5 Snake (3)
6 Subdued grumbling (6)
7 Song (4)
8 Valley (4)
11 Wins (5)
14 Fitting (3)
16 Trudge (4)
20 Expiate (5)
21 Attention (4)
22 Hold out (4)
24 Annul (8)
25 Widened (8)
27 Poles (4)
29 Supplant (5)
30 Landed property (6)
33 Instigate (3)
34 Show contempt (5)
35 Sun-bathe (4)
36 Run (4)
38 Encourage (4)
40 Personality (3)

CROSSWORD No. 3

CROSSWORD No. 4

By D. F. Manley from the *London Evening News*

ACROSS

 1 Prize vessels (4)
 4 Posters (8)
10 Ratify (7)
11 Too (4)
12 Opening (8)
15 Spy on (4)
16 Tidier (6)
17 Image (4)
19 Unit of work (3)
20 Tended (6)
22 One of two (6)
26 Epoch (3)
27 Before (3)
28 Grease (6)
31 Traps (6)
33 Shed (3)
34 Speech impediment (4)
35 Fame (6)
38 Passage (4)
39 Temperature line on map (8)
41 Deserve (4)
42 Absconding (7)
43 Costs (8)
44 Cliques (4)

DOWN

 1 Instrument (8)
 2 Concerning shepherds (8)
 3 Eating clubs? (6)
 4 Blabbed (6)
 5 Cut off (3)
 6 Vindicate (6)
 7 Cover with wax (4)
 8 Disorderly flight (4)
 9 Prophet (4)
13 Biting (4)
14 Venerates (7)
18 Clergymen (7)
21 Individuality (3)
23 Particle charged electrically (3)
24 Something transmitted from
   ancestors (8)
25 Answers (8)
29 Awkward boor (4)
30 Circular frames (6)
31 Tramples (6)
32 Foreigners (6)
35 Fully developed (4)
36 Ceremony (4)
37 Next (4)
40 Small deer (3)

CROSSWORD No. 4

CROSSWORD No. 5

By D. F. Manley from the *London Evening News*

ACROSS

1 Little scamps! (4)
3 Swellings (8)
10 A rope for the artist? (7)
11 Employer (4)
14 Came back (8)
15 Lowest point (5)
16 Stupid (5)
17 Apartments (4)
20 Estranged (9)
21 Dance (3)
23 Weights (4)
24 The truth (4)
25 Work unit (3)
26 Shopkeeper (9)
28 Arrive (4)
30 Performers (5)
33 Goods (5)
34 Lengthen (8)
36 Female (4)
37 Simpleton (7)
38 Sideboards (8)
39 Platform (4)

DOWN

1 Flood (8)
2 Depositing as security (8)
3 Room for a drink? (3)
4 Spoke falsely (4)
5 Pecuniary stakes (9)
6 Stupefy (4)
7 Smooth and concise (5)
8 Bird (4)
9 Flank (4)
12 Tars (7)
13 Ascents (5)
18 Grassland (9)
19 Flower-clusters (7)
21 Unbroken view (8)
22 Demands upon energy (8)
24 Pertaining to central point (5)
27 Extra payment (5)
29 Metal (4)
30 Cupola (4)
31 Incites (4)
32 Excitement (4)
35 Printer's measures (3)

CROSSWORD No. 5

CROSSWORD No. 6

By D. F. Manley from the *London Evening News*

ACROSS

1 Stake (4)
4 Refute (8)
10 Revert (5)
11 Material (3)
12 Asterisk (4)
14 Propose (8)
16 Great terror (5)
18 Gourd (5)
19 Put in (6)
21 Cutting instrument (3)
22 Sing (5)
23 Vehicle (3)
25 Way out (4)
27 Labyrinth (4)
28 Place (3)
29 Dig (5)
31 Lettuce (3)
32 Call for repetition (6)
35 Store (5)
38 Sand-hills (5)
39 Engraved design (8)
41 Disencumbers (4)
42 Single (3)
43 Counterfeits (5)
44 University course (8)
45 Pip (4)

DOWN

1 Patronage (8)
2 Send (8)
3 Weird (5)
4 Greyish-brown (3)
5 Metal (4)
6 First (6)
7 Renovate (5)
8 Precious stone (4)
9 Level (4)
13 Sunburn (3)
15 Gem (5)
17 Weep (3)
20 Volumes (5)
21 Minister (5)
23 Enrol as a Saint (8)
24 Retired (8)
26 Heavy gas (5)
29 Evades (6)
30 Conclude (3)
31 Bird (5)
33 Heals (5)
34 Colour (3)
35 Sibilate (4)
36 Particle (4)
37 Abounding (4)
40 Paddle (3)

CROSSWORD No. 6

It is perhaps ironic that the crossword began in America but that the Americans have mostly got stuck with plain puzzles in the same way that the Victorians were stuck with their acrostics etc. Puzzle 7 is a fairly typical American puzzle.

CROSSWORD No. 7

By Amigo from *Crossword*

ACROSS

1 Coarse Algae
5 Mistake
10 Pardon me!
14 Situs
15 Scene
16 Unaspirated
17 Columbus, e g
19 Ionian Sea gulf
20 Unsound
21 Indonesian coin
22 The abomasum
23 Vehemence
25 Oppose
26 Stud
30 Scion
31 Washington State port city
34 Gracefully delicate
36 Sea duck
38 Healthy
39 US Foreign Policy goals: F D Roosevelt congressional message, 1941 (phrase)
42 Chief Babylonian god
43 Film actor and director: _____ Davis
44 Peepshow
45 Stoat
47 Anchor tackle
49 Tableland
50 Hindu mantras
51 Matrons
53 Corrupt
55 Entangle
56 Bruits
61 Baltic Sea gulf
62 Criticize
64 Hebrew month
65 Impassive
66 Gottfried's sister
67 Confined
68 Import
69 Arabian tribesman

DOWN

1 Moslem judge
2 Emerald Isle
3 Minus
4 South American rodent
5 Jewish ceremonial vessels
6 Surface measure
7 Prosopopeia
8 Grimace
9 Merit
10 Visigoth king
11 Previously
12 Grafted: Her.
13 Metheglin
18 Cape Horn native
24 Activists
25 Peeler
26 Immerse
27 Thomas Tryon novel: *The* _____
28 Calliope
29 Thor's wife
31 Finial
32 Classical dramatic farces
33 Bewildered
35 Nocturnal carnivores
37 Imagine
40 Custom
41 Weir
46 Disclose
48 Bridge hand
51 Italian poet
52 Divot
53 Swathe
54 Assistant
55 Assemble
57 Lawyers' patron saint
58 Vend
59 Irish Gaelic
60 Wound
63 Notes: Mus.

CROSSWORD No. 7

There is an immediate difference noticeable between this and the *plain* British puzzle: obscure words (including proper nouns), abbreviations and prefixes are all OK. In fact any combination of letters is turned into a clue if possible. Even A CAT would be allowed if given a clue of 'Room to swing_____'!

Before we leave the plain puzzle we ought to mention a type of clue which is neither a straight definition nor a cryptic clue. This example from the *Daily Telegraph* (25.5.67) will suffice:

[1.1] 'Has, having, and in quest to have, _____'
    (Shakespeare Sonnets) (7)

Did you know that the answer is EXTREME? If you didn't know, you might have worked it out from E-T-E-E.

[1.1] is a *quotation clue*, which may perhaps be regarded as a particular type of *general knowledge* or *quiz clue*. Although the cryptic crossword solver will benefit from a good stock of general knowledge (and indeed may enhance general knowledge through solving!), the quiz clue is too much like a straight definition to be ranked as 'cryptic'. Nevertheless, there are those solvers who welcome the odd quotation clue in a cryptic puzzle, because it gives them a start.

Some puzzles contain nothing but quiz clues, like this one:

[1.2] He wrote *Ode on a Grecian Urn* (4,5)

The solver can fill in JOHN KEATS and feel like a connoisseur of literature! If you appreciate such puzzles, I recommend the weekly General Knowledge crossword in the *Sunday Express*.

2

A Digression on Diagrams

Although the clueless crossword above is very simple we can use it to define certain terms:

* The letters C, T, W and N are in squares that belong to both across and down answers. These are called *checked squares*.
* The letters A, O, E and I belong to only one answer each and these are in *unchecked squares* or *unches*.
* The words CAT, WIN, COW and TEN are of course the *answers*. When you come to solve a more difficult puzzle with its own instructions you may come across a word that denotes the answers as they appear on the diagram. That word is *lights*. Unfortunately this term is also used to refer to individual letters within words (as C, A, T, O, E, W, I, N, here). The particular meaning is usually obvious from the context, but I now avoid using 'lights' wherever possible.
* The central square is a blank and the whole crossword has a *blocked diagram*. (The diagram is sometimes called the *grid*.)

Now look at the puzzle below:

19

Here the checked squares contain C, T, O, E, W and N, and the unchecked squares contain A, R and I. Letters are kept apart by a bar rather than a block and this is known as a *barred diagram*.

Most crosswords are in fact blocked puzzles, but the most advanced ones are more often barred puzzles—the reasons for this will become clearer later in the book. For the moment look at Crossword 2 on p.5: you can see that there are very few unches and a lot of 'checking'. Crossword 7 on p.17 is even more extreme and has no unches. This means that in theory you could complete the puzzle by solving only one set of clues, Across or Down. In practice though you will need to solve from both sets, since a lot of the clues seem to have more than one possible answer.

Here is an early example of the plain, blocked puzzle. In fact it was the first crossword published in the *Daily Telegraph* on 30 July 1925, and you might like to have a go at it.

CROSSWORD No. 8

From the *Daily Telegraph* 1925

ACROSS

1 Author of 'Childe Harold'
5 Author of tales of mystery
8 Will reveal the hidden
13 Incursion
14 Elizabethan sea-rover
16 Lily
17 Succulent plant
18 Useful in haymaking
19 Nap
20 Where cricketers are trained
21 A distinguished order
22 Adverb
23 Chinese coin or weight
25 A seaside pleasure
28 Cut
30 Soothing; product of Gilead
34 A blemish except in a billiard ball
35 Shakespearian character
37 A word from the motto of the Garter
39 A seaside implement
40 Where Sir John Moore died
41 Travellers' haven
42 Selvage
44 Part of a ship
45 First name of famous American author
46 Unadulterated
47 Petition
48 Beverage
53 King of the Amalekites, who came 'delicately'
57 Military abbreviation
59 That is
60 A measure
63 Cromwell's 'Empty bauble'
64 Island home of an ancient civilisation
66 The germ of a building
67 A volcano
68 Guarded by eunuchs
69 Kind
70 Visionaries
71 Applied to anything perfect
72 A people with unalterable laws

DOWN

1 Often 'snatched from the burning'
2 A seat of learning is the key to this
3 Tumult
4 Poems
5 Bears the burden of youth
6 Tree
7 Supplements

CROSSWORD No. 8

9 Transported
10 Air (mus.)
11 An annual festival
12 A fish
14 Fall
15 Greek god of love
24 Mythical founder of a great Empire
25 Country of Europe
26 Not so well
27 Pronoun
28 Indian lemur
29 A district in South London
31 Conjunction
32 River of France
33 Can pick and strike
34 Note of octave
35 First name of famous Highland outlaw

36 Unit
38 An explosive
43 Thank you
45 Exist
49 A king, both first and sixth
50 A German word not used on Armistice night
51 Consider
52 Depressions
54 Bars and is often barred
55 A skin affliction
56 Changed by motorists
58 Rock
59 Also
60 Recess in a church
61 Lump
62 Would apply to the upper atmosphere
65 Before

Was there anything you noticed about the diagram? The symmetry? Yes, of course—the crossword diagram would look the same if it were turned upside down, a feature we will notice in most diagrams. (This particular diagram will also look the same if turned sideways and if reflected in a mirror.) But what else did you notice? What I noticed was that no sooner had I put a few words together than I came to a stop and had to start again. If you look at the diagram carefully, you will see that there are in fact no less than *nine* crosswords all isolated from each other in the one square. This sort of thing wouldn't be too popular with crossword editors today because one of the requirements of a diagram is that all the answers should be *interconnected*. Totally isolated parts won't do! Times change of course and when we look at p.31 of the *Daily Telegraph 50th Anniversary Crossword Book* we see the diagram below from 1928 (a diagram still used by the *Telegraph* today incidentally).

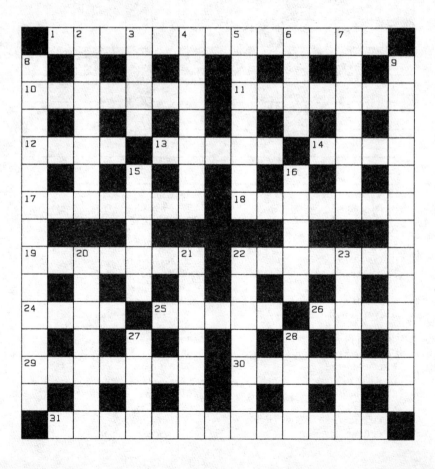

When we come to p.164 you will see that the 1928 clues are slightly cryptic, but for the moment let's look at the diagram and compare it with the diagram for Crossword No. 8. Two features are notable:

(i) The average length of a solution has increased considerably and the number of clues has been reduced substantially. Two-letter solutions have gone, and we have four long solutions of 13 letters each. Crossword No. 8 has 82 clues; the puzzle three years later has only 32 clues.

(ii) In the 1925 puzzle nearly all the white squares are checked, whereas the 1928 puzzle shows a diagram where alternate letters are checked. The 1925 puzzle has a 'closed' diagram with lots of solid white; the 1928 diagram has a latticed appearance, being a much more 'open' diagram. In 1925 you had to solve barely more than half the clues to finish the puzzle; in 1928 you had to solve them all.

We will be looking again at diagrams in Chapter 12, and you will see that even the 1928 diagram has its weaknesses, but for the moment let's recognize what an advance it is over the previous one.

Now we must look at cryptic clues.

3

Beyond the Simple Definition

The first *Daily Telegraph* puzzle had lots of short words of the type that quickly became hackneyed. The solver of the twenties must soon have realized that poems = ODES, thank you = TA, and before = ERE. Yet even in this puzzle there is a hint of the cryptic in 2 Down: 'A seat of learning is the key to this'. The setter is inviting us to think of Yale University and a Yale lock; and he has offered us something a little more interesting than 'An American University'. Now, as it happens, I don't find this a very sound clue because Yale University can't really be the key to a Yale lock—but the setter's heart was in the right place! The Yale clue has a descendant in the modern puzzle called the *double definition*.

An example of the double definition clue might be this:

[3.1] University name on key (4)

The answer is YALE because it is both a university and the name on certain keys. This may not be a very exciting clue, but it shows a degree of trickery absent from the plain clue. Had we wanted simply to offer two definitions on a plate we might have written 'University, name on key', but the omission of the comma is a legitimate trick and we might just be led astray for an instant to think of some poor Oxbridge undergraduate returning home after midnight unable to enter his college.

Now here are some more examples of double definitions which you might like to try for yourselves:

[3.2] Broken part of body (4)
[3.3] Take notice of Gospel writer (4)
[3.4] Oil film? (6)
[3.5] Tumblers producing spectacles (7)

The answers are BUST, MARK, GREASE (remember Olivia and Travolta?) and GLASSES. In [3.5] the two definitions are joined by a *link word* 'producing'. This link word helps the clue make sense, and it is justified because the word for 'tumblers' produces the word for spectacles. More about link words in due course. Were you misled into thinking of the wrong meaning for tumblers and spectacles? Then you have been the victim of what I call the *misleading context*. The clue has provided you with a phrase about acrobats (the straight-forward reading), but the *cryptic reading* has nothing to do with the circus: you are being given a coded (or cryptic) instruction to find a word with two meanings. Isn't that more interesting than 'Spectacles (7)'?

There is no reason why we should not string together a whole series of definitions, as the following clue shows:

[3.6] Left harbour gate bearing drink (4)

The solver may have visions of a sailor sloping off with his rum, but this is simply a series of five definitions for the word PORT.

The double definition can often be entertaining if one of the definitions is fanciful:

[3.7] Sad like the girl who's had a haircut? (10)

Here the answer is DISTRESSED, suggesting that distressed *might* mean having had tresses removed. Because this usage *is* fanciful the clue finishes with a question mark.

Here is an example which yields an idiomatic phrase:

[3.8] Feeling very happy like the mountaineer who's climbed Everest? (2,3,2,3,5)

What phrase suggests that someone is either very happy or at the highest point of Earth? Answer: ON TOP OF THE WORLD.

If it is possible to mislead with two definitions, it may also be possible to baffle the solver with a single *cryptic definition*. My children used to tease me with jokes like this: What do you take the lid off before putting the bottom on? This joke can be turned into a cryptic definition:

[3.9] You take the lid off it before putting the bottom on! (6)

Because this is an outrageous definition we allow ourselves an exclamation mark to warn the solver. The answer? TOILET!

Here's another one derived from a joke book:

[3.10] Will doing them make a scout or guide dizzy? (4,5)

Answer: GOOD TURNS.

We could perhaps define a SKINHEAD as follows:

[3.11] An extremely distressed youngster (8)

A definition such as:

[3.12] A letter demanding money for accommodation (8)

may suggest an unpleasant communication through the post until we remember that it is the LANDLORD (or LANDLADY) who lets out the accommodation. Letter is one of a number of *-er words* often used in a misleading sense; you will meet others.

Here are some cryptic definitions, including one or two 'old chestnuts':

[3.13] A wicked thing (6)
[3.14] A jammed cylinder (5,4)
[3.15] Keen observer of gulls? (8)
[3.16] Presumably one doesn't run after it? (4,5)
[3.17] He was rushed almost from the start (5)
[3.18] 014? (6,5)
[3.19] You won't necessarily see anyone till after this meal (10,5)

The answers to the last seven clues? CANDLE, SWISS ROLL, SWINDLER, LAST TRAIN, MOSES, DOUBLE AGENT (= 2 × 007!), and PLOUGHMAN'S LUNCH.

Notice how in [3.19] 'till' is a verb, not a preposition (a *misleading part of speech*).

To finish with, another clue for the same phrase, published in *The Times*:

[3.20] What expert in share movement wants from the board (10,5).

How wonderfully misleading!

Now you are invited to try a tutorial puzzle based on the ideas in this chapter.

CROSSWORD No. 9

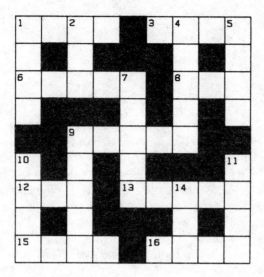

ACROSS

1 This girl is a ruddy gem (4)
3 Roasting device to sputter (4)
6 Marijuana? One notifies the police (5)
8 Six-footer working on a hill? (3)
9 Money for animal (5)
12 Beastly butter! (3)
13 Tree, one of greater age (5)
15 Red wine seen in the marquee perhaps (4)
16 Break? That will do for a card game (4)

DOWN

1 Newspapers showing student pranks (4)
2 Female supporter (3)
4 But it can also play forte! (5)
5 Lyle's partner is displayed in the gallery (4)
7 Parisian flower (5)
9 One like Brutus, upright type (5)
10 Ridge on the guitar may make you worry (4)
11 Holiday accident? (4)
14 Writer of this book, a studious type! (3)

4

The Anagram

In Chapter 3 we saw how fiddling around with definitions could produce an element of 'crypticity' (if I may be allowed to coin a new word). But a word not only has a meaning—or more than one meaning—it has letters too, and these letters offer us many chances for word puzzling. One very popular way of indicating the letters is the anagram, and this is where we begin.

We are forty years on from Don Lemon and his book of puzzles, and we are looking at the *Daily Telegraph* crossword for 21 July 1932. Here is 7 down:

[4.1] 'Meet tired Pa' (anag.)

Although there are millions of ways of arranging these letters, it will only take a minute or two to come up with PREMEDITATE—and of course it may well prove easier if we already know some of the checked letters. Even so, there is something unsatisfactory about this clue because we aren't given any definition of the answer.

However, we must not be unfairly critical when considering clues of over 50 years ago—some progress has been made. The next clue appeared in 1947:

[4.2] Atom plaint farce (anag.) (Yet power can be controlled by it) (3,2,10)

This clue offers us an anagram and a definition—and it is a definition that tries to link up with the theme of the letters to be anagrammed (however vaguely!). The answer is ACT OF PARLIAMENT.

An improvement, yes, but this is still a bit on the clumsy side. How much more elegant is this 1973 *Telegraph* clue:

[4.3] Pure ice broken up for the fussy diner (7)

Here again we have an anagram but instead of '(anag.)' we see the phrase 'broken up'. This phrase serves as an *anagram indicator*, telling us that the letters of 'pure ice' must be broken up to yield a word meaning 'fussy diner'. The answer is EPICURE.

In a 1960 puzzle we have this clue:

[4.4] Arrange to send port (6)

Here the anagram indicator is an imperative verb. We are told to arrange 'to send' so that we can get a word meaning 'port'. We've already seen that 'port' has at least five meanings (p.25), and from the way the clue is worded we're probably thinking of an alcoholic Christmas gift. In fact, however, the port is a harbour and the answer is OSTEND.

Anagram indicators are many and varied. Any words or phrases that indicate a jumbling of the letters will do, so long as the clues are grammatical and make sense: 'terribly', 'excited', 'mixed up' are all warnings to the solver that an anagram might be afoot. Now try this:

[4.5] Dicky came top (4)

Doubtless you will think of a clever boy called Richard who beat his classmates in the examination. However, this is another example of the misleading context because the *cryptic reading* of the clue has nothing whatever to do with a successful male. In the cryptic reading 'Dicky' is an adjective (not a proper noun) meaning 'shaky' and 'shaky came' means an anagram of 'came'. The answer therefore is ACME, meaning 'top'. Again we see an example of how a cryptic clue presents you with a series of words which are ostensibly about a particular theme, but you must ignore the theme and concentrate on the words as a series of 'cryptic' instructions to lead you to the answer.

So far we have looked at two types of cryptic clue: the double definition and the anagram. In the following chapters we shall meet other types.

Before that, though, we are going to have a foretaste of 'clueology' to see how the coded instructions are put together. We are going to analyse all the bits and pieces that actually make up a cryptic clue and label them.

We shan't be doing this for *all* our clues, but if we do it now and then, you will see that there is some sense in the cryptic clue, even if it looks like gobbledegook at first sight! Once you appreciate this, you will know what to look for in a clue when you try to solve it—and this is important.

Into clueology we go then, and first of all we take a look again at clue [4.3] and under its different parts you will see that I have placed some letters:

[4.3] Pure ice broken up for the fussy diner (7)

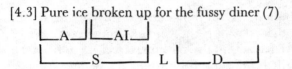

A stands for anagram and AI *anagram indicator*. Together they form S, the *subsidiary indication*. L stands for *linkword* because it links the subsidiary indication to D, which is the *definition* (of EPICURE).

Already in the clues we have seen that A and AI can be the other way round and that L need not always exist, as is the case with:

[4.5] Dicky came top

AI   A

⌊__S__⌋   D

Now it is also possible for D to come before S, as in this example:

[4.6] Fungus in a crag, I fancy

⌊__A__⌋   AI

D   L⌊__S__⌋

The linkword 'in' means 'consisting of' so we are being asked to find a fungus which consists of the six letters of 'a crag I' in a fancy way. The answer is AGARIC.

I hope you have enjoyed your introduction to clueology. What you now need to understand is that *the normal modern cryptic clue nearly always consists of a definition and subsidiary indication.* An anagram, however, is only one form of subsidiary indication, and we shall be looking at some others in the following chapters. In the meantime have fun with the puzzles below. Crossword No. 10 consists entirely of anagrams, so in each clue look out for the AI, the A and the D (and sometimes the L), Crossword No. 11 mixes in anagrams with the sorts of clue covered in Chapter 3. Sooner or later you will have to discern what type of clue the setter has laid before you. At this stage you should be able to recognize a few of the tell-tale signs, but as a help the anagram clues are asterisked.

CROSSWORD No. 10

ACROSS

1 Duet is newly adapted (6)
5 Form of art shown by sailor (3)
6 Re tax—it could be more than is necessary (5)
8 Neat prose translated into universal language (9)
10 Aimed to upset TV, press, etc? (5)
12 Weapon destroyed gnu (3)
13 Modern centre, redeveloped (6)

DOWN

1 Use leather to lash unruly prats (5)
2 *Anti*-beer? I may become drunken! (9)
3 Devour tea possibly (3)
4 Master diverted little river (6)
7 Man out, swinging—what's the total? (6)
9 Weird thing in the dark (5)
11 Female creature featured in odd ode (3)

CROSSWORD No. 11

ACROSS

1 How competitors in dead heat cross the line, nevertheless (2,3,4,4)

8 Evangelist? He scores a couple of points (9)

*9 Reg revamped work unit (3)

10 Distinguished airman is a card (3)

*12 A pith gets messy in a food (9)

*14 Hog, sir, is horrible, monstrous (6)

15 Elegance from Warsaw? (6)

17 Gymnast could be thinking the right way (2,3,4)

18 Prosecute a girl (3)

19 I will, badly (3)

*21 Natural manure makes pod spring out (9)

*24 Broken down floor, note, in historic building (5,2,6)

DOWN

*1 A great school! I get excited—I'm very keen on ancient history (13)

2 Money container? (3)

3 The temptress when night approaches? (3)

*4 Rat, say, could deviate off course (6)

*5 More wrath upsets the gardener's friend (9)

*6 Fish die in agony (3)

7 A period when youngsters come to a full stop? (7,6)

*11 Greet funny little bird (5)

12 One who hangs up half a stocking support? (9)

13 Attempts scores in rugby (5)

16 Start to show to advantage (3,3)

20 Vulgar sound of cow (3)

22 In favour of person being paid (3)

*23 Edward makes a bad end (3)

5

More Common Clue Types

Charades, Container and contents, Reversals

In Chapter 4 we saw how the anagram and its indicator could be used as a 'subsidiary indication' to a definition. We now start to look at a few more ways in which a crossword setter can indicate the letters in the answer. For the moment we must leave the history of crosswords behind, and look at some modern examples.

Charades. Have you ever played the game of charades? In Act 1 someone drops the word 'hat' into the conversation; in Act 2 the word 'red' is dropped in; then in Act 3 someone tries to mention the word 'hatred' without your noticing. You have played this parlour game? Well, the charade clue is just like that; you define 'hatred' as 'hat' and 'red' and tell the solver to put the parts together:

[5.1] Headgear on communist evokes intense dislike (6)

(hat)   CI   (red)   L

CI is a *charade indicator*; the word 'on' is suitable for a down word. The *linkword* L means 'draws out' (i.e. 'provides').

Before we pass on to other examples note how the word 'red' is defined by 'communist'. This is a bit of *crossword jargon* and there are a number of such words that are great favourites with crossword setters. Another favourite is 'ant', which is often defined by 'worker'. You will pick these up as you go along, but some of the more common three-lettered ones appear in Appendix 1.

Now here are some more examples of charades:

[5.2] Man needs essential animal (6)

(Don)   CI   (key)   D

giving don + key = DONKEY. Here is an alternative clue giving the same answer:

[5.3] Stupid person a university lecturer provided with solution (6)

L___D___J   (don)   L___CI___J (key)

[5.4] Discharge of lightning on a Lancashire town (6)

Here the 'discharge of lightning' equals 'bolt'; 'on' is simply equal to itself, 'on'; and the Lancashire town is BOLTON. There is no CI in the clue; the parts just follow on.

[5.5] Dental deposit? Use salt repeatedly (6)

You may use a salt water rinse for that stain on your teeth, but think too much along those lines and you'd be a victim of the 'misleading context'. Think instead of salt as a sailor and use 'tar' repeatedly to get TARTAR.

[5.6] Bridge over loch? That's cunning (8)

This is a down clue and 'arch' (= bridge) is *over* (CI) 'Ness' (a loch). Such ARCHNESS from the crossword setter!

[5.7] It's very warm, the Spanish inn (5)

Very warm is 'hot', the Spanish (i.e. *the* in Spanish) is 'el' and an inn is a HOTEL. Again there is no CI. This is a good moment to warn you that you can expect some simple foreign words in subsidiary indications. EL is another bit of crossword jargon. In addition, LE, LA, LES can all be denoted by 'the French'; 'of the French' would be DU; 'the German' is DIE, DER or DAS. We are concentrating on the 'grammar', but we are also picking up some vocabulary.

Container and contents. The charade clue gave us a formula A *plus* B equals C; the container-and-contents clue gives us a new formula A *in* B equals C:

[5.8] Vegetable to stick in the shelter (6)

CCI

Stop thinking about the wilting lettuce and start getting word conscious! 'To stick' is a definition for 'gum'; the shelter is 'lee'; 'gum' *in* 'lee' gives LEGUME.

[5.9] Finishing with a boxed ear—charming! (9)

CCI

When 'ear' is *boxed* by 'ending' we have ENDEARING. Have you guessed what I mean by CCI? It's the container-and-contents indicator! 'Holds' is a popular CCI and will often tell you what sort of clue you are dealing with:

[5.10] Girl holds information for business programme (6)

'Ada' holds the 'gen' for the word AGENDA.

   'Clutching' is another give-away CCI:

[5.11] Members clutching a rota—they insist on proper procedure (9)

'Members' here are 'legs' because we're thinking about members of the body, not MPs in the chamber—a nice piece of crossword jargon in a misleading context. 'A rota' is 'a list' and 'legs' clutching 'a list' becomes LEGALISTS.

   Reversals. Turn around the word 'peek' and you get 'keep'. This simple fact can be made the basis for a reversal clue:

[5.12] Have a little look round part of fortification (4)

RI

RI is the reversal indicator, telling us that when 'peek' (= have a little look) is put round (around, backwards) we get KEEP (part of the castle).

   For a down clue the reversal word could be said to go *up*, so *up* is another RI as in this example:

[5.13] Bear up: here's a ring (4)

Not 'Cheer up, darling, have a bit of jewellery!', but Pooh (Winnie-the-!) *up* to give HOOP.

   Some words are of course palindromes, and so we could have a clue like this:

[5.14] To-and-fro action (4)

Write the word DEED 'to' (forwards) or 'fro' (backwards) and it is the same.

   Sometimes the reversed clue can be ambiguous:

[5.15] Expert turned evil (3)

Read this as D, S and the answer is DAB; read it as S, D and it's BAD! (If the setter has offered you __A__ with the first and third letters unchecked, he is no dab and is most certainly very bad!)

   You now know about six types of cryptic clue: cryptic definition, multiple meanings, anagrams, charades, container and contents, and reversals. We've still got a long way to go before we've covered all the weaponry at the setter's disposal. Before we go on, however, it's time for you to consolidate what you know; so here's another tutorial puzzle.

CROSSWORD No. 12

(The answer to 14 across is a well-known phrase even though not found in *Chambers English Dictionary*.)

ACROSS
1 Disease boy has got in fifth month (6)
4 Remarks not heard by fellow players when going around team (6)
8 Plump bird's grumble (6)
9 Cat bothered us more (6)
10 Russian cast? They work on a script (9)
14 Gentry receive guests here making Nanny retreat with rapture (5,8)
16 There's scope in the sultanate for a fervent royalist (9)
20 The curse of an old Egyptian city (6)
21 Repay artist on return (6)
22 American general arranging truces (6)
23 More than one door-keeper rushes around (6)

DOWN
1 Faces shown by simpletons (4)
2 Bring up jemmy, for instance—get the swag (4)
3 Wanted gentleman caught in the act (7)
5 Cost I worked out for philosopher (5)
6 Diana's noble disregard (8)
7 Laid importance on sweets being served up (8)
11 Material dug from pit comes to the surface (5)
12 Coasting aimlessly, uncertain of what to believe (8)
13 'These are corpses' vulgar fellow declares (8)
15 In the belfry they play doubles (7)
17 Death is solemn (5)
18 Revolutionary Dutch cheese produced (4)
19 Does funny poems (4)

CROSSWORD No. 12

6

Yet More Common Clue Types

Hidden words, Vocal clues, Subtractive clues

By now you can see that there are lots of ways of writing a cryptic clue by using different techniques to indicate the subsidiary indication. In this chapter we inspect some more weapons in the clue-writer's armoury. Note though that the clue-writer is not out to destroy the solver; rather he is out to tease and amuse.

Hidden words. If you take the letters of a sentence in order, a word will often be found lurking. To show what I mean, I invite you to consider the very sentence you have just read. Look at 'order, a word' and you may see ERA spanning the first two words and RAW spanning all three. Look at 'will often' and you can see LOFT. This phenomenon is the basis of the hidden clue, and it may best be illustrated by an example:

[6.1] Pub in Pinner (3)

    D   HI HW

Pub is INN and it may be found in Pinner.

The word 'in' is our HI (*hidden indicator*) and HW is the *hiding word*. The word 'in' is also part of the HI in this clue, where the hidden word spans more than one word (HP = *hiding phrase*):

[6.2] Rat getting in among children? Egad—exterminate! (8)

    D ⌊____HI____⌋⌊_____HP_____⌋

Another common HI is 'some':

[6.3] Some overenthusiastic kissing—one draws blood (4)

This is nothing whatever to do with a romantic love scene. Some (i.e. 'part of') overenthusiastic kissing is TICK, a bloodsucker (defined by 'one draws blood').

Vocal clues depend on how the answer sounds when it is spoken. There are two sub-categories.

The *pun clue* relies on the fact that some words sound like others, e.g. PAIR and PEAR, HEIR and AIR. They are *homophones*, to use the technical jargon. Here is a pun clue:

[6.4] Feature of Scotland where there was a vicar, we hear (4)

The two words 'we hear' form a very common pun indicator (PI). Where was there a vicar? Bray of course, and it's 'Bray' that we hear when we get the answer which is a feature of Scotland—BRAE.

Can you find the PI in the following clue?

[6.5] Such a range of food is said to be satisfactory (4)

It is the phrase 'is said to be'. FARE sounds like 'fair'.

One more:

[6.6] Shakespeare in speech? It should be precluded (6)

Shakespeare is the 'Bard'. What sounds like 'Bard'? BARRED, meaning 'precluded'. (Would you have spotted the PI?)

The *accent* clue relies on oddities of speech. Such a clue could also be regarded as a special type of two-definition clue. Here are some examples:

[6.7]   Animal is warmer according to 'Arry (5)
[6.8]   Correct, but in a refaned way? Scold angrily (4)
[6.9]   A f-fellow somewhere in Jordan (5)
[6.10] Bird gettin' dressed for ceremony (5)
[6.11] Not thin and thuffering from a complaint? (5)

In [6.7] 'Arry is an 'aitch-dropping cockney' who talks about things being 'otter (hence OTTER). In [6.8] our awfully 'nace' person is never 'right' but 'rate', which prompts us to RATE him. [6.9] is a combination of an accent clue with a simple charade. Our unfortunate stutterer is unable to talk about 'a man'; instead he refers to 'a m-man' (AMMAN is Jordan's capital). In [6.10] 'robing' without the final 'g' leads to a bird (ROBIN) and in [6.11] our lisping (or 'lithping') friend is 'sick' (THICK).

Subtractive clues. In several of our clue types we have been involved in adding words to other words or putting words into other words. In a charade, for example, the formula has been

$$A + B = C$$

Well, equally we can use the idea that

$$B = C - A$$

In the 'average daily cryptic' the most common way of subtracting is by removing a head or a tail and the indicator is usually fairly obvious. Thus:

[6.12] Mama, topless, is something else! (5)

Concentrate on the words please, reader, not the misleading pornography! Mama is mother. Remove the 'top' letter and we get OTHER. 'Topless' is a give-away 'beheading indicator': 'headless' is another. (The suggestion of 'top' means that this clue would probably be suitable for a *down* word, rather than an across one, by the way.)

Here's a clue involving truncation at the other end:

[6.13] Endlessly talk about the field event (6)

Nothing to do with David Vine boring the pants off us ('Remember, he needs 173 metres for the bronze and that is a *big* throw!'). Concentrate on the words, please. When 'discuss' is presented 'endlessly' it becomes DISCUS. 'Endlessly' and 'endless' are give-aways for this type of clue.

If words can lose their first and last letters, they can also lose their hearts:

[6.14] Get the better of the heartless monster (4)

The monster is a 'beast'—remove the heart ('a') to give BEST, a verb meaning 'to get the better of'.

In a *very* sophisticated puzzle you might come across:

[6.15] University lecturer is   an ass   ignoring the solution (3)

⌊_____D_____⌋ L (Donkey) ⌊_SI_⌋   (key)

'Donkey' minus 'key' = DON (SI = subtraction indicator), or even:

[6.16] Arousing affection, having had ear removed, dying (6)

(Endearing)   ⌊_SI(i)_⌋ (ear) ⌊_SI(ii)_⌋ ⌊_D_⌋

Answer: ENDING.

On that gruesome note we are ending this chapter, but not before you attempt another tutorial exercise.

CROSSWORD No. 13

ACROSS

1 Animal sounding like an organ (4)
3 Philosophers? They can't thwim! (8)
8 Title held by certain American (4)
9 Vine-crop is exceptional in particular district (8)
10 Nun's dirge played for parting (9)
14 Looked only briefly—decapitated —killed with a spear? (6)
15 Terrible 'arvest—get desperately hungry (6)
17 A cake before the social function is more than enough (9)
20 Repertory company gets up musical repeats (8)
21 Side of blade useful for cutting 'awthorn barrier? (4)
22 Drunk one coming to entrance? Seek help from the law (8)
23 Requests jobs not using the head (4)

DOWN

1 Sincerely pious outside the home (8)
2 Booze inside worker—one to bring something up! (8)
4 Drug cut short a courageous girl (6)
5 Worked out a route and gave it out (9)
6 Wilderness shelters this eagle (4)
7 Left-wing Tories upset, in a sweat (4)
11 Exhilarating tale given twists (9)
12 See grand exploding bombs (8)
13 Young hares? Permits needed for catching at all times (8)
16 Treasure stored? Not completely, that's most certain (6)
18 Said of country life—it must put aside the past (4)
19 Heartless Jack, who couldn't eat everything, expectorated (4)

7

Non-word Elements in Subsidiary Indications

Abbreviations and symbols, Numbers, Bits and pieces

Over the past four chapters we have looked at all the main clue types, but so far we have used whole words as building-blocks for the clues. We can, however, use letters or clusters of letters as we shall see below.

Abbreviations and symbols. Consider the word PRATTLED. This may suggest 'p + rattled', but can the setter indicate 'p' in a subsidiary indication? The answer is yes, because 'p' is short for 'piano' or 'quietly', so a charade clue might read as follows:

[7.1] Gossiped quietly   in a fluster   (8)

In the world of crosswords there are a vast number of common abbreviations, and you will find a fair number in Appendix 1. This list is by no means exhaustive though, and one of the joys of learning how to solve is in coming to recognize the language of abbreviations and symbols.

In the clues that follow we can introduce only a small number in various types of clue.

[7.2] Miss West embraces novice man

Answer: MALE—'Mae' embraces 'L' (= learner, novice).

[7.3] Good man, a sailor lying on bed, wounded (7)

A good man is a saint (St.); a sailor on this occasion is an AB (on other occasions he's a tar or something else!). Put it all together (in a down clue) to give STABBED.

[7.4] Bob has to study for the exam—buzz off! (5)

A bob is (or was!) a shilling (= s); 's' + 'cram' = SCRAM!

[7.5] Slant in Conservative policy (7)

A simple charade: 'in' + 'C' + 'line' = INCLINE.

[7.6] Poet edited religious education book (6)

This is a bit trickier. Religious education = RE and an (edited) anagram of RE book is BROOKE.

Asking the solver to form an abbreviation which is then incorporated into an anagram is regarded as fair only where the abbreviation is obvious. Even so it is a technique better left to the more advanced cryptics. On fairness and advanced puzzles, more anon!

Numbers. In 'crossword land' we still use Roman numbers when convenient. Thus I = 1, V = 5, X = 10, L = 50, C = 100, D = 500 and M = 1000, with of course the possibility of combinations. Thus:

[7.7] 100, very old and shut in (5)

And glad to get the Queen's telegram ? Forget it! 'C' is a hundred; very old becomes 'aged'. Answer: CAGED.

[7.8] Amiss gets 50 less than ex-Aussie opener (4)

With apologies to those who are unfamiliar with test cricket: the answer is AWRY ('L' less than 'Lawry').

Numbers may be combined with the abbreviations:

[7.9] About 50 inhabiting beautiful Devon village (8)

gives 'C' (=about, an abbreviation which will become familiar) + 'L' in (inhabiting) 'lovely'. Hence CLOVELLY.

'Love' (from tennis) and 'duck' (from cricket) are useful speaking terms for zero which is regarded as the shape of O. Thus:

[7.10] The lady's love is a very brave man (4)

Answer: 'her' + 'O' gives HERO.

[7.11] Cricket ground where there's a duck, 5 and a 50 (4)

Answer: 'O' + 'V' + 'a L' = OVAL.

Bits and pieces. In this chapter we've seen two ways in which the crossword setter can get rid of odd letters. There remains a third, very important way. A letter can be defined by the position it occupies in another word. A few examples will suffice to illustrate this:

More on Crossword Terminology

The 'cross word puzzle' has become the 'crossword' puzzle or plain 'crossword'. But what about the 'realm' of crosswords and the people who participate in it? Could we agree on 'crosswording' and 'crossworders'? Maybe, but neither of these words has found a regular place in the dictionaries.

A word that came into vogue in the 1970s was 'cruciverbalism' (from the Latin *crux, crucis,* a cross, and *verbum,* a word). This would mean 'the realm of crosswords', and a 'cruciverbalist' would be someone interested in crosswords. From there we could also presumably deduce the adjective 'cruciverbalistic'. None of these words has yet gained entry into the dictionaries, though they do seem useful.

'Cruciverbalists' are of course in two categories: those who make up the crosswords and those who solve them. The latter are clearly 'solvers', but what about the former? The word 'compiler' has been much used, but it suggests that puzzle construction only involves *collecting* the material together and underplays the aspect of creativity. What about 'composer'? This is quite good, but would be viewed by some as too grandiose. Many crossword contributors like to be called 'setters', since anyone making up a crossword is 'setting' a puzzle for the solver. 'Setter' therefore seems the ideal word.

[7.12] Look at bee for example round end of cowslip (7)

The words 'end of' will tell us that we want the last letter in the word that follows, i.e. 'p'. Put insect around 'p' to get INSPECT.

[7.13] Craftsman is good initially—then not working so hard (7)

'Initially' is a tell-tale word and 'good initially' gives 'g'. When the craftsman is not working so hard he is 'lazier'. Answer: GLAZIER.

'Finally' is also a tell-tale word:

[7.14] Climbing plant with flower finally providing fruit (4)

'Climbing plant' is 'pea'; 'flower finally' is 'r' ('r' being the last letter of 'flower'). Answer: PEAR.

[7.15] Head of school, many years a wise man (4)

'Head of school' is 's'; add 'age' to get the answer: SAGE.
    Initial letters can often be put together in a charade, as follows:

[7.16] Leaders of firm are terribly obese (3)

Take the three leaders (leading letters) to get FAT. (Alternatively final letters may be joined together, but this is much less common.)
    Now try this one:

[7.17] A bit of trouble with relation's reproach (5)

A 'bit' should always mean the first letter—this is a convention which has become a useful rule. So add 't' to 'aunt' and get TAUNT. There's one other thing to notice about this clue. The apostrophe-plus-s combination denotes a possessive to give the clue sense, but means 'is' when we're thinking about the construction of the clue ('t' with 'aunt' *is* TAUNT).
    Though a bit, a head and an end always have single letters a 'heart' may have one letter or more:

[7.18] Chap with heart of steel, bit of a lion? (4)

The heart of steel is 'e'; add it on to 'man' and you have MANE.

[7.19] Stupid fool in middle of road, beginning to fluster (3)

The beginning to the word 'fluster' is 'f' and the middle of the word 'road' is 'oa', giving OAF.
    Half-words can be useful to the crossword setter:

[7.20] Famous performer is semi-naked (4)

'Semi-starkers' is STAR.
    Now it's time for another tutorial puzzle where you will meet some new 'bits and pieces'.

CROSSWORD No. 14

ACROSS

1 Loud oriental celebration (5)
4 Start to tamper with gun—it's only a toy (6)
9 Girl about ten may receive radio waves (7)
10 Agents bringing food aboard (5)
11 Unusual combination of gunners and engineers (4)
13 One drawing southern vessel, *The Queen* (8)
14 Doctor, endless pain is something monstrous (6)
17 Be a chap like George and start to slay monsters (6)
19 To make one's way takes a very long time in these corridors (8)
21 Five—the age for a girl (4)
25 Make a song about the West—jazz? (5)
26 Grass pots are falling to bits (7)
27 Don't have all the lemonade sister! Leave off! (6)
28 Happening that's not odd at the end of August (5)

DOWN

1 Learner in the amusement park shows instinctive skill (5)
2 Performer is a hundred—over the hill (5)
3 Look after what would now be about 4p! (4)
5 Badge labelled 'First Prize'? It's specially presented to steer (7)
6 Fifty trapped in conflicts—ways of escape needed (7)
7 Makes certain unfavourable judgements, the head having left (7)
8 Note 500 pairs perhaps on Noah's boat (4)
12 Tune is first class? Right! (3)
13 Star in revolutionary students union (3)
14 Deprived of top position (given drugs to capture record) (7)
15 Attacks a ship about to travel (7)
16 Fruit, very large, seen around the open country (7)
17 Public transport almost broken down (3)
18 Salt submerged in Antarctica (3)
20 Former prime minister in the garden (4)
22 Mountain-top home—Jane's taken around one (5)
23 Sailor not at home, abroad (5)
24 Some chap serving in part of church (4)

CROSSWORD No. 14

8

The Orchestration of Subsidiary Parts

Complex clues, Linking clues together

You now should be able to solve the following clues, recognizing a different type of subsidiary indication in each one:

(a) [8.1] Put up with a rude person (4)
(b) [8.2] Goose's mate ruined garden (6)
(c) [8.3] The French shelter is hidden (6)
(d) [8.4] Fast and quiet in sudden attack (5)
(e) [8.5] Show contempt perhaps—gratuities sent back (4)
(f) [8.6] Sea-eagle in her nest (4)
(g) [8.7] Despatched perfume we hear (4)
(h) [8.8] Senior is more daring, losing head (5)

The clue types are:

(a) *Two definitions*	(answer: BEAR)
(b) *Anagram*	(answer: GANDER)
(c) *Charade*	(answer: LATENT)
(d) *Container and contents*	(answer: RAPID)
(e) *Reversal*	(answer: SPIT)
(f) *Hidden*	(answer: ERNE)
(g) *Vocal*	(answer: SENT)
(h) *Subtractive*	(answer: OLDER)

Complex clues. Each of the eight clues above could be described as a *simple* cryptic clue (however hard it is to solve!). A *complex* cryptic clue, on the other hand, includes some combination of more than one technique. Here is a random selection (keyed by the letters above):

(b,c) [8.9] Trails along with legs collapsing after wearisome task (8)

An anagram of 'legs' is 'gles'. Add it to 'drag' and we get DRAGGLES. If you like you can add the S/D notation to see how the clue works, but it's about time you understood the shorthand way that setters use to explain a solution. In this case the solution note would read (drag + anag.). Other notes will be explained as we go along.

(c,h) [8.10] The man has almost finished paved area around a plant (7)

Here the charade incorporates a subsidiary component which has been clued 'subtractively'. The man is 'he'; an 'almost finished paved area' is 'pati' (not quite a patio!) and around is 'c'. The answer is therefore HEPATIC (a liverwort). The note would read (he + pati(o) + c).

(c,d) [8.11] You get dry around bottom of tongue with an American disease (7)

You get 'TT' around 'e' ('bottom' because it is a down clue) with 'an' plus 'US': (e in TT + an + US) gives TETANUS.

(b,d) [8.12] Secular lot are somehow besieging politician (8)

Here we have an abbreviation inside an anagram: (MP in anag.) gives TEMPORAL. Alternatively we could have an anagram inside something else:

(b,d) [8.13] Palatable fruit nasty lice will get into (8)

Here 'nasty lice' = 'elic', and so (anag. in date) gives us DELICATE.

(b,c,d) [8.14] Sweetmeat—kitchenware contains a small amount, cool possibly (5,9)

'Plate' contains 'a' plus 'inch' plus an anagram of cool, 'ocol': (a + inch + anag.) in plate gives PLAIN CHOCOLATE. In this clue we have the formula A contains BC, with both B and C placed inside A. However it is quite possible for A contains BC to mean 'A contains B, then add C' as in this example:

(b,c,d) [8.15] Mathematician worries terribly about Northern fisherman (6,8)

A strange bringing together of concerns? No matter—put an anagram of 'worries' around N, then add 'angler': (N in anag. + angler) gives SENIOR WRANGLER, Cambridge's best maths graduate. You, the solver, would have to sort out whether to put the fisherman inside the anagram or outside. This sort of ambiguity adds a distinct spice to a crossword clue.

(b,c,e) [8.16] Signified dire need after doctor returned (6)

Signified means OMENED and the clue works like this: (MO, rev. + anag.).

(e,f) [8.17] Fairy coming back in dire pantomime (4)

Here we have to look for a word hidden in reverse, and it isn't too hard to spot PERI (hidden, rev.).

(b,h) [8.18] Bread in short supply—unusually scanty (4)

Take (anag. of brea(d)), i.e. an unusual presentation of a short rendering of 'bread', and you get BARE.

(d,e) [8.19] Chaps turned up in the American agency—it should be entertaining (6)

Our note would read (men, rev. in CIA) and the answer is CINEMA.

(c,d,e) [8.20] Women's Libber swallows man up, one man who'd fight (9)

Poor chap! The man is Dan (he could be Les or anybody else, but he isn't). When one (1) is added on and (Ms) Greer does her swallowing, the answer is GRENADIER. Our note would read (Dan, rev. + 1 in (Germaine) Greer). We add the bracketed Germaine, because Ms Greer won't be found in the dictionary.

Clearly we could find yet other combinations of our eight clue techniques, and you can expect to meet others not given here. Deciphering a complex clue is one of the joys of crossword solving.

Linking clues together. In most daily puzzles each clue is separate and independent. The solver has to manage (say) 28 or 32 clues and any linking occurs in the checking of the letters. Sometimes though a setter will attempt to find connections between *clues*. For example, successive clues may be linked together by three dots to suggest a common theme:

[8.21] Now for the give away (7) . . .
[8.22] . . . from me, perhaps, a Spaniard with gold (5)

The answer to the first clue is PRESENT, a simple two-meanings clue—which we would explain in the notes as (2 mngs). Who does a present come from? Answer: a DONOR (don + or). You may not *yet* have learnt that gold = or (the heraldic colour) or possibly Au (the chemical symbol), but I can't tell you everything at once!

Answers may spread across several words at different sites in the puzzle. This was a clue I used in the *Birmingham Evening Mail* (starting at 9 across):

[8.23] 9, 5 down, 1 across, 25 down, 27 across, 22 across. Claim of our paper—exceptional deal, this fine blend reveals many great things (2,3,3,7,7,4,2,3,8).

Three Amazing Stories

The Times did not decide until 1930 to include a daily crossword, and when the go-ahead was given there was no one readily to hand to produce the puzzle. Robert Bell of *The Observer* was approached (he was producing the Everyman puzzle) and he delegated the task to his 28-year-old son Adrian. Adrian had never *solved* a puzzle before, let alone set one! He had ten days to learn and continued setting for over 40 years. Bell's identity was kept secret until a BBC interview in 1970.

One of the early *Daily Telegraph* setters was L. S. Dawe. In 1944 he was visited by members of MI5 who pointed to six suspicious words in his recent puzzles: MULBERRY, NEPTUNE, OMAHA, OVERLORD, PLUTO and UTAH. These words just happened to be code-words for the impending D-Day. Dawe was fortunately able to show MI5 how his crosswords were constructed, thereby convincing them of his innocence.

The Guinness Book of Records tells the story of a lady in Fiji who completed a *Times* crossword in May 1966. What's amazing about that? The puzzle was published on 4th April 1932 and she had been working on it for 34 years!

An anagram of the last eight words gives the catchline on the front page: BY FAR THE LARGEST EVENING SALE IN THE MIDLANDS.

Sometimes there will be cross-referencing between clues all linked by a common theme. Thus, 30 across and 9 down could be linked as follows and the solver may be (mildly) misled into treating 9 as a number in its own right rather than a clue reference:

[8.24] 30. Looked after 9 somehow (6)
[8.25] 9. Separate revolutionary students in rising (6)

9 gives the answer SUNDER (red NUS, rev.) which can somehow give NURSED (anag.), the answer to 30.

This is a simple example. In some puzzles the cross-references can cover half the clues.

It's time for another tutorial. This time you have a complete 15 × 15 with a few complex clues thrown in.

CROSSWORD No. 15

ACROSS

1 Band possibly took horses we hear—route going around city? (4,4)
5 Soul manifest in tipsy cheering (6)
9 Terrible collapse with love deserting—I'm in the operating theatre (7)
10 Fellows in the wrong causing anguish (7)
11 Bit of excitement with a glass of beer he had in frolic? A risky venture (4,2,3,4)
13 Mad artist's characteristics (6)
14 Lessons from the school chaplain? A source of help (8)
16 'Ostel allowed unlimited tea and food (8)
18 Smooth ambassador endlessly getting round (6)
21 Novel with Indian going to America? (5,3,5)
23 Conflict and bombast—what's the justification? (7)
24 Cunning one is turning singer (7)
25 Garden tool has some little worth when brought back (6)
26 Quietly abode—was in the chair (8)

DOWN

1 Concerning the answer you need determination (10)
2 Falls once more upset artist (7)
3 Hate made rip go wild in fit of passion—one should have to make amends (6,3,6)
4 Silver allows metal ornaments to be produced (6)
6 After meal a person gets lively making attempt to do something novel (6,4,5)
7 The scrutineer was a twister in the sixties (7)
8 'Enrietta, a painter (4)
10 Propositions from the session just over half way through (6)
12 Part of watch that isn't new (not seen in digital variety!) (6,4)
15 Start of storm—and oak perhaps will come down on top of the thoroughfare (6)
17 Order to forbid some who grab men turning up (7)
19 A long time before Edward got 'airy'? (7)
20 Examiner of films possibly upset crones (6)
22 Marbles must be given up—prepare for exam (4)

Additional Challenge

Take the word PALE and see if you can use each of the clue types listed on p.48 to write a clue for it. The reverse clue can be a reverse charade *(e,c)*. For good measure, try two charades and a reverse hidden. Then compare your list with mine on p.69.

CROSSWORD No.15

9

The & Lit. Clue

Take a good look at this clue:

[9.1] I'm one involved with cost (9)

Can you solve it? Where is the definition? Well, it reads like one, doesn't it? In that case where's the subsidiary indication? Perhaps it's an anagram of 'I'm one' all mixed up ('involved') with 'cost'—which *would* give nine letters. But if that's the case, where's the definition? Let's pursue the anagram line. Keep juggling and you'll see ECONOMIST. Now read the clue again and you'll see that the whole clue is *also* a definition. If we use our S/D notation we can analyse the clue thus:

I'm one involved with cost (9)

A clue like this is known to crossworders as an '& lit.', and this particular clue would be given the solution note (anag. & lit.). What this means is that the clue offers us an anagram *and* a literal definition all in one. The & lit. clue has a special sort of appeal all its own. Before we consider some other examples let's look at a clue which is *not* an '& lit.':

[9.2] Mint perhaps in gel? It can be refreshing (7)

The answer is SHERBET: (herb in set, v.).
   The letter v. denotes 'verb', by the way. Now the statement inherent in the clue *may be literally true* when you eat a glacier mint, but that does *not* make the clue an & lit. because the part up to the question-mark is S and the remainder D. *Only* clues when the S and D are together are true & lits. What about the following clue, then?

[9.3] Denomination spreading abroad 'Christ doeth much'? (9,6)

The last three words may be spread abroad and we see that they are an anagram of METHODIST CHURCH. The first word is clearly a definition and yet the whole clue also gives a definition—an 'enhanced' definition, in fact. We could analyse the clue as follows:

Denomination spreading abroad 'Christ doeth much' (9,6)

```
|___D___||_____S_____|
|_____D^e_____|
```

where D^e stands for 'enhanced definition'. Since in this clue D^e and S overlap for much of the clue I will term this a 'semi & lit.' rather than a true & lit. It can be turned into a true & lit. though:

[9.4] It spreads abroad 'Christ doeth much' (9,6)

```
|_____D_____|
|_____S_____|
```

In this case I prefer the '& lit.' version to the 'semi & lit.', but the 'semi & lit.' is a legitimate type of clue which may be preferred, especially if the & lit. definition is deemed too vague (more on this later). Now we have seen what an & lit. is and what it is not. We have also seen that there is a sort of halfway-house between a normal clue and the & lit. which we have called a 'semi & lit.'.

Now let's continue the chapter looking at some more 'pure' & lits.:

[9.5] Leaders of various individual congregations (alternatively rectors sometimes) (6)

Take the first letters (leaders) to give VICARS. This is not (anag. & lit.) but (first letters & lit.). A very easy clue, this—not just because it is easy to pick out all the initial letters, but because the definition sense is completely obvious. This is a danger with the & lit. clue—it can sometimes look like a childishly simple definition rather than a cryptic clue.

Another danger with the & lit. clue is that the intended definition sense can be too vague. Here is an extreme example:

[9.6] Andrew could become this (6)

This is a very bad attempt at an anag. & lit. to give WARDEN. Little Andy could become a bus conductor or a brain surgeon (or even a crossword setter!). The definition is somewhat remote, to say the least! But the clue becomes perfectly respectable (even if uninspired) when we stop trying to be too clever and put in a definition:

[9.7] Andrew could become a guard (6)

In the last page or two we have started to criticize clues, and there will be more of this to come in the next chapter. Before we get to that, however, let's have a look at some better & lits. using different clue types. Then it will be time for you to do a little more work:

[9.8] Part of it 'it an iceberg (7)

Answer, TITANIC (hidden & lit.).

[9.9] This language would be strange for Senor (5)

This semi anag. & lit. gives NORSE.

[9.10] One may be found in church (8)

(I in MINSTER & lit.) gives MINISTER.

[9.11] The reverse of a divine fellow? (3)

DOG is the reverse of a god in more ways than one, so this is (rev. & lit.).

Can you spot the & lits. in your next tutorial puzzle?

CROSSWORD No. 16

Games and Puzzles Competition winner by D. F. Manley, June 1977

ACROSS

1 Rooms on view in publishing house favoured by crossword fans (8)
5 Difficulty can be severe, going around centre of maze (6)
9 There's mud—it's a messy sports ground (7)
10 Spiteful woman's dad was primarily a stooge (7)
11 Reptile upsetting a girl a lot (9)
12 Low in generosity to some extent, being in debt (5)
13 Two-faced crook who would spoil his ballot paper? (6-7)
16 True leader of rectors always to be found at the close? (5,8)
20 Something for ploughing an allotment? (5)
21 Disturbances due to unruly brute in horse race (9)
23 Resentment from someone ineffective having gone mad (7)
24 Girl, East European, is dance's centre of attraction (7)
25 Wine can make you reticent about sin (6)
26 Vague notions from learner in fashionable Cambridge college (8)

DOWN

1 Wise man taking vehicle around Bath perhaps (6)
2 I went ahead after girl helped (7)
3 Uses the telephone at that place in the pub—gets through finally? (6,2,3,4)

CROSSWORD No.16

4 Set up a watch maybe—or relax (5)

6 Moon or a star? Ryle would get excited, being this (10,5)

7 Adult w-works vigorously—tries for new job? (7)

8 Imposing old ladies arrange bets (8)

10 Boat specified by Conservative pundit (7)

14 Offer no resistance, confess, having told fibs at first (3,4)

15 Editor, one turning up surrounded by journalists, takes the chair (8)

17 Dreadfully enraged nobleman (7)

18 Fierce character embracing love is a soldier (7)

19 Estimate the worth of a female twit? (6)

22 Tiny chap broadcasting, an Athenian (5)

10

More on Fair Play

In the last chapter we found ourselves criticizing particular & lit. clues. And now we are going to look critically at clues in general. So far we have been learning about different clue types. This is all rather like learning about parts of speech—nouns, verbs, adjectives and so on. Now we must consider something rather like grammar and syntax.

First of all, another historical diversion. We left the history six or seven chapters ago with the advent of the cryptic clue and its gradual development from the twenties and thirties. Is is now time to introduce three famous names. The first is Torquemada of the *Observer*. He is the setter credited with the advent of the cryptic clue. Born Edward Powys Mather, he dominated the scene in the thirties so far as extra hard cryptics are concerned, but at times his puzzles were unsolvable. We shall return to Torquemada later.

While Torquemada was teasing *The Observer*'s readers in the thirties another crossword setter was exploring new crossword possibilities in *The Listener*. Prebendary A. F. Ritchie of Wells Cathedral took the pseudonym Afrit (an Arabian demon), and he too on occasion was able to produce puzzles that attracted *no* correct entries! But Afrit was a pioneer, and when after the Second World War he turned his attention to the theory of crosswords he laid the foundation on which Ximenes was to build so successfully.

Torquemada died in 1939 and his eventual successor was Derrick Somerset Macnutt, a classics master at Christ's Hospital, Horsham, who took the name Ximenes (another inquisitor). We shall meet Ximenes and his successor Azed in Chapter 16. Afrit and Ximenes can be regarded as the 'lawmakers', the codifiers who brought order and discipline to a pastime that might otherwise have got out of hand. Inasmuch as many papers and magazines still 'break the rules' Afrit and Ximenes have not entirely succeeded. Indeed there are some crossword setters who positively delight in being non-Ximenean (unorthodox) against those who are Ximenean (orthodox). Your writer is firmly in the Ximenean camp.

Afrit's book of *Armchair Crosswords* was published in 1949. In a preface Ximenes commends Afrit thus: 'The crossworld world may be trivial, but like greater worlds it needs standards, and Afrit is the man to set them.' The next few pages contain an Introduction by Afrit which mentions *The Book of the Crossword*, an 'exhaustive treatise' which 'has not been written'. In his section on clues we discover Afrit's Injunction, appropriately culled from Alice (how appropriate indeed when Lewis Carroll was such a marvellous forerunner of the modern crossword setter!). This is what Afrit says:

> We must expect the composer to play tricks, but we shall insist that he play fair. *The Book of the Crossword* lays this injunction upon him: 'You need not mean what you say, but you must say what you mean.' This is a superior way of saying that he can't have it both ways. He may attempt to mislead by employing a form of words which can be taken in more than one way, and it is your fault if you take it the wrong way, *but it is his fault if you can't logically take it the right way.* The solver, for his part, is enjoined to read the clues in an anti-Pickwickian sense. This also requires explanation. To take a remark in a Pickwickian sense is not to take it literally; therefore, to read a clue in an anti-Pickwickian sense is to close the mind to the acquired metaphorical meaning of the words and to concentrate upon their bald literal significance. If you do so, you may find you are being presented with an anagram of the solution, or that the solution is 'hidden' in the clue, or a bit of jugglery with its component parts is being done.

In other words: the solver who follows the structure of a clue literally should expect to discover a grammatical set of coded instructions leading to the answer.

A crossword clue is rather like a mathematical sum. The symbolism must be fair to lead the solver to the correct answer. The concept of fairness was further developed by Ximenes through his clue-writing competitions in *The Observer* and his book *Ximenes on the Art of the Crossword*. In fact the post-1949 developments now make many of Afrit's own clues in *Armchair Crosswords* look suspect! We shall follow in Ximenes' footsteps by looking at unfair clues and comparing them with fairer equivalents. Here we go.

[10.1] Small pebbles—English (7)

This is supposed to give an anagram of English, namely SHINGLE, but the clue is a breach of Afrit's Injunction because the clue-writer has omitted an anagram indicator. This is a case of the *unindicated anagram*. The clue may be rendered 'sound' by the addition of a suitable indicator:

[10.2] Small pebbles—possibly English (7)

might do, though 'possibly' is weak—and, incidentally, most Ximeneans would find 'perhaps' too weak. The clue might be better as:

[10.3] Broken English pebbles on the beach (7)

By no means a great clue, but a sound one, and this is important. Indeed it is particularly important for the novice setter who, like an overkeen young fast bowler, may be inclined to lose 'line and length'.

Here is a clue which may look all right at first sight, but which a Ximenean would regard as a no-ball:

[10.4] English mixture on the beach (7)

Two things are wrong here. First we have an *unsatisfactory noun as anagram indicator*. There is no grammatical or syntactical justification to suggest that 'English mixture' can mean 'mixture of English'. In contrast, 'gin cocktail' which *means* 'a mixed gin' could be used to indicate 'ing'. Similarly 'train crash' would be acceptable as a subsidiary indicator for RIANT (an example given by Ximenes himself). Secondly 'on the beach' is an *unsatisfactory definition*. An adverbial phrase (which this is) cannot be used to define a noun. Here is [10.4] rewritten:

[10.5] Mixture of English pebbles on the beach (7)

A clue such as the one following should cause the umpire to have a word with the bowler's captain!

[10.6] Small pebbles possibly coming from the country (7)

This sort of structure has often been referred to as a *clue to a clue* and this particular example is an *indirect anagram*. The solver is expected to equate 'coming from the country' with 'English' and *then* work out an anagram. He may get *the* right answer from the definition and the checked letters but to deduce 'English' and then work out an anagram is too much, because there are simply so many alternatives to English: Turkish and bucolic are just two! And of course any letters already in the diagram cannot easily be fed into the working out of the subsidiary indication. However, some would find the following clue quite defensible:

[10.7] Concerning what diet might become, it's seasonal (5)

Written by your author for the *Radio Times* this clue was meant to suggest TIDAL (i.e. of tide, which is an anagram of diet). Since 'diet' can only become two different words ('tide' and 'edit'), *perhaps* the clue may be deemed fair. [10.7] may perhaps be termed an *indirect definition*.

Here are three more indirect clues sanctioned by *The Times*:

[10.8] Country with its capital in Czechoslovakia (6)

[10.9] Novel sounds as if it will never be read (7,5)

[10.10] Half-hearted robber found in kitchen (7)

The answers are NORWAY (the capital in Czechoslovakia being Oslo); FOREVER AMBER (it will never be 'red'); DRESSER ('robber' becomes 'rober').

Are these fair? Perhaps they are if you consider that they lead to *unique* solutions. I am not personally very keen on the *indirect homophone* (e.g. [10.9]), but it is common, and an unexpected clue type can add spice. Naughty but nice?

There is no excuse whatever for the following clue:

[10.11] What English could produce (7)

The answer is again supposed to be SHINGLE, but we have no indication of the definition—an *undefined answer*! Even worse would be the *indirect, undefined answer* in a case like this:

[10.12] What English could produce (6)

where the setter intends the answer to be GRAVEL. The inexperienced clue-writer might argue thus: '"English" could produce "shingle", and "gravel" means "shingle". What's wrong with that?' Let me tell my hypothetical friend. (1) There is no definition to the clue, and (2) the subsidiary indication leads not to the answer but to a clue to the answer. All *very* unsatisfactory!

Here are two further clues with unsatisfactory definitions:

[10.13] Brief affair with a lassie? (8,5)

The answer is supposed to be HIGHLAND FLING. This would be a clever idea for a subsidiary indication but the true meaning of 'Highland fling' is 'Scottish dance' and something like that would have to be incorporated into the clue. [10.13] is what I would term a *spurious definition*.

[10.14] HIJKLMNO (5)

This clue consists of the sequence H to O. Say 'H to O' and it sounds like 'H_2O', which everyone knows is WATER. This may seem ingenious, but to my mind this *indirect pun* is simply a nonsense. That sequence of eight letters simply cannot define WATER, and it does not pass muster in the same way that clue [3.18] does, in my opinion. I know that one or two crossword editors have quoted [10.14] as their favourite clue, but I must part company with them.

Sometimes a clue-writer will provide an *inaccurate definition*. One way of doing this is by *false generalization*. A couple of examples will suffice to illustrate this:

[10.15] Month in East for the saint (9)

clearly gives Augustine (August + in + E), but now look at this clue:

[10.16] Dreadful stain produced by Augustine (5)

The intended answer is SAINT, but this won't do because while 'saint' can define a particular saint (i.e. Augustine), 'Augustine' cannot define 'saint'. Because the saint (who produced this mysterious stain!) might have been Matthew, Mark, Luke or John, we must qualify 'Augustine'. Three common ways of doing this are:

[10.17] Dreadful stain produced by Augustine? (5)

[10.18] Dreadful stain produced by Augustine maybe (5)

[10.19] Dreadful stain produced by Augustine perhaps (5)

Another way of providing an inaccurate definition is by indicating an *incorrect part of speech*:

[10.20] What's hidden by Fred afterwards? He must be stupid! (4)

The S part of this clue is straightforward. The answer is DAFT. But what about the last few words? They suggest a definition that is a noun rather than an adjective—say TWIT or FOOL. A clue-writer will often want to 'dress up' his clue to make sense but won't know how to tie in the D with the S. In difficulty he adds extra words ('He must be'), then tries to convince himself that the clue is really quite good by sticking an *unnecessary exclamation mark* at the end (an additional fault in itself). When you think about it, clue [10.20] is indeed daft. If we must stick with this idea, though, and we want to produce a sound clue we could try this version:

[10.21] What Fred afterwards conceals is stupid (4)

Clue [10.20] is evidence of another affliction suffered by the inexperienced, the *redundant word syndrome*. The following clue is supposed to give the answer DORSET:

[10.22] Strode out to where Hardy lived (6)

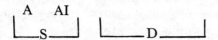

The trouble is that 'to' fulfils no syntactical function in the clue. It is not a legitimate link word between the S and D parts denoting equivalence (such as 'for' or 'in'); it is merely there to make the whole clue read better. A better version is:

[10.23] Strode out where Hardy lived (6)

Before we leave the subject of redundant words, let's take a fresh look at two clues from an earlier chapter:

[7.3] Good man, a sailor lying on bed, wounded (7)

The answer, remember, is STABBED (St. + AB + bed). Isn't the 'a' redundant? In a sense it is, but by a long-standing convention we may allow ourselves to introduce the indefinite or definite article when defining a noun.

[7.4] Bob has to study for the exam—buzz off! (5)

SCRAM consists of S + cram, and here we have defined cram by 'to study' in the way that a dictionary might. In fact the 'to' in the infinitive could be deemed redundant, but convention allows us to use it.

Here is another wide delivery from our overkeen and wayward fast bowler:

[10.24] Sykes is found in the United States of America (4)

This hidden clue to ERIC can't justify all those extra words where our comedian *isn't* lurking, so let's make it snappier:

[10.25] Sykes is found in America (4)

If a crossword setter can put too many words in his clue he can also put in too few:

[10.26] Fred in a bad way? A mate is required (6)

An anagram of 'Fred in' suggests itself fairly quickly: FRIEND which means mate. But look carefully. The word 'in' is doing *double duty* as part of the phrase to be anagrammed *and* the anagram indicator. The clue should really read 'Fred in in a bad way'—it is 'Fred in' that is 'in a bad way', not just Fred. What about the right-hand side of the clue? After all I have said about redundant words, wouldn't 'mate' suffice? Yes—but the extra words can be justified syntactically. The solver is telling you 'You require a word meaning mate,' so the extra words do fulfil a function as a legitimate instruction to the solver. If we want to rewrite the clue soundly let's try this version:

[10.27] Fred in muddle. A mate is required (6)

At first sight this may look like another example of double duty: 'Fred in' in (a) muddle. Or it may look as though we have an unsatisfactory noun as the anagram indicator (see [10.4] above on p.60). But this clue *can* be justified: 'muddle' is an *acceptable intransitive verb*: the words 'Fred in' muddle, i.e. 'potter about', to produce the answer.

Contrast [10.27] with this:

[10.28] Fred in difficulty—a mate is required (6)

A clue-writer might try to argue that 'in' is *not* doing double duty. The clue is meant to suggest that there is difficulty with the words 'Fred in'. This is not Mr Macmillan's 'little local' difficulty but a 'Fred in' difficulty. A true Ximenean will regard this as stretching the language too far: the clue suffers from the same fault as [10.4].

Here is another way in which an anagram could be improperly indicated:

[10.29] The East has lad striking a bargain (4)

The word 'striking' is the anagram indicator and we are supposedly asked to form an anagram from E and lad to give DEAL. The word 'has' is quite unfairly misleading however. It is true that East is somehow 'involved' with lad in the anagram, but 'has' is grammatically misleading.

It's easy to make the clue sound:

[10.30] Eastern lad striking a bargain (4)

and

[10.31] Lad involved with Eastern bargain (4)

are both possible.

In [10.30] we have treated 'has' as a redundant word; in [10.31] we have integrated the anagram letters with the anagram indicator in a syntactically accurate way.

The unsatisfactory anagram indicator is a particular example of what we might call *word abuse* (for want of a better phrase). Types of word abuse are best illustrated by individual examples:

[10.32] An accomplishment indeed to be beaten (8)

This is supposed to give FEAT in DEED = DEFEATED. Ximeneans say that 'indeed' in a clue does not equal 'in deed' (two separate words). Not all setters agree (alas).

Here are two clues with similar difficulties:

[10.33] Peruse in Gateshead—or somewhere in Berkshire (7)

The intended answer is READING (read in g) but Gateshead = G is taking too great a liberty with the language say Ximeneans (even if G is head of the word 'gate').

[10.34] The cold season now in Bury (5)

This is supposed to suggest INTER (winter with no W). The Ximeneans rightly assert that 'now' cannot equal 'no W' in a clue. Notice too that Bury has a capital B which it shouldn't really have. The *false capital*, is a very minor offence (if it is an offence at all), but see how we can overcome the difficulty and the 'now' problem by putting Bury at the beginning of the clue:

[10.35] Bury in the cold season, no hint of warmth (5)

The cold season (winter) with no hint of warmth (w) gives INTER.

The same convention applies to 'hint' and words of that type as applies to 'bit' (see p.45). It should indicate *only* the first letter. Similarly with the tail. Ximenes has an amusing example of an unsound clue where this is not so:

[10.36] There's a horse in the stable with a lion's tail (8)

The answer is STALLION (stall + (l)ion), but as Ximenes says, 'why should a lion have a tail three times as long as the rest of him?'

Middles must be precisely middles, too, says Ximenes, so this would not pass muster:

[10.37] Active learner at heart of Universe (4)

The supposed answer is LIVE (L + (Un)ive(rse)) but the *heart* of UNIVERSE is 've' or even 'iver', *not* 'ive'.

The next example is perhaps the most oft-quoted of all clues adjudged unsound by Ximenes:

[10.38] I am in the plot, that's clear (5)

The intended answer is PLAIN ('i' in 'plan'), but 'I' is the letter, not the pronoun. To overcome the deliberate ambiguity we can change the form of the verb and of course we can change 'I' to 'One'. Here are just some of the ways by which [10.38] can be rendered sound:

[10.39]

$$\left\{ \begin{array}{c} I \\ One \end{array} \right\} \left\{ \begin{array}{c} \text{will be} \\ \text{must be} \\ \text{can be seen} \\ \text{should be} \end{array} \right\} \quad \text{in the plot, that's clear (5)}$$

Curiously enough, though Ximeneans do *not* allow the word 'I' to assume a personal status, a word or cluster of words can develop human characteristics:

[10.40] Rescue reviled drunk (7)

The word 'reviled' is 'drunk', i.e. in a disorderly condition, giving the answer DELIVER. Notice how 'reviled' is an adjective in the meaning reading of the clue and 'drunk' is a noun—but in the actual cryptic reading these parts of speech are reversed. This is a nice example of Afrit's Injunction.

One very common error is that of the *wrong direction*. Consider this clue for example:

[10.41] Dull poet coming back (4)

This is all right for an *across* clue but *not* for a *down* clue. The letters of 'bard' are 'reversed' to form the answer DRAB, but they should go back in an across word and up in a down word. So a better version for a down clue would be:

[10.42] Dull poet turned up (4)

If for some reason a crossword setter had a brilliant clue involving 'up' (and 'back' would not do), he could change the diagram by making all the across words 'down' and down words across. A drastic measure, but one which your author has resorted to a few times.

In some crosswords you will find almost any Roman numeral defined by 'many' (L possibly, C, D and M certainly). Thus:

[10.43] Many aged suffering from hypothermia (4)

Here, 'many' is supposed to suggest C (=100); C+old=COLD. But by what criterion is a hundred equal to 'many'? Ximenes certainly didn't like this practice, and I don't think he would have liked this clue either:

[10.44] Note ancient brave (4)

Here you are presumably invited to take cognizance of a revered figure by his tepee, and B + old = BOLD. But a note could be A, B, C, D, E, F or G (not to mention DO, RE, MI, FA, SO, LA, TI with all their variant spellings!). If notes are plentiful, so too are directions:

[10.45] Direction to have a meal—get a chair (4)

It's quite easy (S + eat = SEAT), but there are lots of directions if you box the compass from N, NE, round to NW. I haven't got a name for what is wrong with these last three clues. Shall we call it the *many/note/direction syndrome*?

This clue shows another offence against the spirit of Ximenes:

[10.46] First chap, aged, frigid (4)

This time 'first chap' is supposed to indicate 'C', but grammatically this just doesn't work—'first chap' cannot mean the 'first letter of chap'. But it isn't difficult to write a *sound* clue:

[10.47] Leader of chaps, aged, frigid (4)

Not exciting, but an accurate clue for COLD.

Next a few words on punctuation. You will already have noticed how the D and S parts of a clue can be juxtaposed without any punctuation (as in [10.40] above). The Ximenean convention is to allow the omission of punctuation but not to allow inaccurate punctuation. This would amount to word abuse. The presentation of 'Gateshead' for 'gate's head' could be deemed an example of this, but there are other dreadful possibilities usually reserved for the more difficult cryptics with the words 'Punctuation may be misleading' in the preamble.

Watch out for this sort of thing:

[10.48] Stage love-in—Shakespeare setting initially? (6)

'Stage' is the definition for BOARDS (O in bard + s). The addition of the hyphen and the dash undoubtedly helps to make sense of a sequence of the six words, but this constitutes a case of *unfair* punctuation in breach of Afrit's Injunction. The clue must be recast to make it sound.

I have left until last the type of clue that is sound but meaningless. It is quite possible to write a clue which is 'fair' under the conditions laid down in this chapter) but which is still unsatisfactory.

[10.49] Floor covering fish—and Parisian! (6)

The answer is CARPET (carp + et). Yes, this is fair in terms of its construction, but in what *context* would this gibberish mean anything—and does the clue-writer hope we will enjoy this nonsense by adding an exclamation mark? Here is the *nonsensical clue*, and it is a type that many crossword clue-writers (especially novices) find difficult to avoid. Clues must make sense, or even semi-sense, but not *non*sense.

We have dwelt on the matter of fair play at some length, because the crossword solver who aspires to become a crossword setter often gets into great difficulty in creating a sound clue. If you should ever attempt clue-writing for yourself, I hope this chapter will point you in the right direction. Now try the tutorial puzzle, where I *hope* all the clues are sound.

A filler on fillers

This little article is a filler, an extra topic slotted in to fill an awkward gap. Some words in crossword grids could also be described as 'fillers'.

Imagine the crossword setter filling in the grid. At the outset, everything looks possible – nice long phrases (OVER THE MOON, OUT FOR THE COUNT), long and interesting words (STAGE-WHISPER, POWER-STATION). All too soon, though, the setter is faced with E–T–A. It has to be EXTRA, a word he or she has written a clue for several times before (usually something to do with an extra run at cricket or a jobbing actor). EXTRA is a filler, a word that the crossworder can't escape from. Here are some more five-letter words beginning with E in the same category: EASEL, ELAND, ELOPE, ENSUE, ERASE, ERATO, EVOKE. And what can you do with I–A–E? IMAGE, INAME, IRATE (and IRADE, if that isn't too hard a word). And look – here's R–D–O. Last time it was RADIO, so this time we'll fill in RODEO (oh, not rode+O again, *please*!). If you are a setter, beware of the five-letter words beginning with E! No one likes coming up with a sixth clue for ENSUE – one is bad enough.

Grids are, of course, to blame – but, as we note elsewhere (p. 86), –A–E– and –R–T– would seem to offer the solver too many possibilities. No doubt about it – five-letter words are a problem.

There are fillers of other lengths too. Expect to find ELEMENT and EVEREST frequently, especially along the edge. And in barrel puzzles you'll soon learn about EATH (an old word meaning 'easy') and EALE ((*Shak.*, Hamlet I, iv, 36) *n.* various conjectures, generally supposed to be for evil, but perhaps a misprint).

Dear solver, forgive the setters their fillers. Learn to regard them as old friends.

TEN CLUES FOR PALE
(see Challenge on p.52)

(a) Whitish stake of wood.

(b) Leap frantically looking ill?

(c) Soft drink wanting in colour (p + ale).
Friend needs a bit of expertise to make part of fence (pal + e).

(d) Albert in Physical Education is not looking well, maybe (Al in PE).

(e, c) Eastern circuit goes around wooden post ((E + lap), rev.)

(f) Sup ales—partly making you lose colour? (pale, verb).

(f, e) Wooden post in hotel apparently rejected (rejected = sent back).

(g) Whitish bucket, we hear ('pail').

(h) Bill coming out of palace looking ashen (palace minus a/c, a/c = account, bill).

CROSSWORD No. 17

By Duck from *The Hamlyn Book of Crosswords No. 1*

ACROSS

1 The French doctor and essayist (4)
4 A cricket club's umpire saying 'Exit sir'! initially points the finger (7)
10 Possibly a group of extremist pop fans is coming around the party afterwards (9)
11 See nurse rummaging to some extent for fluid to inject (5)
12 See thin fragments in food being obtained beside a street—this sort of food? (7,8)
13 There's a shortage of salt passing through a plant (6)
14 A boy stuck in marsh plant used logic (8)
16 Whole large tin exploded (8)
18 Nothing in swimming pools? That's an anticlimax (6)
21 A long struggle. Representing us: Edward R. and a Henry (7,5,3)
23 Ignorant learner must have external restraint (5)
24 Firm newspaperman, anything but apathetic (9)
25 Relax almost completely in lodgings and introduce red herrings (7)
26 Artist left cathedral city (4)

DOWN

2 Rousing a fellow in a side-section of the building (9)
3 He produces booze in a little brown jug (6)
4 Satisfy an appetite perhaps with grilled sausage (7)
5 Actors we hear in the class (5)
6 Sign of future developments in London street appearing round top half of window, ghastly white (5,2,3,4)
7 The dog will reform someday (7)
8 Endlessly talk about a field event (6)
9 Party putting up for election makes 'class' the issue (6, 8)
15 Tries messing about with wall—a difficult region for the home decorator (9)
16 A bloke at first opulent, losing head—the glory has departed (7)
17 Forcibly removes tar on pipes (7)
19 Violins producing sort of jazz on board (6)
20 Plant's a sensation with double dose of nitrogen in (6)
22 Mountain range, head of Glencoe—make journey round (5)

CROSSWORD No. 17

11

Crossword Lingo

**Definitions, Anagram indicators, Other indicators,
Some 'give-away' words**

We have now covered all the main clue types that you can expect to
meet in a 'daily cryptic' crossword. Much of our attention has been
focused on the 'grammar' of crossword clues. In this chapter we are
going to focus briefly on vocabulary. When faced with the series of
words in a clue you need to know what to look for. You will ask
yourself lots of questions: Are these words the definition? Is the setter
telling us to put one word inside another? What does 'about' mean
here? The comma comes here, but is this where the definition and
subsidiary indication are divided? Why has the setter used a question
mark here? And so on.

  Definitions. For the most part we have concentrated on subsidiary
indications and taken the definition for granted. Take the word
CAPTAIN. A dictionary definition begins thus: 'a head or chief
officer: the commander of a troop of horse, a company of infantry, a
ship, or a portion of a ship's company.' In providing a definition for a
cryptic clue we can either (i) provide a *straight definition:*

[11.1] Commander with army in awful panic (7)

(TA in anag.)

or (ii) provide a *cryptic description* (based here on a cricket captain's
function):

[11.2] 'Pa, I can't! That's wrong!' he may declare (7)

(anag. with the misleading context of George Washington?)

or (iii) provide a *definition by example:*

[11.3] Cook? Starts to prepare the added ingredients to be put into
container (7)

(ptai in can with another misleading context—think of Captain
Cook).

[11.3] shows us how the crossword setter's lingo often relies on
double meanings. Vocabulary may be specially selected to mislead—but
only within the framework of Afrit's Injunction!

Anagram indicators. It is not long before a crossword solver learns
to recognize anagram indicators. There are hundreds of words at a
crossword setter's disposal: 'strange', 'unusual', 'terrible' are common
adjectives; also used are the corresponding adverbs ('strangely' etc.).
A setter may refer to 'a mixture of' something or talk about
something being 'cooked' or 'ruined'. And so on. But beware of
'upset' which can indicate reversal in a down word.

'Upset' is indeed an ambiguous word as the following examples
show:

[11.4] Light at night has upset these rodents (4)

Answer: RATS (star, rev.).

[11.5] Rats upset Russian emperor (4)

Answer: TSAR (anag.).

'Around' and *'about'* are likewise ambiguous—even more so in fact.
Consider these clues with 'about':

[11.6] Banter about a fibber (4)

Answer: LIAR (rev. of rail).

[11.7] The manner shown by chaps about one (4)

Answer: MIEN (I in men).

[11.8] Fastening device about source of light (5)

Answer: CLAMP (c. + lamp).

[11.9] About to get single girl, being lax (6)

Answer: REMISS (re + miss).

In these four examples we see how the word 'about' can indicate
two types of clue or be part of a subsidiary indication.

'In'. This too can be a troublesome little word, which the solver
must learn to interpret:

[11.10] Girl found in cloisters (4)

Answer: LOIS (hidden).

[11.11] Mean not to go in the river (6)

Answer: DENOTE (not in Dee).

[11.12] Setter let loose in thoroughfare (6)

Answer: STREET (anag.) with 'in' simply acting as a link word between the subsidiary indication and the definition.

Other indicators. You know now that 'we hear' means a pun and you will spot reversal indicators such as 'returning' and 'coming back' quite easily. Something 'getting' something might suggest a charade and something 'outside' something could suggest a container-and-contents clue. Recognizing the indicators, like everything else, comes with practice.

Some 'give-away' words for short subsidiary components. Attempt a daily cryptic and you will enter a world preoccupied with directions (north = N, etc.), numbers (hundred = C, etc.), and a more-than-usual interest in the French (LA, LE, LES). American soldiers may have gone home after the War, but the good old GI still appears in the back pages of our papers. Indeed there is something of a military preoccupation with gunners (RA), engineers (RE), volunteers (TA) and so on. Crosswords may be square, but they often have sex-appeal (IT or SA) which may please a sailor (AB or TAR usually). A worker is regarded as less than human (ANT), but great consideration is shown to the doctor (DR, GP, MB, MD, MO—a health centre practice where you don't know which one you will get). 'Political' neutrality is achieved with a fair balance between left (L) and right (R), though the Conservative (C) party has more seats in the grid than Labour (LAB) which still lags behind the Liberal (L) party.

If you want a longer vocabulary, look at Appendix 1. The bibliography (Appendix 2) also includes crossword dictionaries. It is impossible, however, to tell you *everything*—and I only hope that I haven't told you too much, for one of the joys of crossword puzzles is to learn the language for yourself. I've got another tutorial for you on p. 76.

Letter to *The Observer*, 11 July 1971:

XIMENES

'It just won't do,' said the angel crew,
'To go on with our present compilers:
It's getting much harder for Torquemada
And Afrit can no longer beguile us.

'The judging, too, has gone all askew
And the lists grow quite absurd;
A crafty sinner was last month's winner,
With God's clue only third.'

'I'm on your side,' St. Peter cried,
'I'd hoped for a V.H.C.,
And the last bit of luck for old Habakkuk
Was in 1953.'

So loud and long the heavenly throng
Debated some fresh nominees:
Then with one voice they agreed on a choice—
And sent for Ximenes.

N. C. Dexter (Oxford)

CROSSWORD No. 18
By Quixote from *The Independent*

ACROSS

1 Put upon others, little devil does wrong (7)
5 Old soldier detained in Newport Hospital (7)
9 Note friend hardly at all (9)
10 Virginia's not well inside the house (5)
11 Golf course—after a little time man gets a round in (5)
12 Mediocre journalist announced requirement to be trite (9)
14 Tar making one tarry! (7,7)
17 Where records of matches are kept (8,6)
21 Luminous fish, one six-footer! (9)
23 A green? He wants to _____ eco-disaster! (5)
24 Get to know Edward by name (5)
25 Thy crimes found out? The forensic bods use this! (9)
26 Give back to stock again (7)
27 Beast making the lady gasp at first (7)

DOWN

1 Favoured friend, someone imprisoned (6)
2 Is this card game bridge? Yes and no (7)
3 I'll help make the meaning clear— but I can't mess about! (9)
4 We offer spectacular entertainment—see lad hop in air acrobatically (11)
5 Money received brings a little power always (3)
6 Sailors will hang around an avenue for a bird . . . (5)
7 . . . Henry's caught that peaceful bird (7)
8 Flag to be situated overlooking a road (8)
13 Some top chap spouted a lot of rubbish! (7,4)
15 Increase in business has someone in the family collecting francs (9)
16 A footballer from the cradle? (8)
18 Could they render airs with gut? (7)
19 Sounds like a dishonest boundah, a beast! (7)
20 One to keep trying—gets part of the way to the top, we hear (6)
22 Performed slowly in sullen tones (5)
25 Line needing to be heard? (3)

CROSSWORD No. 18

12

More on Diagrams

In Chapter 2 we defined what we meant by 'checked' and 'unchecked' squares and we saw how the cryptic puzzle moved quickly from a closed diagram to an open diagram. It is time to look at diagrams in a little more detail and in doing so give you the chance to have a few more tutorials.

The most common size for an everyday cryptic is 15 × 15 and the diagram will usually be based on the lattice shown below:

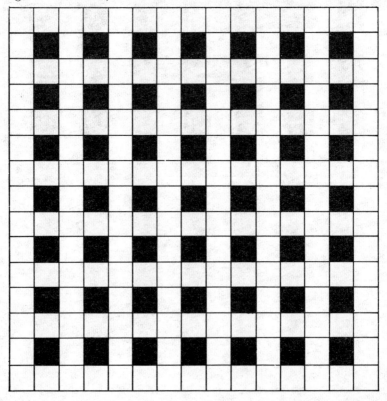

Extra squares will then be blocked out to divide words off and the result will usually be a puzzle of 28, 30 or 32 clues. The 28 formula is regarded as ideal because it offers four long words or phrases and a range of answer lengths down to 4 or 5 letters. It is also possible to blank out the squares in either of these ways:

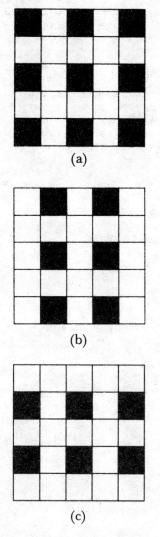

(a)

(b)

(c)

(Diagram (c) amounts to the same thing as Diagram (b) turned through 90 degrees.) The two puzzles which follow show grids based on these lattices.

CROSSWORD No. 19

By Quixote from *The Independent on Sunday*

ACROSS

7 No summer in guest-house would be complete without this cake (8)

9 Each flower is placed in dry kitchen vessel (6)

10 Dress is needed by the Spanish star (5)

11 Ate bits of nut ground extra small within fancy diet (8)

12 Lets out a secret and causes a problem in the kitchen? (6,3,5)

15 Useless beer—died after a couple of rounds (2-4)

16 What did Henry swallow? (Think of King, in pain!) (6)

18 Scientist to perform with hesitation when there's another (similar?) scientist around (14)

20 What 18 down could be? It's arrived (6,2)

22 There's little right in a fever—it makes one get heated maybe (5)

24 Soft further on in the day? That'll suit poor horse (6)

25 Disgusting mince pies—one rejected sample (8)

DOWN

1 Prefab in tract of land (parking included) (8)

2 Enclosure must be sound (4)

3 Fairy shut up to die (6)

4 Guns set up for animal to be hunted (4)

5 New gold chairs? Disgusting! (10)

6 You'll get wind when accompanying uninteresting person (6)

8 Endoscopy now helps surgeon remove it—Galen lost out! (9)

13 Reason US soldier is stationed in a particular place (10)

14 Amazon weapon? (9)

17 Domestic device makes runny marge set (3,5)

18 One provides cover by bringing in bread (6)

19 Upper section of pillar shows tribute (6)

21 Female artist needing work initially (4)

23 Endless dirt is unpleasant (4)

CROSSWORD No. 19

CROSSWORD No. 20

By Duck from *The Hamlyn Book of Crosswords No. 4*

ACROSS

7 Builders, etc. hang around a monument in Scotland (9,6)
10 Symbol displayed by 'Arry's picnic basket at the seaside? (9)
11 Kind but terribly green (5)
12 Master to make a study of wine (5)
13 Rows with beet sown by middle of patch—and here's a place for the runners (3,6)
14 Airmen stayed up endlessly—a chancy business (6)
16 Powerful joke about Henry (6)
17 Form of art—while there's this there's hope (5,4)
19 Rascal in Society party (5)
21 Pervert asked for more (5)
22 Author—one to sample but only a minor literary figure (9)
23 Get very angry wanting insect removed from part of machine (3,3,3,6)

DOWN

1 Bring stillness to city area, bring stillness around (6)
2 Fairy appearing in October only (6)
3 Introductory comment—blame rep if it's wrong (8)
4 Advertisement in exhibition for spirit (6)
5 Father going to inn got drunk somewhere in Devon (8)
6 Riding up on the green, turn back (6)
8 Climb tricky with ice? A pity—faultlessness will be required (13)
9 Showing feeling for what a nice lettuce should be? (6-7)
15 Almost entirely deceitful Welshman, character created by Shakespeare (8)
16 Comes before President goes back (8)
17 Directions given to gent to begin journey (3,3)
18 Charge mischief-maker with upsetting trade union, leader of extremists (6)
19 Beetle making mark on seaman (6)
20 Hospital worker providing beer (6)

CROSSWORD No. 20

Sometimes a pattern will have different lattices clashing into one another, so that rows and columns appear to be dislocated. In the grid of Crossword No. 21, for example, there are examples of answers where two checked letters sit together and two unchecked letters sit together.

CROSSWORD No. 21

By Quixote from *The Oxford Times*

ACROSS

1 Some French bigwig in charge is tyrannical (8)
9 On the wing cloud is causing panic (8)
10 Band in the heart of New Orleans (4)
11 Warn that dear loony it spells out 'no hope' (5,7)
13 Beer for college servant (6)
14 Be hugging the monster? *I'd* get rid of the devil (8)
15 Flower Circle involved in arrangement for Easter (3,4)
16 Food cases with meat half one's own (7)
20 Leading character not what you'd expect—I may be confused with another (8)
22 Helical pairs formed life originally? (6)
23 River with waters swirling into specially designed hydroelectric plant maybe (5,7)
25 Two little islands in river (4)
26 Mocking lecturer in car is naughty (8)
27 Is the sacked worker not sure what to do? (8)

DOWN

2 It could make one hear with plug initially inserted (8)
3 Need MP retire if found out? Settle in advance (12)
4 You get a form of art in these, possibly (8)
5 Sack employee of NatWest? (7)
6 Rock has unpleasant smell—get basin for washing (6)
7 I am in city, a South American capital (4)
8 Laws providing conditions to restrict trade union (8)
12 Tie inspector—absurd office worker conscious of public image? (12)
15 Very good saint? Only if his mouth is sealed off first! (8)
17 Gold and fragrant substances as omens (8)
18 I care not about the response (8)
19 Ruler abandoned Roman church (7)
21 Member of sect: 'The most important thing is to oust the Conservative' (6)
24 Fighting dunce, a child who needs special care (4)

CROSSWORD No. 21

Whatever basic grid is used the setter should try to keep to certain standards of fairness:

1 *No part of the grid should be completely cut off* from another part of the grid (remember the nine mini-crosswords on p.21).

2 *The number of unchecked letters (unches) in an answer should be a half of the total or less.* It won't matter much if 7 letters out of 13 are left unchecked, as here: _ R _ S _ O _ R _ V _ R _ .

Knowing that the answer should give you a football team (7,6) you will soon get BRISTOL ROVERS. In the diagram on p.22, though, one may be left trying to solve e.g. 13 across with _ A _ E _ and this can simply pose too many possibilities for comfort. (It should be added that lattice (a) makes the observance of this convention easier than (b), (c) or (d).)

3 *The triple unch (and worse!) should be avoided.* This means that no answer should contain three consecutive letters not checked by crossing letters.

4 *Normally the diagram should be symmetrical if given a half-turn* (i.e. through 180 degrees). Some diagrams also give symmetry if turned through 90 degrees. Sometimes a mirror symmetry will be preferred to a half-turn symmetry, as in the final tutorial puzzle for this chapter.

CROSSWORD No. 22

By Don Manley from *Church Times Crosswords*

ACROSS

1 Hymn tune which could make Sid feel sedate (6,7)
7 Wise man to draw breath in amazement on arrival (6)
8 Small number having happy Christmas (6)
9 Tempts everybody with devilish ruse (7)
11 Fellow of generous disposition— now there's good news for all . . .! (7)
13 Boy, 8 (4)
15 Love to people shown in a sign (4)
21 Anger so out of control—not fruit *of the Spirit* (7)
22 '. . . thou goest I will go' (Ruth 1: 16, AV) (7)
23 Relating to a morning service in which mum can feature (5)
24 Girl's song now being heard? (5)
25 Gin now on sale maybe to bring seasonal bonhomie? (9,6)
28 Cheap and ostentatious like Christmas tree decorations? (6)
29 Like the Pope, free from coarseness (6)

DOWN

1 God's messengers held by gang elsewhere (6)
2 Methodist preacher using rambling prose? (5)
3 Sin brings an element of terror (3)
4 Fashionable northern bar with limited accommodation? (3)
5 A chap may have red wine—but avoid the extremes! (5)

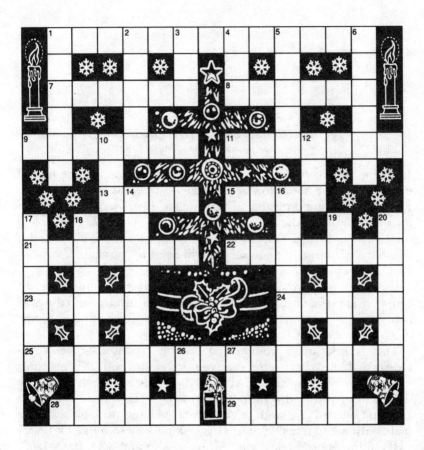

6 This night we celebrate as 24-singers—enlist for wandering around (6)
10 Vessel from Abraham's city, last thing found in excavation (3)
12 The family makes one of the three travellers stop short (3)
14 Strains go out from church musicians perhaps (9)
16 Bishop's cope is silly on friend (9)
17 Some rays are funny when placed round head of saint (6)

18 Letter from bishop of bygone days (spoken) (8)
19 Strange arch, very French, in cathedral city (8)
20 Alter introduction to 'Messiah' in arrangement for band (6)
26 Peter e.g. with yen to follow master (3)
27 Present, very big, put up on piano (3)

13

Mountaineering with Chambers

It is time now to progress from the blocked diagram to the barred diagram. We are about to scale the heights of Crossword Mountain. Farewell to Definition Plains and farewell to *The Times* Foothills. Ever on, ever upward to the rarefied atmosphere of Azed, *The Listener* and the Crossword Club. For our journey we need a guide book, and if you have not already done so you will need to purchase a copy of *Chambers English Dictionary*.

Hitherto we have used common knowledge, common words, common abbreviations. From now on we will meet unusual words and ancient language that rarely survives in a single-volume dictionary—except *Chambers*.

This is not just a commercial for my 'sponsor'—*Chambers* is indispensable. Where else can you so easily find the probable misprint in Shakespeare (EALE)? Where else, in such a concise volume, can you find a supposed 'cross between a male yak and a common horned cow' with ten different spellings (though some are male only, some female only)? If you don't believe me, look under ZHO in the big red book where you will also find: ZO, DSO, DZO, ZHOMO, DSOMO, JOMO, ZOBO, ZOBU, DSOBO. Also in its 1500-odd pages you will find everything from ancient words for 'grievous' (DEAR, DEARE, DEERE) and a Scotticism for a hanging clock (WAG-AT-THE-WA') to WORD PROCESSOR (a cryptic definition of a clue-writer?). If you pause to *read Chambers Dictionary* while solving a puzzle, you may also find some quirky definitions in the best Johnsonian tradition: try ECLAIR and MIDDLE AGE for example.

As you progress to the barred puzzle you will need to learn the abbreviations in Chambers. You will still be meeting MA indicated by 'master', but that abbreviation may also be clued by Morocco, the International Vehicle Registration. Copper may still be Cu, but you had also better know that beryllium has the symbol Be. And so on.

gaff¹ *gaf, n.* a hook used esp. for landing large fish: the spar to which the head of a fore-and-aft sail is bent (*naut.*). — *v.t.* to hook or bind by means of a gaff. — *adj.* **gaff'-rigged** (of a vessel) having a gaff. — **gaff'-sail** a sail attached to the gaff; **gaff'-topsail** a small sail, the head of which is extended on a small gaff which hoists on the top mast, and the foot on the lower gaff.   [Fr. *gaffe.*]

gaff² *gaf, (slang) n.* a low theatre: a fair.   [Origin obscure.]

gaff³. See **gaffe.**

gaff⁴ *gaf, (slang) v.i.* to gamble. — *ns.* **gaff'er; gaff'ing.**   [Origin obscure.]

gaff⁵ *gaf, (slang) n.* humbug, nonsense. — **blow the gaff** to disclose a secret, to blab.   [Prob. connected with **gab²** or **gaff³**; cf. O.E. *gegaf-sprǣc*, scurrility.]

gaffe, rarely **gaff,** *gaf, n.* a blunder.   [Fr. *gaffe.*]

gaffer¹ *gaf'ər, n.* originally a word of respect applied to an old man, now familiar (*fem.* **gammer**): the foreman of a squad of workmen: (orig. *U.S.*) the senior electrician responsible for the lighting in a television or film studio.   [**grandfather,** or **godfather.**]

gaffer², **gaffing.** See **gaff⁴.**

gag¹ *gag, v.t.* to stop the mouth of forcibly: to silence: to prevent free expression by (the press, etc.): to choke up. — *v.i.* to choke: to retch: — *pr.p.* **gagg'ing;** *pa.t.* and *pa.p.* **gagged.** — *n.* something put into the mouth or over it to enforce silence (also *fig.*), or to distend jaws during an operation: the closure applied in a debate: a nauseous mouthful, boiled fat beef (*Lamb*). — *n.* **gagg'er** one who gags. — **gag'-bit** a powerful bit used in breaking horses.   [Prob. imitative of sound made in choking.]

gag² *gag, (slang) v.t.* to deceive. — *v.i.* to practise imposture. — *n.* a made-up story, lie.   [Possibly **gag¹.**]

gag³ *gag, (coll.) n.* an actor's interpolation into his part: a joke: a hoax. — *v.i.* to introduce a gag: to joke. — *v.t.* to introduce a gag into. — *n.* **gag'ster** (*coll.*) one who tells jokes, a comedian. — **gag'man** one who writes gags: a gagster.   [Possibly **gag¹.**]

An extract from *Chambers English Dictionary*, showing lots of definition possibilities for the crossword setter.

Buy your *Chambers* then—and buy a few more books if you can, as indicated in Appendix 2. But if you only have money for one reference book it must be *the* Dictionary. Use it and enjoy it. End of commercial!

The tradition of using bars was established in the early days of British crosswords and became the hallmark of Torquemada, mentioned briefly in Chapter 10. One of his puzzles from his 1934 miscellany *The Torquemada Puzzle Book* is shown overleaf.

I provide the grid with the answer because in my humble opinion no one in his right mind should be expected to attempt a solution! By today's standards this is a work of misdirected genius with its unsound clues and difficult references. Note too the lack of symmetry and reversed words which strike us as very odd.

TORQUEMADA PUZZLE

ACROSS

1 Bunny gets a head on him and becomes peevish
7 American law-giver sets a Scottish standard
12 Waited for by Brutus but not by Pilate
14 I wrote Terminations when I started and The Trimmed Lamp when I ended
15 *rev.* 36
16 I take those who do not take themselves
17 37's
19, 21 Confirm officially
20 City found in a town
23 I'm already fashionable and if you add the difference between six and sixteen I'm an erroneous overcoat
24 Genus of worms in a heretic
25 *rev.* French fleet in English waters
27 Shepherd's bad companion
29 11
30 You may discover us in a trick but you had better shake to make sure
31 34 dn
32 *rev.* Shortened
34 Relying on a large scale
38 Trim is my county town
39 Epitaph in bad verse
40 I can hold a candle—to 26

DOWN

1 Behead this old clothesman for a murderer
2 Bisected drawback
3 e.g. squire
4,11 One boot that helped another to dish a cake
5 Clouded with brown from unfaces it
6 Walked on by people in coloured shirts
7 Solomon's eight-bottle man
8 *rev.* I said: "The purple flowers droop: the golden bee Is lily-cradled: I alone awake"
9 A German might associate this piece of lead with 22
10 Novelist not encouraged to write at Cambridge
13 *rev.* Scottish stout that becomes musty when it crosses the border
18 Next will help in
22 Should come after 27
26 *rev.* 29
28 *rev.* Noah's care has become anyone's old care
32,33 All but the play by Maugham
34 31
35 My first is unchecked in 13 and my second in 11
36 *rev.* 15
37 One 17

TORQUEMADA PUZZLE

¹F	²R	³A	⁴B	⁵B	⁶I	⁷T	⁸J	⁹E	¹⁰D	¹¹G	E

| ¹²R | E | P | L | ¹³Y | N | ¹⁴H | E | N | R | Y | R |

| ¹⁵I | T | ¹⁶H | U | F | F | E | R | O | ¹⁷A | P | ¹⁸S |

| ¹⁹P | R | E | C | ²⁰F | U | N | ²¹O | N | I | ²²S | E |

| ²³P | O | S | H | U | ²⁴S | A | B | E | L | L | A |

| ²⁵E | D | I | ²⁶R | T | ²⁷C | R | O | O | ²⁸K | ²⁹E | R |

| ³⁰R | U | S | E | ³¹S | A | ³²L | A | ³³T | R | U | C |

| ³⁴S | C | ³⁵U | ³⁶T | ³⁷A | T | E | ³⁸M | E | A | T | H |

| A | ³⁹T | R | I | P | E | ⁴⁰T | O | R | C | H | E |

Notes

Across: 7. Two meanings; 12. Julius C., III, 2, 37; Bacon, Essays, Of Truth; 14. Henry (James), (O.) Henry; 23. Posh-teen, posteen; 24. Sabell(i) a(n); 25. *rev.* French borrowing; 30. R-us-e, anag.; 39. T-R.I.P.-e; 40. Candelabrum when put to 26.

Down: 1. Jack the (f)Ripper; 2. Draw back; 3. Esquire; 4 and 11. Wellington, Napoleon; 5. Anag.; 6. And others; 7. I Kings, xii, 28; 8 *rev.* Tennyson, O., 28; 9. Trail; 13. *rev.* Two meanings; 28. *rev.* C-ark; 32 and 33. (The) Letter.

It would be very easy for us to write off this puzzle completely, but two aspects of it have survived: the difficult vocabulary and the barred diagram. Clue-writing has become more disciplined, and this has allowed the difficult solution to be more solvable (thanks to the pioneering work of Ximenes); the barred diagram has become more orderly. A typical 12 × 12 Azed diagram is shown below.

The basic permitted parameters for the 12 × 12 'plain' puzzle were laid down by Ximenes in his book *On the Art of the Crossword*:

1 Number of unches in a word:
   4 and 5 letters, 1 unch
   6 and 7 letters, 1 or 2 unches
   8 and 9 letters, 2 or 3 unches
   10, 11 and 12 letters, 3 or 4 unches
2 Number of words in a barred puzzle: 36, usually with six rows and six columns containing one word and the other twelve two words. 'Four of the twelve one-word rows and columns will contain your four long words: the other eight will be reduced in length by bars to fit shorter words.'

Note how the Ximenean formula leads to a tidy balanced-looking diagram with no 'multiple unches'. You can see that there is more checking in a Ximenean diagram than in a blocked diagram, and this is a distinct asset for the solver. Suppose you are faced with a clue such as this:

[13.1] Vegetable, very black inside—it grows in the tropics (6)

and you have all the crossing words to give you

LEB__E__

By the time you get that far you should be able to work out BB in leek = LEBBEK, but if you cannot you can always look up *Chambers*, find the only word that will fit and work backwards to see how the clue works. With L__B__E__ or __E__B__K it would be a shade harder.

For the most part, clues in plain barred puzzles are similar in concept to those in blocked puzzles, but to give you a flavour of the different language due to *Chambers* here are some examples and answers all from Azed and his competitors (we shall look at the Azed competition again in Chapter 16):

[13.2] Pour out Jock's shin-bone soup (5)

Answer: SKINK which has two meanings—hence the note reads (2 mngs). Skink is a Scottish word for that form of soup—hence the label 'Jock's'. Jock is a familiar person in Azed!

[13.3] Zinc sulphide to mix with einsteinium (6)

Answer: BLENDE (blend + E). You've been warned about abbreviations.

The next clue won S. L. Paton first prize in Azed No. 1:

[13.4] Before the heart ensnares one, one likes to go on a binge (7)

Answer: ORGIAST (a in or + gist). Note two things: (1) before = or, a rare usage which would be too obscure for the average cryptic: (2) one = a (quite justifiable but in less advanced cryptics 'one' = 'I' usually).

[13.5] Campaigner in old company holding steadfast to right (8)

Answer: CRUSADER (sad in crue + r, 'semi & lit.'). This too was an Azed first-prizewinner from M. L. Perkins. Note the use of 'old' for the obsolete word 'crue'. Many words in *Chambers* can be labelled 'obsolete', 'stale', 'traditional' or 'as before'. In this clue also note 'to' meaning 'beside', a useful 'throwaway' in a charade.

[13.6] Gee surrounded by at least four more dashes (6)

Answer: SPANGS (g in spans). 'Gee' is a spelling of the letter 'g' (as well as a suggestion of a horse). Look out for el, em, es and others!

[13.7] Oily swimmer has success on lake–goodness me, born genius (9)

Answer: GOLOMYNKA for a down clue (go + L + O my! + n + ka). An interesting assemblage of obscure bits and pieces combining to make an obscure word—but genius = ka is soon learnt with experience!

In 'advanced cryptics' the answer often describes itself in the first person. This prize-winning clue from C. O. Butcher uses this convention to achieve an & lit:

[13.8] I form bulges erected on a defence's sides (9)

The answer is GABIONADE (I bag (rev.) + on a d e & lit.).

This *personification* goes back to the Victorian riddle (see p.2). This sort of thing is definitely allowed, even if the personal I cannot be allowed in the plan (see p.65)!

Solvers of an Azed puzzle will need to know that familiar words can take on unfamiliar meanings when used as indicators. If you are familiar with the hymn 'There is a green hill far away', you will know that 'without' can mean 'outside' as well as 'lacking'. Here's an example from Ximenes:

[13.9] Rural spot without excitement (8)

giving MOFUSSIL (fuss in moil).

Did you know that 'on' can mean 'getting drunk' and that 'over' can suggest a word being *rolled* over (i.e. reversed)? No examples here, but you will meet them soon enough!

From unusual words and unusual usages of usual words to unusual word order. Most of us think and write like this:

I hate people who flatter me with lies.

But a poet does not always write his sentences in the order 'subject/object/verb'. Thus William Cowper:

The lie that flatters I abhor the most.

And thus William (W. J. M.) Scotland, an Azed prizewinner demonstrating another verbal art form, that of clue-writing:

[13.10] The jungly mass one cleaves (7)

The answer is MACHETE (anag. in m ace, because in fact 'the jungly' is cleaving 'mass one').

B 8

beveller -s	biparous	Blenheim	blushful -ler
beverage -s	birdbath -s	Blennius	-lest
bewailed	bird-bolt	blessing -s	blushing -s
bewetted	birdcage -s	blighted	blustery -rier
bewigged	birdcall -s	blighter -s	-iest
bewilder -s,-ing	bird-eyed	blimbing -s	boarding -s
-ed	bird-lice	blimpish	boarfish -es
bezonian	bird-lime	blindage -s	boastful -ler
bheestie -s	birdseed -s	blind-gut	-lest
biannual	bird's-eye	blinding -s	boasting -s
biassing	birdshot -s	blinkard -s	boatbill -s
biathlon -s	biriyani -s	blinking	boat-deck
bibation -s	birthday -s	blissful	boat-hook
biblical	birthdom	blistery -rier	boat-load
bibulous	biscacha -s	-iest	boatrace -s
bick-iron	Biscayan	blithely	boat-song
biconvex	bisector -s	blizzard -s	boattail -s
bicuspid -s	biserial	bloating -s	bobbinet -s
biddable	bisexual	blockade -s,-d	bobby-pin
bidental -s	bistable	-ding	bobolink -s
bien-être	bistoury -ries	blockage -s	bobstays
biennial -s	bitchery -ries	blocking -s	bobwheel -s
bifacial	bittacle -s	blockish	bob-white
bifocals	bitterly	block-tin	bodement -s
bigamist -s	bivalent -s	bloncket	bodiless
bigamous	bi-weekly	blood-hot	bodywork -s
Bignonia	Bixaceae	bloodily	Boeotian
bijwoner -s	bizcacha -s	blood-red	bogeyism
bilabial -s	blabbing -s	blood-tax	bogey-man
bilander -s	blackboy -s	blood-wit	bog-Latin
bilberry -rries	blackcap -s	bloomers	Bohemian
bile-duct	black-cat	bloomery -ries	boldness
billbook -s	black-fox	blooming	bollocks -es,-ing
billeted	blacking -s	blossomy -mier	-ed
billfold -s	blackish	-iest	boll-worm
billhead -s	blackleg -s,-ging	blotched	bolt-head
billhook -s	-ged	blotting -s	bolthole -s
billiard	*black-neb	blowball -s	bolt-rope
billowed	blackout -s	blowdown -s	bomb-site
billyboy -s	blacktop -s	blowhole -s	bombycid -s
billy-can	bladdery	blowlamp -s	bona-roba
bilobate	blah-blah	blowpipe -s	bonassus -es
bimanous	blamable	bludgeon -s,-ing	bondager -s

An extract from *Chambers Words*, compiled 'for the benefit of all who play in fun or in earnest with words'.

Finally a subtle pair of clues from Azed linked by leader dots:

[13.11] Cunning but timorous if losing head . . . (5)
[13.12] . . . To these fools, given which they *would* have heads (5)

[13.11] gives LEERY and [13.12] OAVES. Transfer the L from the first clue to the second and you would have 'eery' (timorous) and 'loaves' (heads). Clever stuff!

The time has come for two small tutorial puzzles. Then we must look at some of the more sophisticated clue types common to barred puzzles. Are you using your oxygen yet?

CROSSWORD No. 23

ACROSS

1 Poppy and a stone in Jock's gutter (8)
7 Greek character will shortly become invalid (4)
8 Arsenic arrives from geological formations (4)
10 Source of hope in troubled times? (6)
12 One in old age not yielding milk for Mac (4)
13 Fruit giving dog energy (4)
16 Man at table shows orange stain (6)
17 Unit attached to bit of sound (4)
18 Scottish boy shows spirit (not square) (4)
19 Watching over five couples on the floor? (8)

DOWN

1 Pa eats nut rudely rejecting superior old appetiser (8)
2 Flower that's tender, hurt when upset? Not entirely (4)
3 Bard puts touch of magic in E.lang. and E.lit. (7)
4 Master sermon amplifies a message from the heavens maybe (5)
5 One in love is secure (4)
6 Die with a tear destroyed in shoot out... (8)
9 ...killed with gun outside American institute (7)
11 Workers appearing before newspaper boss complained as before (5)
14 Instrument with nothing in order (4)
15 Touches of obvious talent in crossword in 'The Listener' (4)

CROSSWORD No. 24

ACROSS

1 Plant tissue shows tree is 2000 roughly (8)
7 Dedicated man retired, no longer with us (6)
8 Bird's old garment (4)
9 Townsmen linger endlessly around (4)
11 Do is producing an old-fashioned racket (4)
12 What Jumblies went to *sea* in—or river we hear (4)
15 'urried along and declared (4)
16 Poet heard to be in prison? (4)
17 Girl gets hold of hard Azed—36 lines of skilled writing? (6)
18 The old weaken and come in about to die (8)

DOWN

1 I am great, fantastic—superior's right! (8)
2 Beetle story upset Her Majesty (6)
3 Heartless bird's mutter (4)
4 Fallen angel, one with happiness curtailed (5)
5 Bird eating a wee portion (4)
6 A month in old Paris requires my French, second language, right? (8)
10 Cordyline has two birds in it (6)
11 Old city governor is in the city (5)
13 A bit of mutton to devour? (4)
14 Expert turned up admitting learner's lacking in literary style (4)

14

Advanced Clues

Moving, Substituted and Alternate letter(s), Subtractive container-and-contents

Ximenes once recommended that hard words should have easy clues and easy words hard clues. Much of the 'hardness' in clues is due to the subtlety of wording, but there are clue types used in advanced puzzles that you probably will not meet in the everyday cryptic. The examples that follow are culled from Azed puzzles and Azed clue-writing competitions in *The Observer*.

The moving letter(s). In this clue type the solver is invited to find a word and then move a particular letter (or letters) to discover a new word:

[14.1] See me in N. European water, tail moving? (6)

N. European water is WASSER: move the tail (r) to get WRASSE. Note that an '& lit.' effect is also achieved since a wrasse is a fish.

[14.2] I disapproved of the unseemly skunk, tail foremost (4)

Move the c of atoc (a skunk) to the front to obtain the censor CATO.

The substituted letter(s). Here you are invited to find a word and substitute one letter (or set of letters) for another. Thus in this clue:

[14.3] Vigorous? Love yielding to East in source of drowsiness (5)

We find a source of drowsiness (poppy) and substitute e for o (love) to arrive at PEPPY (meaning 'vigorous').

Here is another example, a first prize in one of Azed's competitions, from J. P. H. Hirst:

[14.4] Given unconventionally for Jack's head (7)

Jack is tar. Replace his head ('t') with 'vineg' (anag. given) to give

VINEGAR, which you will remember was accompanied by brown paper (hence the '& lit.'). But see p.136 when you get to it.

Alternate letters. The solver is asked to discard every other letter in a clue such as the following:

[14.5] Outings in which you find chain keeps losing odd bits (5)

A ride on a shaky bicycle? Maybe—but forget the 'misleading context' and remove the odd letters ('bits') from 'chain keeps'. The result is HIKES.

The words 'odd bits' and 'even bits' usually give the game away but here is the technique given a new subtlety by Azed:

[14.6] Ancient Syrian one regularly placed among king and troops (8)

Place A alternately among R and MEN and you'll get ARAMAEAN.

In the following clue (which won a first prize for N. C. Dexter in a 1984 Azed competition) the alternate letters are anagrammed:

[14.7] By it 'truth' and 'lie' looked alternately interchangeable (11)

An anagram of BITUHNLEOKD is DOUBLE-THINK (another & lit. of course).

The missing-words charade is best illustrated by some examples:

[14.8] Opening gambit at parties is hard if shyness _____ inhibits one (7)

The first word here provides the definition. The remainder is a sentence into which you must insert some words which make sense. The words required are 'or if ice' ('ice' meaning 'reserve'). Put them together in a charade and the answer is ORIFICE.

[14.9] 'Adam's _____ ', said archaic Eve, *very* old crone? (6)

The answer is RIBIBE. Can you see why?

Sometimes the charade provides a 'letter formula' telling you how to get from one group of letters to another:

[14.10] Highland cattle put with this will become quiet (4)

The answer is NOUT (Highland cattle) because 'put with no ut' equals 'p' (an abbreviation for 'quiet'). A relatively unusual type of clue this, and the example given threw more than one solver when perpetrated by Azed.

The subtractive container-and-contents clue is a combination of techniques (*d*) and (*h*) in Chapter 8. Here's an example of my own, hitherto unpublished:

[14.11] This minor when put in bed is happy (4)

It's nothing to do with a compliant child when you read the clue cryptically. You want a word which when put in bed gives you 'blessed': hence LESS.

Here's one from Azed:

[14.12] What'll those enthralled like us in Market get? Mare's-nest (5)

The word you want, hidden in the 'mart' (or market) in 'mare's nest' is ESNES, who are enthralled as slaves. Quite simple really!

The composite anagram was revived by Don Putnam in a *Games and Puzzles* magazine article in 1975 (how sad the demise of that monthly which for ten years provided some splendid advanced puzzles). He described a clue from Afrit's book which read as follows:

[14.13] You could make this whale seem quarrelsome, but hold it up by its tail and it begins to laugh (7)

Forget the words after 'quarrelsome' and concentrate on the first seven words. Afrit is saying take 'this word for whale' plus 'seem' and you could make 'quarrelsome'. The answer is RORQUAL (hence the 'lau' in the reversal, the beginning(!) of 'laugh'). Quite soon after Putman's article Azed and *Listener* puzzlers were faced with the rediscovery of the composite anagram. The clue-writer was saying in effect 'If A won't form a decent anagram, I'll add B and define it as an anagram of C.' A way had been rediscovered of combining the anagram with the subtractive clue.

This type of clue normally appears as an & lit., as the following examples illustrate:

[14.14] Ecuadorans, broke, might produce a _____ and nothing else (5)

ECUADORANS is an anagram of 'a, _____, and, o'. The missing word is SUCRE.

[14.15] Some sprinkling with this could give a tame meal gusto (9)

This won B. Franco a first prize from Azed in 1977. The word 'some' has to be sprinkled with a word to give 'a tame meal gusto'. Answer: MALAGUETTA (look up its meaning in *Chambers* if you don't know it).

4 -UZZ

stay	bley	Esky ®	ismy	espy	oosy	gazy
quay	fley	yuky	fumy	I-spy	posy	hazy
away	gley	paly	cany	nary	rosy	jazy
M-way	sley	waly	many	oary	upsy	lazy
sway	joey	ably	wany	vary	busy	mazy
tway	drey	idly	zany	wary	maty	vizy
baby	grey	rely	deny	scry	city	cozy
gaby	prey	ugly	reny	adry	mity	dozy
inby	trey	lily	miny	aery	pity	fozy
goby	stey	oily	piny	eery	doty	oozy
go-by	quey	wily	tiny	hery	arty	Z
toby	defy	ally	viny	very	duty	Geëz
upby	affy	illy	winy	airy	cavy	chez
orby	cagy	inly	bony	miry	Davy	trez
ruby	edgy	only	cony	wiry	navy	oyez
lacy	eggy	holy	mony	skry	wavy	phiz
pacy	bogy	moly	pony	dory	bevy	whiz
racy	dogy	poly	tony	gory	levy	friz
ricy	fogy	duly	puny	lory	envy	quiz
fady	orgy	guly	tuny	pory	movy	swiz
lady	hugy	July	awny	rory	yawy	Günz
wady	achy	puly	gyny	Tory	dewy	lutz
eddy	ashy	ruly	ahoy	spry	nowy	Druz
tedy	caky	owly	pioy	'Arry	towy	jazz
tidy	laky	gamy	cloy	bury	waxy	razz

An extract from *Chambers Back-Words for Crosswords*, a reverse-sorted word list, ideal for the crossword fan who is stuck with (say) _____ TZ: LUTZ is the only answer here, but it just could be RITZ!

My own prize-winning Azed clue for PICKLE (which can mean 'steal') read as follows:

[14.16] Kleptomaniac: a man to _____ indiscriminately?

(Incidentally 'A man to pickle indiscriminately' is a rather good clue for KLEPTOMANIAC, don't you think?)

The composite anagram does not *have* to be part of an & lit. clue; as in this case of mine 'very highly commended' by Azed near St. Valentine's Day:

[14.17] A little romance? Such fun with cryptic letters may show it is
        fourteenth.

In other words take a word possibly meaning 'a little romance', combine it with 'fun' 'cryptically' to give 'it is fourteenth'. The answer comes out as HISTORIETTE (a short story). In the first of your next tutorial puzzles all clues are based on the clue types described in this chapter. Quite often though you won't find a single example of any of them, even in an Azed—but there are just a few in the full-size puzzle. Remember, too, that the setter will always be looking for a new and subtle way of telling you how to deal with the letters in front of you.

CROSSWORD No. 25

ACROSS

1 Might _____ malfunction to make light smear? (5)
5 This snake with ring around is making grating sound (3)
8 Fragments to classify, first to last (4)
10 Work of art's loud, not soft and languishing (8)
11 Plans—utter odd bits showing what man's made of? (5)
12 Plundered—one gets a hanging (dead towards the end) (5)
17 Offering amnesty—a little time given for four (8)
18 Jock's cattle oddly shifting round—it's a habit (4)
19 An unseemly place like this could be nasty (3)
20 Bell sounds pierce, start to finish (5)

DOWN

1 Look fit selecting odd bits in the attic (4)
2 It's Bahrain: see _____ in this setting? (4)
3 Dot boozes with a touch of sadness coming to the fore (7)
4 See girl ruin tea—odd bits served (4)
6 Numbers switching ends in ecstasy (4)
7 Horror writer has a bit of ghastliness for his middle bit of book (4)
9 Special errand: _____ might be attracted to Mr Electron! (7)
12 Ogres half twisting into fabulous birds (4)
13 Lean sceptic may interject with _____ (4)
14 Write in _____ or . . . alternatively presented as 'orient'? (4)
15 _____? It is possibly to sing (4)
16 Big _____'d produce bad sting possibly (4)

CROSSWORD DINNERS

Crossword dinners have been held in honour of *The Listener* and *The Observer*. At *Listener* dinners the solvers meet the setters, but at *Observer* dinners solvers meet *the* setter. *Observer* dinners have celebrated Ximenes Nos. 100, 200, 500, 750 and 1000, Azed Nos. 250, 500, 750. Azed 1000 was celebrated with a lunch in 1991. The 'D-AZED' menu is shown below for the Azed 500 held in Oxford in 1981. The conventional menu is on p.110.

D-AZED MENU

Ten common beers? No! (8,8)

★ ★ ★ ★

Eel's fins? Tell no fool! (6,2,4,6)

★ ★ ★ ★

A crab trifle left? Come often! (11,2,4,7)

Heat a cat-toe soup . . . (7,8)

. . . Ill at our tea? (11)

Boil croc (8)

★ ★ ★ ★

Mum's choice lemon cheese (we'd hot treat) (9,6,4,5,2,6)

★ ★ ★ ★

The finer men ate stiff cow-rind (6,4,5-6,5)

ACROSS

1 Look around mountain pass—it will have hard mass of igneous rock (9)
10 Chemical coming from a chimney in Glasgow? (4)
11 Black crew in underground layer (8)
12 Tropical dish maid can cook—not all right, fantastic! (9)
13 Strong liking for eating a bit of garlic and salad (6)
14 Black mineral has resistance? This will pierce a hole (5)
17 Feminine English woman's felt hat (6)
19 Small cask in pub attracting glance, not half! (7)
20 Hobo languishes holding a coin not worth much (4)
22 Advance payment for penniless pre-1971 poet (4)
24 Artist put back silk in cupboard (7)
26 You can't play cricket without _____ ball! This intruder's taken possession (6)
29 Praying not to get gee-gee as present (5)
30 Garbled matins—one only *appears* to pray (6)
31 A learner needs library service—never on a permanent basis? (9)
32 Cold sea bit tricky, around zero? Such may be the answer (8)
33 Account by army for the official minutes (4)
34 Softly touching woman—not entirely kind to be a grasper (9)

DOWN

1 Bean produced in the biologist's workplace repeatedly? (6)
2 A loser primarily, an 'orse not finishing sadly (7)
3 Water-carrier wasn't fit, with wooden joints somehow? (12)
4 In room a ghost lurks somewhere in Ireland (5)
5 Antiseptic appearing as yellow crystals—ten sufficient for the chemistry class? (8)
6 Wife featured in educational paper organised communities (6)
7 Mother 100—having modern technology around one is key to prolonging life (12)
8 I don't go to matins *and* evensong —what'll do for collection? (5)
9 A time in Israel with actors turning up (4)
15 Torment losing every other part —allowance for waste required (4)
16 Fish become frightened—I had *one* caught (8)
18 Be a success? Ali was with his (4)
21 Wine that's yellow I vote 'nasty' (7)
23 Where you'd see British go on jaunt—and the king? (6)
25 Some of the fens, earthed, dry up as before (6)
27 Fine French child for rude eruption after meal? (5)
28 Would a non-conformist Scot primarily inhabit me? (5)
29 Handle of kettle perhaps or bucket (4)

CROSSWORD No. 26

15

Special Crosswords

All the crosswords so far have had 'normal' clues (however complex) and the words have been entered in a 'normal' diagram. In a special crossword something is abnormal—either the form of clue *or* the grid you are presented with *or* the way you must enter letters in the grid. In extreme cases you may be faced with several forms of abnormality. There are a number of standard special crossword types and beyond that there are the 'special specials'! In this chapter we shall look at some of the well-known specials. In each case we shall look at the standard 'rubric' which accompanies that type of puzzle and then illustrate with a tutorial.

Printer's Devilry. This form of puzzle was invented by Afrit (see pp.58–9). Here is the rubric in its classical Ximenean form:

> Each clue is a passage from which the printer has removed a hidden answer, closing the gap, taking liberties sometimes with punctuation and spacing, but not disturbing the order of the remaining letters. Thus in the sentence *Now that it's so much warmer, can't I let the boiler go out?* MERCANTILE is hidden. The printer might offer as a clue: *Now that—it's so much wart, the boil : ergo, out!* Each passage when complete makes some sort of sense.

The clue Ximenes chose has an extreme case of shifting word breaks along the line. A PD clue with a simple break and no shifting letters is also possible, as in this beautiful example which won Mrs E. M. Pardo a first prize from Ximenes:

[15.1] Children taking piano lessons soon learn the sign ff (6)

The break occurs in ff giving the undevilled version '. . . for a clef', and the answer is therefore ORACLE. In Azed competitions this additional advice is given to PD clue-writers:

> N.B. Preference is given to PD clues in which breaks before and after the word omitted (before *and* after omission) do not occur at the ends or beginnings of words in the clue.

Hints to solvers. Sort out any obvious space shifts. Then try to find the point at which the clue looks strained and insert a pencil stroke. See if you can add new letters to the 'stranded' letters either side of the stroke to produce a word which fits in with the theme of the clue. In the Ximenean example above you should be able to see 'the boiler go out'. In that context a 'wart' doesn't make much sense. By trial and error you might decide to break thus: war/t. In the context of the clue and perhaps with some help from checking letters you should arrive at 'warm' and 'warmer'. Then if all else fails, you can look up the 10-lettered MER words in *Chambers Words* and work backwards. Solving PD clues can be very hard, but this tutorial puzzle offers generous checking and should present few problems.

CROSSWORD No. 27

Printer's Devilry

1	2	3	4
5			
6			
7			

ACROSS

1 Royal Academy will only display the bet (4)
5 If you're going in for driving, Tess, son might help (4)
6 Got a big success? Banks should be pleased! (4)
7 In a gale you might see town (4)

DOWN

1 Towards end of game do play 'ere (4)
2 Sleep's needed by one living in busy street-bus? 'Tis impossible with traffic noise (4)
3 Cats are crossbred by American ranchers (4)
4 Ties—dress in the latest fashion (4)

Misprints is a form of puzzle invented by Ximenes, and the rubric explains all:

Half the clues, both across and down, contain a misprint of one letter only in each, occurring always in the definition part of the clue: their answers are to appear in the diagram correctly spelt. The other half, both across and down, are correctly printed: all their answers are to appear in the diagram with a misprint of one letter only in each. No unchecked letter in the diagram is to be misprinted: each twice used letter is to appear as required by the correct form of at least one of the words to which it belongs. All indications such as anagrams, etc., in clues lead to the correct forms of words required, not to the misprinted forms.

The Ximenean rubric does not give an example of a misprinted clue, but we can illustrate from Ximenes himself:

[15.2] Rummy sort of girl—see the old-fashioned bun (6)

The answer is GINGAL (gin + gal), and the misprinted word is 'bun' which should be 'gun'. It is a curious feature of the misprinted clue that it always makes much better sense than the so-called 'correct' version!

Correctly printed clues are like any other clue but you need to work out by process of elimination where the misprint occurs.

Hint to solvers. Fill in unchecked squares in ink, but divide the checked squares diagonally, putting the across letter in pencil in the top corner and the down letter in pencil in the bottom, thus:

$$\boxed{^I\!/_T}$$

When you have settled the priority work out the implication for the crossing words, inking in where possible. And if two letters agree, use ink straight away. Put a pencil line through each misprint in the clues, and beside the number of each misprint clue mark C (for *clue* misprint). If the misprint is in the *diagram*, mark D. Thus a sequence may read as follows (supposing that 'work' is a misprint for 'word'):

Down
C 1........work.......
D 2....................
D 3....................

In each section of clues you will probably be looking for nine Cs and nine Ds. This may help you categorize some of the clues as you tussle with the last one or two.

In the tutorial puzzle that follows, checking is generous, which should be helpful.

CROSSWORD No. 28

Misprints

1	2	3	4	5	6
7					
8					
9					
10					
11					

ACROSS

1 Here's a little to eat and a little to drink, dear (6)
7 Dagon has limb in the drink (6)
8 Jock's mysterious disease—the unemployed won't get it (6)
9 With five rings perform a touch of oriental magic (6)
10 Ale not bad? I get tight coming in (6)
11 Leaves again being terribly restless—ship sails off (6)

DOWN

1 Corn Street, somewhere in Bucks (6)
2 Dean produces sort of tract about the Old Testament (6)
3 Sheep perhaps beginning to play before long on mountain range (6)
4 Community work interrupts footballer (6)
5 Musical composition rendered by for example French artist, not English (6)
6 Claps a lot, one with half-century having been caught (6)

Playfair. The Playfair code was invented by the famous Victorian scientist Charles Wheatstone (you may remember his famous electrical bridge for measuring resistance if you took physics at school). But it was his friend Lyon Playfair who publicized it: hence the name. Used by the British Army in the First World War, this code is rather more difficult than the simple substitution code where one letter is replaced by another. Afrit it was who introduced Playfair codes to crosswords, and this is the now-familiar rubric using the sample code-word favoured by Azed:

MENU

CONSOMMÉ BRETONNE

★ ★ ★ ★

FILLET OF SOLE NELSON

★ ★ ★ ★

CONTREFILET OF BEEF CLAMART

CHATEAU POTATOES

RATATOUILLE

BROCCOLI

★ ★ ★ ★

CHOCOLATE MOUSSE WITH CRÊME DE MENTHE

★ ★ ★ ★

COFFEE WITH AFTER-DINNER MINTS

Wine kindly provided by *The Observer*

(see page 103)

In a Playfair word square the code-word (in which no letter recurs) is followed by the remaining letters of the alphabet, I doing duty for I and J (see below).

```
O  R  A  N  G
E  S  T  I  C
K  B  D  F  H
L  M  P  Q  U
V  W  X  Y  Z
```

To encode a word split it into pairs of letters, e.g. CR IT IC AL. Each pair is then seen as forming the opposite corners of a rectangle within the word square, the other two letters [at the corners of the rectangle] being the coded form. Thus CR gives SG (not GS which RC would give). When a pair of letters appears in the same row or column, the coded form is produced from the letters immediately to the right of or below each respectively. For last letters in a row or column, use the first letter of the same row or column. When all pairs are encoded the word is joined up again, thus: SGCICEOP. Answers to clues are to be encoded thus in the diagram. Solvers must deduce the code-word from pairings determinable by cross-checking letters, thus enabling them to complete the diagram.

This rubric nowhere states that the remaining letters are in alphabetical order, but this is always evident from the example. In a typical Playfair puzzle there are four words to be encoded. Often they are of six letters each with two pairs of letters checked for coding and one pair unchecked.

Hints to solvers. The first stage is to solve the Playfair clues—without help from any checked letters! Because of the lack of checking the setter should give you easy clues (e.g. a hidden word, a simple anagram, a two-part charade all help). For solving these codes Scrabble® tiles can be a great help, enabling you to shift around the letters more quickly than with pencil and paper. The setter should give you some straight line coding and once you can decide whether the straight line is a row or column you are well on the way. Remember always to point your diagonals consistently upwards or downwards rather than sideways (see the note about CR above).

If you come across a sequence such as PQR, you may reasonably assume that it comes horizontally among the 'remaining letters'. This can be a great help. *Expect* to find XYZ on the last line—but beware the tutorial puzzle that follows!

CROSSWORD No. 29

Playfair by Duck from *Games and Puzzles* (see rubric on p.111)

Coded words are asterisked

ACROSS

1 The Devil's old catalogue (6)
6 Hamlet, for example, is mostly tragic in retrospect (5)
10 That is associated with rugby (masculine, rough game?) (9)
11 Showing ribs weakened, lacking energy (7)
12 Front half of gym shoe can make you swell (4)
13 Somehow became lower once (6)
*15 Leave a club perhaps and join up again? (6)
17 Epic dual is thrilling (6)
18 Introduced quietly, showing embarrassment and hiding effrontery (8)
22 Organ's something awful—it may be full of sand (8)
24 Yarn found in old magazine? (6)
*25 Gate—it often falls on sports field in summer (6)
27 Local girl collecting seaweed in abundance (6)
29 One with little height, circling, came down (4)
30 Delay coming through old Czech province (7)
31 A number could be revolutionary in combat (9)
32 Remain b-bad, old, backward (5)
33 Inflicted injuries—horrific—with weapons (6)

DOWN

1 Not in sorrow as previously—start afresh (5)
2 Salt drink, sort of soup, taken about noon—Sal usually has it (9)
3 There's semblance of disorder as before with shortage of oil (4)
4 Plant with two currents? One must have *a*! (6)
5 French lady in ermine, etc.—they can provide material for heat (8)
*6 Mace-bearer has to live with raw deal (6)
7 Schoolboys' punishments— bottoms must turn over. It's a handicap (6)
8 Bitterness is slightly excessive? You can do this to wine (7)
9 New horses in mire are slithering around (6)
14 Restaurant's dreadfully lurid inside and lifeless according to Mac (9)
16 A pet lamb? Mickey isn't half taken in school (8)
19 Riding over Somerset ditch is likely to make you sneeze (7)
20 Man who supposedly demonstrates 'god-power' upsetting conventions in party (6)
21 Drawing no. 50 at least? (6)
*22 Inwardly hard, outwardly spiteful, inclined to gossip (6)
23 Region in South Africa where men were tough (6)
26 Mass of flowers round top of loom once used for weaving (5)
28 Dice game without name initially—did Caesar go to work on it? (4)

CROSSWORD No. 29

Letters latent. Here is the appropriate rubric:

> From the answer to each clue one letter must be omitted whenever it occurs in the word, before entry in the diagram. Definitions in the clues refer to the full unmutilated answers; subsidiary indications refer to the mutilated forms to be entered in the diagram. Numbers in brackets show the full lengths of unmutilated words.

Then usually is added something like this:

> The letters omitted, read in the order in which the clues are printed, form an appropriate message/quotation from the *Oxford Dictionary of Quotations*.

Curiously a sample clue is rarely provided, but that is no reason for you to be deprived:

[15.3] Politicians monkey with society repeatedly (8)

The diagram (from Azed) shows that the mutilated form has five letters, so we are looking for a word with three letters the same, all missed out. The SI consisting of the last four words gives us 'sai' + S + S = SAISS and since 'ists' looks like a possible ending for a word meaning politicians, we try to find some way of constructing a word with three t's. There is one, STATISTS, so we put a T in the margin to contribute to the message or quotation.

The generous checking in the puzzle that follows should make your task reasonably easy. The missing letters spell out a name to which we must all be grateful, but there is one proper name missing from *that* book!

CROSSWORD No. 30

1	2	3	4
5			
6			
7			

ACROSS
1 Burglars finally grab a bit (5)
5 Orchestra completely English (5)
6 Navy'd name rowing boat (6)
7 Measured part of carpet edge (5)

DOWN
1 Times for bringing up a sword (5)
2 Right and left, with hints of national tragedy, soften (6)
3 Tree, possible supplier of deal (5)
4 Jock's vaulted passage to shed (5)

9 EEE

eeenprrst	eeffoprrr	eefhoorrs	eefinorst	eefoprrrv
presenter	profferer	fore-horse	firestone	perfervor
represent	eefforstt	foreshore	forestine	eefoprrty
eeenpprrtv	off-street	eefhoortt	eefinprsu	ferrotype
preventer	setter-off	three-foot	superfine	eefprssuu
eeenprsuv	eefghiorw	eefhorrtu	eefinrrst	superfuse
supervene	foreweigh	three-four	renfierst	eegghorsw
eeenpssst	eefghirrt	eefhrrrtu	eefinrstu	whore's-egg
steepness	freighter	furtherer	interfuse	eeggiilnt
eeenqrssu	eefgillnr	eefiillnp	eefioprrt	gelignite
queerness	refelling	fillipeen	profiteer	eeggiklnr
eeenrrstw	eefgillny	eefiilmtx	eefioprrw	Greekling
westerner	feelingly	flexitime	fire-power	eeggilmnr
eeenrrsuv	eefgilnnu	eefiilnrt	eefiossuw	gemel-ring
unreserve	unfeeling	infertile	sousewife	eeggilnnt
eeenrssst	eefgilrss	eefiilqru	eefipprrr	negligent
terseness	griefless	liquefier	fripperer	eeggilnss
eeenssstw	eefgimruv	eefiilrst	eefiprstu	legginess
sweetness	vermifuge	fertilise	stupefier	eeggiloos
eeeoprrtv	eefginorr	eefiimnty	eefiprsuv	geologise
portreeve	foreigner	femineity	perfusive	eegginnpu
eeeoprsst	eefginrrr	eefiimrrt	eefirrrtt	pug-engine
poetresse	referring	metrifier	fritterer	eegginnrv
eeeorrstv	eefginrrt	eefiinrss	eefirrrtu	revenging
oversteer	ferreting	fieriness	fruiterer	eegginrrs
eeeorrtvx	eefgiortv	eefiiprtw	eefirrstu	sniggerer
overexert	forgetive	tripewife	surfeiter	eegginrst
eeepprrtu	eefgiprru	eefiirrsv	eefirrttu	gee-string
puppeteer	prefigure	versifier	fruit-tree	eegginrtt
eeeprrrsv	eefglnrtu	eefiirstt	eefkllttu	gettering
preserver	refulgent	testifier	kettleful	eeggiorsu
eeeprrrtv	eefglrrtu	eefiklmrv	eefknoort	egregious
perverter	regretful	milk-fever	foretoken	eeggoorrv
				overgorge

An extract from *Chambers Anagrams*, for those who are solving in a hurry perhaps.

The Common Theme. Perhaps this is the most common of all special puzzles. The rubric simply reads as follows:

The unclued answers have something in common.

(Sometimes the word 'lights' is used instead of 'answers', but since this word has also been used on occasion for actual letters, I have avoided using it in this book.) If you finish solving all the clues you might be left with a set of unfilled answers as follows:

CAL_IO_E, CLI_, ER_TO, EUT_RP_, _ELP_MENE, PO_YH___NIA, TE_PSI_HOR_, THA_IA, _RANI_

It should not be difficult to spot that these are the nine muses (Calliope, Clio, Erato, Euterpe, Melpomene, Polyhymnia, Terpsichore, Thalia, Urania). The following puzzle is a fairly typical example from *The Spectator* (though the diagram isn't quite 'Ximenean'!).

CROSSWORD No. 31

Looking Up by Duck from *The Spectator*

The unclued answers have something in common. A clued answer could be said to have given them a start.

ACROSS

9 Going in for comp again and making deeper impression? (10, hyphened)
14 Boxer landed one short (3)
16 Part of empire—gold carriage (6)
18 Some benzole ICI supplied—oily (5)
20 Burning is constant hazard known to Lloyd's (7, hyphened)
22 Interferometers and other things assigned to Head of Science (7)
24 One (late) taken aback by certain heavenly bodies? (7)
25 Tangle—what fools must finally suffer (5)
26 Valley with coal-dust, black (5)
28 Terrible ordeal around noon in controversial play (7, two words)
31 He may travel in it over it unconsciously (7)
33 Cowper's work has Greek character endlessly blue (7, two words)
37 Dead serious crime? Answer's hanging (5)
39 Stale vinegar is penetrating fish—end of meal (6)
40 Narrow projecting part 'urt (3)
41 Ixtle's been woven and elastic (10)
42 Secluded lanes with hollow tree among other trees (6)
43 Wyatt rejected eminences—magistrates (8)

DOWN

1 Blades in country cycle, dress and hat carefully arranged (13, hyphened)
2 Go off having relaxation without hint of anxiety (5)
3 Punch is nothing after sharp pain (6)
4 What's in poisonous air showing up somewhere in Paraguay (5)
6 Alluring commander is incompetent (7)
7 Boy to remain cuddling Dad, upset (6)
8 Some bypassed Amsterdam—to go here? (4)
10 What's this—is seen possibly? (6, two words)
11 Bird in wavy bit of déshabillé with few people around (9)
12 Mean women fool these society suckers (13)
13 Canine sight—peer hard (8, hyphened)
15 Beautifully thin having eaten nothing (7)
21 Element of thrillers produced by South American writers with energy (8)
29 Obliquely, like philosopher (6)
30 Rivers in depressed old pasture (6)
32 Bring down medic—to free from pain going round (6)
34 Soft, pure, terribly superior (5)
35 Prison dance (5)

CROSSWORD No. 31

Looking Up

Theme and Variations. A development of the 'thematic' puzzle is the theme and variations puzzle, for which the rubric is as follows (the numbers may vary):

> Four theme words have something in common. Each of them has two variations connected to it, though the nature of the connection differs with each set of variations.

In the puzzle some of the clues read 'Theme-word A',' Variation of A', and so on. To give you some idea of how this works, here is a listing of some answers from an early Azed puzzle:

Theme: 4 Stomachs of ruminants
Theme-word A Rumen. Variations: Lions, Wasps (R.U.men)
Theme-word B Reticulum. Variations: Bonnet, King's hood (alternative names, see *Chambers*)
Theme-word C Bible. Variations: Vinegar, Breeches (names of famous bibles)
Theme-word D Read. Variations: Solve, Study (definitions)

A theme and variations puzzle appears as No. 53 on pp.192–3.

Carte Blanche. With this sort of puzzle you are presented with a blank diagram, usually 12 × 12, and asked to fill in the bars as well as the letters. Instructions are in the form:

> The symmetry of the diagram is such that it would be the same if turned upside down, but not if given a quarter turn. The proportion of checked to unchecked letters is about normal. The clues are in their correct order.

In other words you have a normal Ximenes/Azed diagram of 36 clues with the usual conventions on the number of checked letters (see p.92).

Hints to solvers. You would be well advised to avoid using the printed diagram initially. Start solving the puzzle on a large sheet of squared paper, until you have defined the tops of the diagram's two sides. Concentrate very carefully on the first three or four across clues, and a few down answers will suggest themselves. When you are able to fill in a bar, fill in the one symmetrically opposite. Remember that the nth across clue will be in a symmetrical position with the nth counting from the end, but the same is not true of the downs. By the end of the sixth row of the diagram there should be space for nine across clues since there are usually 18 in total.

Jane Bown, *The Observer*

Ximenes
wearing his Ximenes tie, 1971

The Headmaster, Wells Cathedral School

Afrit
Headmaster of Wells Cathedral
School, 1948

Rob Judges

The author
wearing the Azed tie and displaying
the Azed Cup, 1992

Simon Murison-Bowie

Azed
cutting the cake in celebration of
his 1000th puzzle, 1991

CROSSWORD No. 32
Carte Blanche by Duck from *Crossword*

The clues appear in the correct order. Solvers are asked to fill in the bars (but need not bother with the numbers). Symmetry is such that the diagram would appear the same if turned upside down but not if given a 90 degree turn.

Clamorous priest stirred up the Northern worker
A talent to contain what's original, not going to an extreme?
Some speeches drag out in Shakespeare
Violent poetry translator's immersed in
Field of activity—what the book records in this place
River needs raised bank, removing rapid current in duct
Scottish observer—creeps nervously about, very Scottish
Poisonous plant from Uruguay, thin short one
Genus of monkeys—see returning missionary with one
The most evil character in Indian police station detained by security force
Part of opera: what's central in it?
Note aphis spurting . . . what comes from a _____?
Look in farm vehicle, see old peasant
Bashed lout in revenge
Communist always rejected Thatcher
The prize in old game
Onset of crisis and I go a greeny yellow
The pan is shaken in the specified place—is this a precious ore here?
Group of armadillos look heavy coming up round end of plateau
Animal in tangle with short tree, right between the branches
'To the garçon' (He got a _____ split up?)
Old woman wanting common time in the gutter
Aquatic organisms lunge uncertainly in canal
What the intrusive newsman says: Here's a monetary advance
As before you should stifle onset of excessive laugh
Eye cut with lancet and chemical often used in cutting
What laugh may produce, we hear, spreads
Murmuring softly instead of loudly in excessive nicety
Marine creature from old civilisation kept in an American city
Certainly old Duck is not absurdly hard . . .
. . . Eagerly aimin' to provide what overstressed solvers need?
What you get in *Private Eye*? It bores
Porgies—what one receives aboard?
Low character in airship
Public shelter keeping out the cold . . .
. . . Nevertheless one . . . one probably won't feel it!

CROSSWORD No. 32
Carte Blanche by Duck

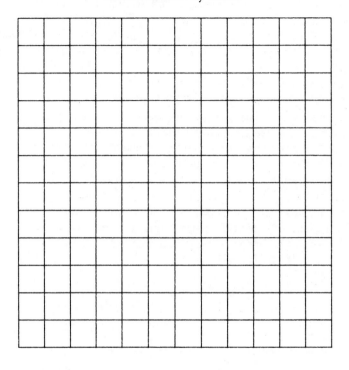

Right and Left was invented by Ximenes, who also set several examples under his other name Tesremos for *The Listener* (for the uninitiated Tesremos is the reverse of Somerset, Macnutt's middle name). The rubric says all:

> Apart from 1 across, which is normal, each clue is really two clues, side by side but not overlapping, leading to two answers, one for the numbered space on the left of the central line and one for that on the right: the clue for either side may come first. The division between clues is not necessarily marked by punctuation.

Hints to solvers. It is worth spending several minutes on 1 across. Quite often it is a straightforward anagram clue and it may be related to the peculiarity of the right and left puzzle. Solve as many clues as you can in the upper half of the puzzle and expect the break to be cunningly concealed in many cases. If the worst comes to the worst, arrange clusters of answers together on one side of the central divide and be prepared to transpose the letters across the divide when everything becomes clearer. Alternatively you might consider using a copied diagram before working on the printed one.

The puzzle below is one from Ximenes:

CROSSWORD No. 33
Right and Left by Ximenes

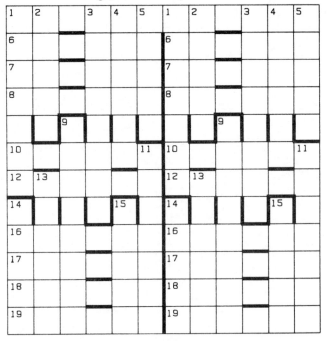

CROSSWORD No. 33

Right and Left by Ximenes from the *Observer*

ACROSS

1 Fruit bolter being terribly sick in rowing-boat (12)

6 Every one of these fish is to pass the Rear Admiral safe and sound—a close shave (6,6)

7 There's starchy stuff in half the arm-bone and in half the guts—in half of each more than a pound (6,6)

8 With pride old Nelly embraces an Apollo with a head of gold caught like Apollo himself on the rebound (6,6)

10 Slow down: there's a danger signal about road-surfacing with lumpy projections not firm edging second-class road (6,6)

12 This predatory bird hasn't quite got the dash to catch carp, or scarlet-backed carp-like fish (6,6)

16 Mum, a mercenary Venus, needs to be got up in the old, old way, i.e. long curls innumerable (6,6)

17 A thing which stands for Britain, with what's British in it, to provoke a shy creature around America (6,6)

18 Preserve one bed for each: this fertiliser is not quite at full strength (6,6)

19 A dark blue cloth—something unique I got in jumble-sale—a short yard, with a margin to spare (6,6)

DOWN

1 Jet flyer crashes bridge—G.W.R. link with east disorganised: single line remains—verb. sap. (7,7)

2 It's the Cup—grand—half the second half's gone—all the tricks —blaze away—the ball's in—it's a goal (5,5)

3 Spanker's near me! I've terrible Latin, little Greek—I'll be kept in—not well up in courses about oxygen: we're downtrodden, but na tanned the noo (8,8)

4 I stagger along: I might remind you of the cricket tests—those paragons of patient effort (6,6)

5 Great violinist, having to give a recital among you, renders no less than fifty odd pieces (5,5)

9 A night-flier with strength to diminution can hardly fly at all—pulls up, being about to fit sails (8,8)

11 Saintly man in France has his prime interrupted by the Nine wild and eery busting the clerical domicile (7,7)

13 She'll advise you, for example, up the river to go slowly and take it easy with little work (6,6)

14 An Admiral, born to be on the water, that's to say a fatherly man where there are ships (5,5)

15 The organ stops: part of the woodwind has perished and rings sharper: some of the cellos elope (5,5)

Definition and Letter-Mixture.

In a DLM puzzle each clue consists of a sentence which contains a definition of the answer and a mixture of the letters (beginning with the beginning or ending with the end of a word in the clue) of the required word.

That, more or less, is the normal rubric. A typical clue might read as follows (without the underlining provided of course!).

[15.4] I can't sleep 'cos I'm an insecure sort of person (9)

The first three words here give the definition and COSIMANIN is a mixture of INSOMNIAC.

Here is a DLM clue where the mixture ends at the end of a word:

[15.5] Tango theme is rendered by octet (9)

Can you see a mixture of EIGHTSOME working back from the 's'?

Unlike with strictly hidden clues, a certain amount of verbal 'cottonwool' is encouraged to produce an interesting context. Often three DLM clues are run together and an example of this from Azed is given below. A puzzle consisting entirely of DLM clues becomes quite easy once a few words have been put in, because you soon learn exactly where to look for the answer.

CROSSWORD No. 34

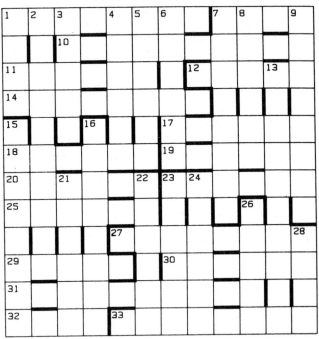

CROSSWORD No. 34

Radio Times by Azed from *The Observer*

Each 'programme synopsis' contains both a definition (one word or more) and a mixture of the letters (beginning with the beginning or ending with the end of a word in the clue) of the three words indicated by the clue numbers (in the correct order). Both indications of the first word precede both indications of the second, and so on. In each case either the definition or the letter-mixture may come first.

ACROSS

1 } *The beat glides up.* George Melly
7 } shows how rhythm has been put
10 } on disc and film since the Beatles were seen prancing through Yellow Submarine land (8, 4, 10 (2 words))

11 } *What were we wearing?* A panel of
12 } fashion experts examines how to
14 } get back those old styles, i.e. rare clothes from the clothes-horse, or make copies of old garments ('U', of course) (6, 5, 8)

17 } *The Stage is Set* (play). Country
18 } shepherd cannot refuse scheming
19 } city bird, abandons sheep, ewe lambs and all, in exchange for the inevitable lost innocence (6, 6, 6)

20 } *Lifting the veil.* In a downright
23 } uncompromising look at what is
25 } going on in a modern convent, Rory Pinstripe seeks to explain unceasing devotion to the 'habit of centuries' (6, 6, 6)

27 } *Pins and Needles.* See Charmian
29 } Purl knit a shawl from yak hair
30 } (matted) and sew a flimsy dress in bombazine (her class assisting in this) (8, 5, 6)

31 } *Punk—Inspiration or Babel?* Lower
32 } end of music scene scrutinised
33 } by Ted Grope, a chap with no liking for glib appraisals or easy slants (10, 4, 8)

DOWN

1 } *Comic Book Art—Pop or Op?*
2 } Examining the role of
3 } Superman, Penny Numbers checks on what may be salvaged from the original concept (4, 10, 5)

4 } *Lines in Maroon Ink.* Dundee poet
5 } Hamish Thible seeks to bare his
6 } soul and thus give a Gaelic ring to the phrase 'go metric' (6, 6, 6)

7 } *A 'Pink' or a 'Purple'?* Giles
8 } Painter's talk is not so rash as to
9 } try to get at what liberalism really means but it should help to clear the system (8, 6, 8)

13 } *Everything About it is Unfeeling.*
15 } Representing show business in
16 } declamatory lingo, puts off the comic mask, warning of that elusive 'slot in the bill' (10, 8, 8)

21 } *New Arrangements.* A conducted
22 } tour through the maze of
23 } modern dance orchestrations by that skilled Scot king of the ballroom pas, Hew McOrnes (6, 6, 6)

24 } *Here let me lie.* Panel-game in
26 } which contestants repair to the
28 } Truth Booth to see flagrantly fictitious experiences dispensed with as objects of fun (6, 5, 4)

Wrong Number. This, perhaps, is the least common of the standard specials, and it is very hard to start off. Here is the rubric:

> Each clue includes a one-word definition of the word required at the number where it stands but belongs as a whole to a word of the same length elsewhere. Method recommended is to find, after solving a clue, a definition of the solution in one of the other words of its length: this will show where the word is to go.

Here are two clues from such a puzzle by Azed:

[15.6] 28 across. The old woman's blue over end of relative (5)

[15.7] 9 down. Glum youth soft-headed, one kept in trim no longer (5)

It turns out that the answer belonging to 28 across is UNCLE (the clue for which is at 25 down and the definition for which at 28 across is 'relative'). 28 across gives ANILE (anil + e) which means soft-headed, so the answer fits in at 9 down. The answer to 9 down is PROIN (p + i in Ron—remember Ron Glum in the radio programme 'Take It from Here'?). This fits in at 2 down which contains the definition word 'prune'. Thus each WN puzzle consists of a number of circular chains, one for each word length.

See how you get on with this one from Ximenes:

CROSSWORD No. 35

1	2		3	4	5	6		7	8	9	10
11							12				
13			14								
15		16					17				
					18					19	20
21											
			22		23						
24								25			
26	27					28					
29							30				
31					32						
33						34					

CROSSWORD No. 35

Wrong Number by Ximenes from *The Observer*

Each clue includes a one-word definition of the word required at the number where it stands but belongs as a whole to a word of the same length elsewhere. Method recommended is to find, after solving a clue, a definition of the solution in one of the 5 other clues to words of its length: this will show where the word is to go.

ACROSS

1 Grape contains centre of pulp, a conical body (5)
5 I'm from the isle—I'm too small to pull a coach (7)
11 I'm fleecing a bird that's swallowed champagne, perhaps: you can have a slice (7)
12 To take prolonged looks at a TV is to flounder (5)
13 The Navy in America are used in state elections (4)
14 Rail being far from broken is together in one piece (8)
15 East China must slough off N.America and welcome in minor officer, Turkish official (6)
18 What's divine about novelist revered a good bit (7)
21 Crown, and less valuable coins, contain a mineral coated with copper carbonate (9)
22 To intrigue disloyally with her is horrific, just a bit (9)
24 Held head in an awful state, covered with blood (7)
28 Have a crack at the French in the hollow (6)
29 Putter-in of good work in bar, being in debt, behaves like bird-fancier off to Gretna (8)
30 Aromatic condiment kept in pukka vases (4)
31 Fastener—here's part of the clasp right in view (5)
32 Meal dear in Paris: he'll pinch your pony and sock you (7)
33 Socialist votes stuck together—shows herd instinct (7)
34 The flower of creation, its appetites and its food (5)

DOWN

1 Unusual ernes in flight, to reach which one must cross part of the Channel (8)
2 The activity of a fly-by-night round that location could be learnt as the result of a pick-up (8)
3 If it luxuriates on a lawn, spray is in vogue (5)
4 Take sly measures, lacing one tea with another (9)
6 Hiding-place on shore where seceding party receives envoy representing Navy (6)
7 This cherry split's nice, not 'arf—swell (6)
8 Affected by storm tortile tellurium is laminated (9)
9 Rising prima donna, wanting meals supplemented (4)
10 Make declarations and talk rubbish in the 'ighlands (4)
16 With endless rush I beat: my force fairly staggers (9)
17 She's in arch, short shows never filmed by BBC—they gave lots of people the sack (9)
19 ITV arias out of tune must have got the bird (8)
20 Once passionate wench in only part of garment (8)
22 Ham recipe is wrong—result's slimy, often salt (6)
23 Product of juice of red fruit spoils a metal (6)
25 Lobe of whale's tail's eaten mashed—that's lucky (5)
26 To separate brawlers, flushed with start of drink (4)
27 Economised—only half keen—in a limited edition (4)

Other specials. In addition to the specials just described there are a number of other specials which have become standard (e.g. Justyn Print by Zander, see pp.224–5). Some, though, are very much 'special specials'. A 'special special' may exploit a different clue type, a different way of entering words on the diagram, a different shape of diagram—or even all three. Some advanced solvers feed on such a diet of puzzles almost exclusively, and their needs are well catered for by the Listener crossword (now in *The Times* every Saturday) and the Crossword Club—not to mention the occasional new special from Azed in *The Observer*. (Roughly one puzzle in six from Azed is a special, but new specials are usually reserved for particular occasions.)

In difficulty such puzzles vary enormously, and the setter can overload the dice against the solver by leaving too many possibilities for the answer's mode of entry on to the diagram. 'Special specials' lie at the top of Crossword Mountain. Only you will ultimately decide how far up that mountain it is worth going and whether the setter is launching an unfair blizzard directly at you. But keep trying and you will soon conquer some exciting new peaks!

7 j☐g☐i

jagging	Jenkins	Jezebel	knitted	knowing	leafbud	Lockist
jigging	jangler	jazzily	knittle	knock-on	leap-day	luckily
jogging	jingler	jazzman	knitter	knock-up	llanero	lock-jaw
jugging	jinglet	khanate	kajawah	knocker	loathed	locular
jiggish	junkman	khaddar	kakodyl	kroo-man	leather	loculus
juggins	jannock	knavery	kikumon	knotted	loather	locally
jigajig	juniper	khalifa	kellaut	knotter	loathly	lace-man
joggled	janitor	kyanise	kilobar	kippage	leading	lockman
juggler	jonquil	kyanite	kilobit	kip-shop	leafing	locoman
jugular	janizar	knavish	killcow	kip-skin	leaning	lacinia
jog-trot	jeopard	klavier	killdee	kurbash	leaping	laconic
jugfuls	jeofail	knacker	kiln-dry	kursaal	leasing	Lychnic
Johnian	jookery	knapped	kolkhoz	Kurhaus	leaving	lacunae
johnnie	jap-silk	knapple	Kallima	Kartell	loading	licence
Jehovah	Japonic	knapper	killing	kermess	loafing	license
joinder	Jupiter	knarred	killick	kirmess	loaning	lacunal
joinery	jury-box	khamsin	killjoy	kerygma	leaflet	lacunar
joining	Jericho	Kabbala	kalends	kerogen	learned	lychnis
Jainism	juridic	kebbock	killock	kernite	learner	lock-nut
jointed	jarring	kibitka	kiloton	Karaite	leasowe	lucency
jointer	Jersian	kebbuck	Kalmuck	Karling	lead-out	lactose
jointly	jerking	kibbutz	kamichi	karting	Liassic	lich-owl
jejunum	jurally	kachcha	kamseen	kirking	liaison	lockout
ju-jitsu	jarkman	kacheri	Kommers	kernish	leaguer	lycopod
juke-box	juryman	kick-off	kemping	Kurdish	libbard	Lacerta
jellaba	jurymen	kimboed	kimboed	karakul	lubbard	lucarne
jellied	jargoon	kidding	kampong	kirtled	labiate	lucerne
jellify	jerquer	kidling	kamerad	keramic	librate	lockram
jellily	jarfuls	Kaddish	kumquat	kirimon	library	locusta
jollify	jessant	kiddier	Kannada	Koranic	lubfish	lichtly
jollily	jessamy	kiddies	kingcup	Karenni	Librium®	licitly
jollity	jaspery	kid-skin	kingdom	keratin	labella	Lactuca
jalapic	jestful	keelage	kinless	kirkton	lobelia	lecture

An extract from *Chambers Crossword Completer*, a helpful crossword reference book for the 15 × 15 puzzle solver.

16

Crossword Competitions

Although solving crosswords is often a solitary occupation, it is possible to introduce a competitive element. Many periodicals limit their competitions to the level of chance, by inviting solvers to send in their solutions and then awarding prizes for the first three 'out of the hat'. This at least reassures the editor that there is someone 'out there' solving the puzzles—though it is surprising how many of Afrit's *Listener* puzzles in the 1930s attracted no correct entries. The best competitions, though, must be those that have an increased element of skill. The best-known of these is undoubtedly *The Times* Crossword Championship (which is currently sponsored by InterCity). Here one has to solve a standard puzzle plus a very hard elimination puzzle in *The Times* before progressing to a regional final and the national final. Speed of solving and accuracy are the keynotes.

If *The Times* championship is the best-known competition, then the *Observer* clue-writing competition is probably the most significant in terms of 'good done for crosswords'. Started in 1945 by Ximenes it continued until his death in 1971, then resumed under Azed in 1972. Solvers are required to solve the puzzle, then write a cryptic clue for a specified word (usually replacing a definition-only clue in the puzzle itself). Through the competition Ximenes developed the theory of cluemanship from Afrit's basic ideas to a fine art (culminating with the publication of *Ximenes on the Art of the Crossword*). Azed is the pseudonym of Jonathan Crowther, who is an editor at Oxford University Press. He has carried on where Ximenes left off, and although he takes his name from the reverse of a Spanish inquisitor (the reverse of Deza) he is no more tolerant of latter-day 'heretics'!

Associated with the *Observer*'s competition have been annual honours lists and periodic celebrations to salute the setter. As the competition now stands, the submitters of the three clues judged best by Azed are rewarded with book tokens and 2 honours points; the next 20 or so best are labelled VHC (very highly commended) and gain one honours point; and a further 70 or so are deemed HC (highly commended). A cup passes between first-prizewinners and a silver salver between annual champions. Prizewinners and VHCs are listed in *The Observer*, and in a competing year there are 13 competitions (12 monthly, plus one at Christmas when VHCs are awarded 'extra prizes'). Solvers sending a stamped addressed envelope receive slips detailing successful clues plus a commentary from Azed on the competition, often with details of clues that didn't make it and why they didn't.

For the rest of this chapter we will look at some extracts from the slips, with the comments of Ximenes and Azed. Some of the prizewinners became celebrated for turning out brilliant clue after brilliant clue. Sadly C. Allen Baker, Mrs L. (Norah) Jarman and D. P. M. Michael are no longer with us, but N. C. Dexter and C. J. (Sir Jeremy) Morse have provided gems for nigh on 40 years. Your author has had a measure of success himself, but is still quite a 'new boy', having begun as recently as 1970!* (In this second edition I am happy to thank Colin Dexter for his kind comments, but acknowledge that some even newer boys such as R. J. Hooper are also stars in the firmament.)

Ximenes No. 79
SALOME—1. Maj. G. W. Shepherd (Scarborough): Perplexed damsel wanting a head and requiring nothing more (*amsel-o* and *literal mng.*) . . .
. . . An interesting point of 'cluemanship' was raised by a regular and expert solver. Was 'insist' for 'in sist' without a hint of division, sound in the clue to SISKIWIT? . . . the practice had better stop. . . .

Ximenes No. 148
FILIBUSTER—1. A. N. Clark (Portsmouth): I rifle tubs at sea . . . Mr Clark's *multum in parvo* is, I think, superb; he has brilliantly seized a rare chance.

Ximenes No. 162
TITANESS . . . 'A hardy girl to go against a goddess.' Unsound in *many* ways! It is meant for 'Tess anti' anag., but no anag. is indicated, the wording being vague and unhelpful: this is particularly unfair in an *indirect* anag., the actual anag. words not being given: on top of that Hardy loses its capital—this is deliberately unfair, as it *cannot* be a true clue; the converse process is allowable—a writer may *give* a word a capital for his own purposes without incorrectness. . . .

* This and other diffident statements here do no justice to DFM's importance in the crossword field. Over the past decade it is he himself who has been the undoubted star in the Azed competitions, for which he has produced a stream of clues to 'fill the eye' (as the judges say of champion dogs at Crufts!). NCD

Ximenes No. 229
MASCOT—1. C. Allen Baker (Milnathort): Up in the morning and with the sun and early bed is said to bring good fortune. . . . May I repeat what I have said before several times, that when I quote unsuccessful clues, I do so not to hand wooden spoons to the authors but to help not only the authors but the competitors, especially the newcomers.

Ximenes No. 275 (Printer's Devilry)
ESTOVER—1. J. B. Filburn: True! Man's fasts are inconsistent even with Lent here to inspire. . . . COMMENTS—375 entries, 354 correct . . . I must repeat two principles about devilled clues. (1) The formal sense must *not* be sacrificed to the devilled sense . . . (2) The hiding can be *too* well done. An example is 'A good coke heats water in no time' . . . *Very* difficult . . . no fun at all. . . .

Ximenes No. 460
ASTONISHMENT (Misprints)—1. H. S. Tribe: Open winder? Then no mats is shaken (*wonder*). . . . By the way, my wife assures me that Mr Tribe's delightfully neat clue presents a strong household hint . . . Indication of anagrams. There were a good many which I couldn't accept as sound, e.g. 'fraught', 'separation of', 'critical', 'it appears'.

Ximenes No. 634
BEDSTEAD—1. C. J. Morse: To be still is not enough here: both sides of the sheet must be tucked in (be-d-st-ead '& lit.'). . . . It seems clear that posting on Friday is no longer safe, even in London itself. One solver has written, he tells me, to the P.M.G. to complain, and has so far received no satisfaction but a brief acknowledgement.

Ximenes No. 647
MADCAP—1. E. Gomersall (York): Cake with nuts on top (*cake = madcap, Chamb.*).

Ximenes No. 690 [A 'trick' puzzle for 1 April]
ASCERTAIN—1. Miss D. W. Taylor (Worthing): Find the right answer? Sure—the first of April's over! (A-'s-certain) . . . 263 entries, 229 mahoganies . . . the leg-pull was far, far more successful than I meant.

Ximenes No. 945
OBLITERATE—1. N. C. Dexter: (Biol.) Treat defective end of a tube (*anag. plus e '& lit.'*) . . . R. Postill: Wipe out Beatle and disorganised trio remains . . . [Mr Postill] says in his note 'out, vb'; that leaves 'blot' [sic] alone as the definition, and I don't think it will quite do without 'out'.

Ximenes No. 967
CREMOSIN—1. N. C. Dexter: Colour of the Skie, perhaps, with
Morne [sic] breaking (*anag. '& lit.'*, *F.Q.* 11, 3 '*Early before the Morne
with Cremosin ray*') [F.Q. = Faerie Queene.]

Ximenes No. 1000
THOUSAND—1. C. J. Morse: Up-to-date product of X and C. . . . All
the dishes on the 'Millenu' (and most of the speakers) began with M.
. . . One thing I forgot to say, so I'll say it here—how greatly I
appreciate the sporting way in which you never dispute my often
doubtful umpire's decisions . . .

Ximenes No. 1115
FLESHPOTTERY—1. Mrs B. Lewis: Product of the Tory's pelf,
snarls the prosy left (*anags. '& lit.': snarl = tangle*)... COMMENTS—
Just under 300 entries, nearly all correct. Was it too hot? Am I, quite
unconsciously, becoming more difficult? Or were people upset by not
finding Jethart staff (s.v. Jeddart)? This arbitrary omission of
cross-references in C is annoying (and, I think, inefficient). . . .

Azed No. 70
. . . If the misprinted clue is as much a definition as its original it
cannot be considered to be misprinted. Ximenes made the point in
the slip to No.1131 for those who keep scrap-books.
. . . I would always regard 'a bit of', 'a piece of' as coming from the
front of the word. . . .

Azed No. 92
BRAINWASH—1. L. May: Bust down reason? (bra in wash).

Azed No. 100
CENTENARIAN:—1. D. F. Manley: An ancient the Queen may get
excited (*anag. '& lit.'*, *royal telegram*) . . . 'Azed achieves his for when he
drives around Muswell Hill chased by two?' (EN TEN (N.10) in
CAR + I + AN (1 + 1 = 2)). Dreadfully unsound, I'm afraid, and
virtually unsolvable. There is no indication of the part of speech
required; 'When he drives' will never do for 'car'; Muswell Hill is only
one part of N.10; and 'two' for I + AN is surely unacceptable.

Azed No. 430
TEGULA: 1. C. G. Millin: What the fiddler might have played on, in
the film (*gu in tela '& lit.' Fiddler on the Roof*) . . . Is a tela a film? I
examined this question very carefully . . . *Chambers* definition

somewhat inadequate . . . turned to the new *Collins English Dictionary* for the reassurance I needed . . . Finally a reminder that I still have small stocks of Azed ties, all three colours. The price is now £3 each inclusive of V.A.T. . . .

Azed No. 482

BODY-SNATCHER: 1. C. J. Morse: Stiff collaring, that's my trade—shows what can be done by starch (*2 mngs and anag*).

Azed No. 500

BEFOOL (with 2 extra D's): 1. D. Ashcroft: Admass imperative: get fund at others' expense (*be-fool* imp. form of am-ass). . . . Very few of you noticed that the style of the down clues was such that they made reasonable sense with and without the superfluous D's. . . . The Azed 500 Dinner was a spectacularly successful affair . . . I look forward to meeting many of these friends at No. 750.

Azed No. 662

BARGE-COUPLE: 1. R. J. Hooper: Sawyer's contribution to topping story shows the lighter Twain (barge-couple; ref. Mark T.) . . . [This following clue] is probably the most unsolvable clue I've ever received. ' "O Attic shape!" Sounds like naughty Keats may have been involved in this.' Explanation (I quote): 'Quotation from "Grecian Urn" by Keats. Naughty = no "T"'. Keats without T sounds like KEYS. Keys open locks, as do couples on a barge.' Need I say more?

Azed No. 679 (see also Ximenes No.275, p.131)

ESTOVER ('P.D.'): 1. T. J. Moorey: 'Dry' minister organising party left-winger. . . . COMMENTS:—A mammoth entry—702 in all. . . . I also failed to notice that Ximenes used ESTOVER as a P.D. competition word over 30 years ago (his No. 275), and there are still regular solvers who remember that earlier occasion . . . the Ximenes competition attracted a much smaller entry.

Azed No. 904

VOETGANGER: 1. J. F. Grimshaw: Boorish promenader's against reggae not being represented (*v. + anag.*). . . . An interesting point of principle arose in a number of clues using the appealing 'a Green Govt' anagram. Is wording along the lines of '. . . could produce a Green Government', with or without 'shortly' to indicate an abbreviation of 'Government', fair to the solver, or is it tantamount to an indirect anagram, involving a two-stage decoding process? I tend to the latter view (especially as 'Govt' is only one of the abbreviations given for 'Government', at least in *Chambers*). Repeated use has given acceptability to the convention of including in anagrams single-letter abbreviations indicated by the full form of the word abbreviated, especially when such abbreviations are in common use, but there is a difference, I think, between the practice and expecting the solver to unscramble larger and perhaps less familiar abbreviations. . . . Comments welcomed.

Azed No. 917
HOOLIGANISM: 1. M. Barley: Trouble Italy has looming (*anag. incl. I & lit.; ref. World Cup*). I hope my choice will be seen as consistent with my remarks on the use of abbreviations in anagrams in the recent VOETGANGER slip. One or two solvers have expressed misgivings about the use of IVR abbreviations, especially those rarely encountered on cars in Europe, but this one is surely common and familiar.

Azed No. 1000
ONE THOUSAND: 1. D. F. Manley: The Sun. No. specially launched with a do (*anag. & lit.; ref. AZ 1000 lunch*) . . . it had to be ONE THOUSAND since Ximenes got competitors to clue THOUSAND. . . . The celebratory lunch in Oxford was a joyous occasion blessed by beautiful weather. . . .

Over the past forty years N. C. Dexter has probably been the most brilliant clue-writer, but C. J. Morse has been the most *consistent*. If you want to know what makes a good cryptic clue, simply look at his two clues above (Ximenes No. 634 and Azed No. 482). One is a great '& lit.'; the other shows how a clever definition can be combined with a subsidiary indication in a totally misleading context. Aspiring crossword setters would do well to enrol in Azed's correspondence school.

17

Yet More on Fair Play

The last chapter gives some indication of how Ximenes and Azed have worked out the rules of fair play through the *Observer* clue-writing competitions. Some of the 'rules' have come easily, but we've seen how there may still be some tricky areas. The slips of Azed 904 and 917 demonstrate that we are operating under case law.

In one slip, Azed dared to confess that 'I must be becoming more tolerant with the passing years'. We now look at a case when he seems to have become *less* tolerant, and this again will show that 'fair play' may not be as cut-and-dried as we once imagined.

Let's look again at [10.20]:

[10.20] What's hidden by Fred afterwards? He must be stupid! (4)

In the clue the part of speech defining the answer was clearly wrong, but *must* the definition *always* be defined by the appropriate part of speech? The answer to this isn't as obvious as you might think. For example, you may reasonably define a noun by a verb as here:

[17.1] One party after another is really dead! (4)

Here 'party' = 'do' and do + do = DODO. The definition consists of the three words 'is really dead' with an 'it' understood:

[It] is really dead.

Here is a prize-winning clue from M. Barley in an Azed competition in the *Observer*:

[17.2] Bears cope (10)

Sophisticated stuff this, so pay attention! 'Bears' = 'balus' (the animals) and 'cope' = 'trade'.

Hence the clue as a whole spells out BALUSTRADE. And the two words are also a definition of a balustrade if one is prepared to accept an ellipsis of an 'understood' and necessary subject, namely 'it':

[It] bears [a] cope.

I must admit it's stretching the language, but the clue does seem to me to be fair.

Now look at this clue, which is another Azed first-prizewinner from 1972 (and which we met on p.98):

[14.4] Given unconventionally for Jack's head (7)
with its note, (anag. for t in tar & lit.).

In the definition sense we are being asked this time to take as understood:

[It was] given unconventionally . . .

Should this be allowed? In 1988 Azed said no. He disowned his earlier judgement, claiming that it was unsatisfactory to define a noun by a past participle, which is effectively an adjective. One sympathizes with the wish to discourage setters from defining 'glass' by 'transparent', but if one can swallow [It] why cannot one swallow [It is] or [It was]? It could be argued, in fact, that the ellipsis of [It is] is more common than the ellipsis of [It] in the history of language—certainly [14.4] seems more understandable than [17.2].

The debate is continuing, even among the Ximeneans. Analysing this clue for SIMKIN (hidden & lit.)

[17.3] Among wines I'm king

Azed makes a similar criticism:

'Although in the "& lit." [= definition] reading the pronoun "I" clearly indicates a noun solution, in the *cryptic* reading [= subsidiary indication] all we have is an adverbial phrase which can't as it stands indicate a noun.' He then recommends the sounder version:

[17.4] It is among wines I'm king.

At this point it is very interesting to look through the old Ximenes slips. Here is the clue to SISKIN that won A. R. Fraser first prize for Ximenes No. 87:

[17.5] Among St. Francis of Assisi's kindred.

This is a very early hidden '& lit.' in which the extra words are necessary and forgivable (see [10.24] and [10.25] on p.63). And the clue has a lovely idea, conjuring up a picture of Francis and the birds. But that clue was pre-Azed.

Here is another clue that found favour with Ximenes, one of many winners for N. C. Dexter:

[17.6] Fantastic warblers do it—sew leaves! Here's one among them.

The answer is TAILOR-BIRD (*anag. minus sew incl. i, & lit.*). In case you didn't follow that note, it works like this: take an anagram of 'warblers do it', remove 'sew', and insert 'i'. You'll get the right letters and a surprisingly good definition.

But, faced with this clue, Azed would have reservations. He argues that the departing letters should be in the same order as they are in the word or phrases to be anagrammed, although they do not need to be contiguous. To make [17.6] acceptable, where 'w, e, s' are leaving 'warblers do it' and not 's, e, w' he would probably suggest 'somehow sew'. It is arguable, though, that one could choose to make the anagram such that the letters would fall into the correct order ready to drop out. Readers may decide for themselves, but those entering Azed competitions will now know where they stand.

The examples in this chapter show how difficult it can be on occasion to apply the rules of grammar rigidly to crossword clues. There are likely to be contentious areas, and one has the utmost respect and sympathy for Azed in the difficult position of clue-judge. One should not, however, resort to the attitude that it is all a question of hair-splitting and that it really doesn't matter. The underlying attitude of Afrit, Ximenes and Azed is that grammar *does* matter, and I believe that the best clues will always come from those clue-writers who aspire to sound grammatical style.

18

Crossword Setting: a Case Study

So many people ask me how I go about setting a puzzle for the dailies that I've decided to let you in on the secret. I shall show you how to go about a 15 × 15 puzzle. I have been fortunate enough to set for *The Independent, The Independent on Sunday, The Guardian,* and *The Times*. In each case I have a choice of grids so I had better choose one and find some letters to fit.

A *Guardian* grid (their no. 49) sits on my desk. Suppose I put MOTORWAY MADNESS at 1 across. With help from *Chambers Words* and a trusty old *Modern Crossword Dictionary* (the 1967 edition as it happens) I've soon got the outside answers written in.

GUARDIAN GRID No. 49

Nice finishing letters on the right-hand side, but the O at the bottom of 20 and the I at the bottom of 23 are less than ideal. Never mind—let's tackle 23 down straight away—LORELEI is an old favourite—in it goes.

Now I'll tackle 29 across keeping an eye on 21 down. An R would be nice to start with because TANTRUM could go in at 21 down. Out with the Franklin Spellmaster: R___L___E and press ENTER: REDOLENCE (horrible word), REGULABLE (even worse), REPULSIVE (*not* repulsive, but let's keep going), RESALABLE (not today, thank you), RESOLUBLE (mm, maybe), RETALIATE (best yet), END OF LIST. RETALIATE it is. And so it goes on and the answers go in in the following order (if you want to follow them through):

7 down (ELABORATE), 22 across (GALLEON), 22 down (GHETTOS—check 'OS', not 'OES'), 24 across (ASH), 26 across (ENRAGES), 27 down (GRAIN). The nasty SE corner is done—let's go to the SW. 19 across (HIDEOUT—hope that U will be OK!), 20 down (OREGANO—what, again?!), 25 across (NUCLEON—it's time we had some physics!) and 28 across (IBIZA—horrible last time, no better now I've got to find a new clue). 15 down has several possibilities starting with 'addiction' but let's try SEDUCTION this time (didn't I clue 'addiction' somewhere else recently?). Better look at 16 down. Try TAU. Then 14 across (RESTATE), 3 down (REPLICA), 9 across: 'stamp something'? No, try SANDPIPER. If 4 down is APPEASE, 11 across can be 'partita' and 2 down 'tenor', but I've clued 'tenor' a lot recently. Try TON-UP and PAPRIKA.

Only the top NE corner to go! 17 across suggests EYEWASH, YEA? (18 down), and MIRACLE quickly follows at 5 down. 13 across is SOL. We're nearly there having shown a lot of FLAIR (10 across). Let's have American defence for a change (DEFENSE at 6 down). We could have 'concoct' or 'contort' at 12 across but let's have CONSORT. I've simplified the process slightly (there *were* a few blind alleys!) but not much. That took less than an hour and probably not more than 30 minutes.

So on to the clues. I've got some ideas already, but one or two worries as well. Never mind. Let's try taking the clues in order and see how it goes.

1 across: MOTORWAY MADNESS. A clever definition and an anagram? Could be tricky. Let's think about a cryptic definition. Idiots who crash in the fog (and the innocent victim too) may be driving one minute and finding themselves at the pearly gates the next, so let's try:

The sort of idiocy that makes folk drive up to the pearly gates? (8,7).

9 across: SANDPIPER. Almost the same as 'sandpaper'. In fact, they'd sound the same 'down under' surely:

Bird sounding abrasive in Melbourne? (9).

10 across: FLAIR is L in fair. 'Fair' is 'blonde' and 'flair' is talent. I'm going to take a chance with the feminists here:

Blonde, about 50, shows 'talent' (5).

11 across: PAPRIKA. Awkward letters here. 'Papa' looks nice but I don't like the 'rik'. A bits-and-pieces job I think:

Condiment makes Dad consume only half the rice, ending with 'Yuck!' (7).

12 across: CONSORT. A gift, this: con + sort. I don't suppose I'll upset too many *Guardian* readers with this:

Tory type, a tagger-on? (7).

13 across: SOL. Isn't 'sol' an alternative for the note 'soh'? Yes, it is—and Sol means 'Sun' too. Not an exciting clue, this, but it's OK:

Note source of illumination (3).

14 across: RESTATE. Another charade, surely: rest + ate. Hmm, I think I've done that before, so let's try R + estate:

Once again affirm king must be given the property (7).

17 across: EYEWASH. I can remember a nice *Times* clue for this: 'English trees rot', I think it was (E + yew + ash). I'd better not pinch it. I'm saying the word to myself, desperately searching for a new idea and suddenly it sounds like 'I wash':

What sounds like claim to keep clean is nonsense (7).

19 across: HIDEOUT only differs from 'hideous' in the last letter. Ideally we should perhaps signal the exact substitution, but I think this clue is fair enough:

Den with nasty decor maybe changed finally (7).

22 across: GALLEON. Surely gall and eon, but how can we link that with a ship? Here's an idea which seems to work:

Rancour goes on a long time—one may have wanted calm waters (7).

24 across: ASH. A dull little word inviting a double meaning, but I've done that before. What about 'as H'? But how can we like 'H' to wood? Simple!

Like rugby post made of wood (3).

25 across: NUCLEON. It's a particle in the centre of a nucleus, either a neutron (not charged) or a proton (charged). Try linking *that* to an anagram of 'on uncle'. No thanks! I'll go for a cryptic definition with a misleading context:

I play a central role, but I may or may not be charged (7).

26 across: ENRAGES. One of those dull seven-letter words ('element' is another, not to mention 'oregano'!) that keep cropping up in dense diagrams like this one. No good ducking it—time for an anagram. Whatever the definition, the answer could be as 'green as' could be. Let's try a theme of jealousy. To enrage X is to get X very cross, so here goes:

Gets very cross, being as green as could be (7).

28 across: IBIZA. A pain! Why did I allow it? Because I'm equally disenchanted with 'idiot' and 'idiom'. Since 'biza' is 'bizarre' minus 'rre' (= err, rev) and 'i' is a half of 'is', let's try something contrived and pass quickly on to the next clue:

Island is not half bizarre—go wrong turning to leave it (5).

29 across: RETALIATE. Only one anagram so far. Time for another:

Treat shamefully with a lie to wreak vengeance (9).

30 across: NON-COMMISSIONED. Oh, lousy word to define! Oh, horrible letters! Surely a candidate for a cryptic definition if ever there was one. Think for a moment! NCOs have stripes; COs have pips. Got it!

Give someone the pip and he won't be this any more (3-12).

On with the Downs:

1 down: MISAPPREHENSION. Try an anagram. 'Perhaps' comes out nicely, and I quickly find 'some perhaps in in'. I'm going to be rather more devious than usual for this level of puzzle. Make 'in in' into 'doubly in' and use 'muddle' as a transitive verb. And of course 'perhaps' looks almost too innocent to be part of an anagram. The gerund definition should help though:

Some, perhaps, doubly in muddle, taking things the wrong way (15).

2 down: TON-UP. If I wrote 'ton' up, I would get 'not' surely? So if I suggest that the answer is a *clue* I can put the answer to the answer in the real clue! Who said I have a devious mind?

Not, as you would deduce, very fast (3-2).

3 down: REPLICA. My trusty *Chambers* defines this as 'a duplicate, properly one by the original artist'. Don't artists produce 'pics'? Here's an anag. & lit. then:

Real pic re-created (7).

4 down: APPEASE. I've clued this before, and obviously it is a + pp + ease. Looking in Chambers for a new twist I can't help noticing that ease is quiet (n.) and appease is quiet (v.)—not to mention p and p. If 'a' is one, the rest of the clue can consist of quiets!

One needs to get quiet, quiet, quiet—QUIET! (7).

5 down: MIRACLE. Not an anagram of 'reclaim' *again*, please, but I can see car, rev. in mile so let's try this, suggesting the latest model with the powerful brakes:

Wonder vehicle pulled up within the distance (7).

6 down: DEFENSE. It's not inconceivable that the boggy 'fens' would have a river round them and this time the *Concise Oxford Dictionary* helps me with the definition:

US military resources in boggy area with river around (7).

7 down: ELABORATE. The adjective looks slightly more promising than the verb from the definition point of view and an anagram comes easily (the fourth—we'd better not use many more!):

Complicated tale a bore spun out (9).

8 down: SCRATCH ONE'S HEAD. Phrases that offer a literal and a metaphorical meaning are a gift:

What can a person do without a comb? Be perplexed (7,4,4).

15 down: SEDUCTION. I've used s + educ(a)tion before but never 'du' in 'section'. Think of those naughty folk across the Channel:

Tempting act of the French in part (9).

16 down: TAU. Ta + U or T + Au. Not very interesting, let's face it, but it's almost 'taut', and we can conjure up a Saturday night in Athens with the retsina flowing ('retsina' is an anagram of 'nastier', did you know? I avoided it in 3 down):

Greek character little short of being tight (3).

18 down: YEA. Let's use 'indeed' as the definition and bring it alongside a statement of the obvious, so start with 'The old' for 'ye' and finish with 'indeed'. Then it's not too difficult:

The old will need a bit of assistance, indeed (3).

20 down: OREGANO. I've already grumbled about this. I suppose I've only got myself to blame. I'm going for O + anag. this time with October brought in for autumnal plausibility:

Herb leaves turning orange after beginning of October (7).

21 down: TANTRUM. So much French drink (tant + rum)? No, I must do something different. We haven't used a hidden word yet, have we?

Ill-temper brought by constant rumours (7).

22 down: GHETTOS. I'm getting perilously close to my maximum number of anagrams, but I can't resist 'get shot'!

Get shot going astray in slum areas (7).

23 down: LORELEI. I won't be the first (or the last!) to clue this by lore + lei, but we can't *always* be original!

Fabulous singer in folk stories given garland (7).

27 down: GRAIN. I see that this can be defined by 'fruit', something which we should encourage everyone to eat, of whatever age. Put in a 'perhaps' because it's possible to be a gran at 32:

Old lady perhaps eating one fruit (5).

So there we have it: 2 or 3 hours work, showing you how it's done. I haven't in any way saved up my best clues for this puzzle, and I haven't provided equal numbers of all types of clue (there are rather more cryptic definitions than usual, for example), but I hope it was enjoyable enough for *Guardian* readers on 25 January 1992.

Here is the puzzle, clues and grid together:

GUARDIAN CROSSWORD 19,313

Set by Pasquale

ACROSS

1 The sort of idiocy that makes folk drive up to the pearly gates? (8,7)
9 Bird sounding abrasive in Melbourne? (9)
10 Blonde, about 50, shows 'talent' (5)
11 Condiment makes Dad consume only half the rice, ending with 'Yuck!' (7)
12 Tory type, a tagger-on? (7)
13 Note source of illumination (3)
14 Once again affirm king must be given the property (7)
17 What sounds like claim to keep clean is nonsense (7)
19 Den with nasty decor maybe changed finally (7)
22 Rancour goes on a long time—one may have wanted calm waters (7)
24 Like rugby post made of wood (3)
25 I play a central role, but I may or may not be charged (7)
26 Gets very cross, being as green as could be (7)
28 Island is not half bizarre—go wrong turning to leave it (5)
29 Treat shamefully with a lie to wreak vengeance (9)
30 Give someone the pip and he won't be this any more (3-12)

DOWN

1 Some, perhaps, doubly in muddle, taking things the wrong way (15)
2 Not, as you would deduce, very fast (3-2)
3 Real pic re-created (7)
4 One needs to get quiet, quiet, quiet—QUIET! (7)
5 Wonder vehicle pulled up within the distance (7)
6 US military resources in boggy area with river around (7)
7 Complicated tale a bore spun out (9)
8 What can a person do without a comb? Be perplexed (7,4,11)
15 Tempting act of the French in part (9)
16 Greek character little short of being tight (3)
18 The old will need a bit of assistance, indeed (3)
20 Herb leaves turn orange after beginning of October (7)
21 Ill-temper brought by constant rumours (7)
22 Get shot going astray in slum areas (7)
23 Fabulous singer in folk stories given garland (7)
27 Old lady perhaps eating one fruit (5)

GUARDIAN CROSSWORD 19,313

19

The Complete Solver; The Complete Setter

The Complete Solver

In this book I've taken you through definition puzzles, 15 × 15 plain cryptics, and then suggested that you go mountaineering with *Chambers* to tackle the 12 × 12 barred puzzles and eventually the advanced specials. This manual is designed to help you do just that and when you get to Chapter 20 you will be invited to romp up to the greatest heights. Inevitably, though, you may find the pace of the romp rather hard going, so use the newspapers to work out where you are as a solver and move up when *you* are ready. The easiest 15 × 15 puzzles are those in *The Observer* each Sunday under the title Everyman. My rival Quixote puzzles in *The Independent on Sunday* are broadly similar but perhaps a little spicier if you're more than a beginner. Among the quality broadsheet dailies *The Daily Telegraph* has traditionally been regarded as the easiest with *The Guardian, The Times* and *The Independent* rather harder. Some of the puzzles for *The Times* that are used in their championship are deliberately on the hard side and you may like to test yourself against the finalists. By now I am disappointed if I cannot finish *The Times* in 20 minutes, but the Everyman rarely takes me more than 10 minutes.

There are three Sunday papers offering 12 × 12 barred puzzles among which Beelzebub in *The Independent on Sunday* is probably the easiest. Mephisto in *The Sunday Times* is a shade harder, but Azed in *The Observer* is usually the trickiest. The Saturday puzzle in *The Independent* offers a relatively gentle introduction to the barred special and has plugged a gap between the plain 12 × 12 barred puzzle and the more difficult specials. Azed's specials are significantly more difficult than his plains, but generally not as hard as those published under the heading of *The Listener Crossword*, now appearing in *The Times* (Magazine Section) on a Saturday. *The Listener* went out of business in 1990, but The Listener Crossword lives on and continues to explore the frontiers of novelty and difficulty. Anyone who aspires to be a setter should ideally solve puzzles one level harder than the ones he or she sets (unless he's a Listener setter of course). I would recommend that anyone who wants to be a regular 15 × 15 setter should enter the Azed competition, but at the same time recognize that the clue styles and vocabulary for daily puzzles will often need to be simpler. Incorporating an obscure abbreviation with an anagram for an Everyman-style puzzle would *never* do.

If you are in the USA look out for *Atlantic Monthly* (see puzzle no. 65 in this *Manual*) and *Harper's* (puzzles by Ed Galli and Richard Maltby Jr). These are barred puzzles. If you want the equivalent of a *Times* puzzle try *Games* magazine edited by Will Shortz.

I end this section with ten tips for solvers:

1 Don't spend all day on 1 across! If I am solving a 15 × 15 standard cryptic, I read through the clues in order, spending no more than 15 seconds (roughly) on each and solving where I can. As I start on the down clues I can expect help from checking letters. After this first run-through I concentrate on clues relevant to a particular part of the diagram and follow wherever that leads.

2 Remember that the definition will always be at the beginning of the clue or at the end. If you can separate it out easily, the remaining words in the clue may suggest the clue type.

3 Hidden words and anagrams offer beginners the easiest start. Some crossword jargon shouts 'Anagram!' (as we have already discussed on p.73.

4 Look out for other crossword jargon. Something 'going around' something may alert you to a container-and-contents clue. The worker may well be an 'ant'.

5 Look out for opportunities to fill in individual letters on the diagram in pencil. The definition of a plural may allow you to fill in an 's'. Similarly you may see opportunities for 'ing', 'ed' and other common endings.

6 Don't be afraid to use a dictionary, especially when you are learning. It is *not* 'cheating'!

7 In addition to a dictionary you may find other reference books helpful, especially a one-volume encyclopedia and an atlas. (More about this on p.298.)

8 If you get desperately stuck, have a break. Let your brain tick over on 'automatic pilot' and after a night's sleep the answer may be obvious.

9 If you fail to finish a puzzle, try to learn something by reading the answers.

10 Keep a sense of proportion, and don't let solving crosswords dominate your entire existence!

The Complete Setter

The would-be crossword setter has to face two challenges: (i) locating an outlet for puzzles, (ii) doing a decent job.

I must say a word about (i) first. When I was a teenager setting puzzles for the *Radio Times* I received a letter from the Crossword Editor of the *Daily Telegraph* returning my puzzle and telling me that 'Fleet Street is not normally reached in one leap'. Quite so. There have been one or two spectacular under-20 crossword setters since then, but on the whole you must work your way up. It is just possible that *The Modern Lady's Weekly* (my invention) may want a puzzle, or the *Agricultural News*, but don't think you can start with *The Times*. That way lies disappointment. Look for openings, local and national, but recognize that you're at the bottom of the ladder. If the only way to get on the ladder is to set a definition puzzle for *The Barchester News*, go for it.

Let's suppose that you're going to set a 15 × 15 puzzle. Perhaps it's for the good folk of Barchester or perhaps it's for your college mag. I suggest that you (like the solver) need ten tips:

1 Get the diagram settled first. If you want to devise your own diagram, take note of the points I make in Chapter 12 (especially p.86). As a novice, though, you would do better to use a grid from one of the dailies (but preferably *not* one of those which has five-letter words with only the second and fourth letters checked). The experienced setter can make up the diagram as he goes along and choose it to fit the selection of long words and phrases he wants to use. This is the ideal situation—something the complete setter should eventually aim for. Ideally your diagram should have answers with several different lengths. Words with 3 letters are not often used but they do provide an opportunity for the 11-letter answer that is otherwise likely to be forgotten.

2 Keep a good stock of dictionaries, encyclopedias and reference books (see Appendix 2, but also see 5 below).

3 Use a pencil, and be careful about word endings. There aren't many 9-letter words ending in J, so be prepared to use an eraser and don't be stubborn.

4 Use an interesting variety of words and phrases and fill in the long answers first. Avoid words that are boring to define and/or difficult to break up (e.g. STRENGTHLESS). You will often be forced to have dull words, but there is no need for you to make life difficult for yourself. Make sure that any *phrase* used is standard, i.e. either in the dictionary, in common parlance, or well known as a title. YELLOW SHIRT is not acceptable, but YELLOW FEVER is. YELLOW SUBMARINE wouldn't have been acceptable before it became a Beatles' hit, but it could be appropriate in some crosswords (if the Crossword Editor allows song titles).

5 If you are setting for a periodical and dealing with a Crossword Editor, you must know what she (or maybe he) does and doesn't allow on the grid. Several dailies will not allow the names of living people on the grid, for instance, and *The Times* doesn't like names of products or 'words with unpleasant or non-drawing-room associations (e.g. leprosy, semen, carcinoma, incontinent)'. For a 15×15 puzzle you will want your *Chambers*, but also use the *Concise Oxford Dictionary* to check that you have an 'everyday' word if in doubt.

6 As you write in your words and phrases log up a few ideas on how you will clue them later on. If you have ten words that can only be clued by anagrams you could be in trouble. For the sake of variety you will only want about half a dozen anagrams at most.

7 When you write your clues, put into effect all the principles outlined in the *Manual*. Ask yourself these questions for each clue:
Is the definition fair?
Is the subsidiary indication fair?
Can all the words in the clue be justified? (What about the link word(s)?)
Does the clue as a whole make some sort of sense or is it only a zany mixture of subject, verb and object? (See [10.49] as a terrible warning.)
Don't try to be too clever. Err on the side of simplicity, and don't write a 'clue to a clue'.

8 Check your crossword carefully and get it checked by others if possible. If you know someone else who is a 15 × 15 solver, ask that friend to try and solve the puzzle. When you check your puzzle, check one thing at a time—the clue numbers, the clues, even the numbers in brackets. You can easily make mistakes by trying to check everything at once.

9 If you are having your crossword published by a Crossword Editor, try to establish a dialogue if possible. The Editor may be able to help you, but (if you've read the *Manual* carefully) you might even be able to help the Editor. If an Editor doesn't like your clue, do not allow him or her to inflict a non-Ximenean alternative if you can help it. Instead suggest a new clue yourself. Always ask to see proofs.

10 If you publish crosswords regularly, you may get much less reaction than you had hoped for. Solvers often overlook mistakes, so don't get too many hang-ups about them. They are much more likely to complain that a puzzle is too hard. It's one thing to set a really hard 'advanced' puzzle, another to set a 15 × 15 standard. You don't want your puzzles to be a push-over, but in the contest between setter and solver you must expect to lose graciously.

It is just possible that some readers of this *Manual* will want to go on to set advanced puzzles. For a 12 × 12 Azed-type puzzle, study once again Chapters 13–17. If you do set advanced puzzles for a periodical you will almost certainly be able to choose your own diagram and you will have the freedom to shift bars around to get the words to fit—this can be a great help. If you move on to advanced specials, you will need to have lots of original ideas or gimmicks. You will have the opportunity to construct imaginative new grids with letters entered in fanciful new ways, and you may even invent your own type of clue. Not many of you may get that far, but specialist publications such as the *Crossword Club* will take puzzles from all comers solely on merit—and The Listener puzzle in *The Times* is still open to all. There will always be room for new talent.

The Social Dimension

Solving and setting crosswords can be a lonely occupation—and that can be one of its attractions. But it doesn't have to be like that all the time, as many Azed solvers will testify. If you can, find others with whom you can discuss your ideas, and you may help each other up Crossword Mountain. For the truly complete crossworder the social dimension is essential.

20

A Crossword Romp

This final chapter contains 49 puzzles ancient and modern. Some are easy; some are hard; a few might seem impossible. They have been chosen within three different categories: (i) 'historical' puzzles, (ii) representative puzzles of the modern era, and (iii) some of my own puzzles reprinted for a larger audience. Since I am writing the book, I had better contribute at least half the puzzles overall, but this proportion by no means reflects my significance as a setter! Not all the clues printed here will necessarily match Ximenean standards (though I hope my own will not be found wanting); but all the puzzles should have something interesting about them, so I hope you will enjoy the romp.

Nos. 36–38 take us back to the early days. No. 36 was a discovery in a second-hand Oxford bookshop while I was writing the earlier chapters of this book. In 1924 C. Arthur Pearson of WC2 published a book of 'word squares', but these were in fact primitive crosswords. Our No. 36 was Word Square No. 12. The individually numbered squares, overlapping words and unclued pairs (e.g. 49–50) are evidence of a new word-puzzle form coming alive. The idea of a pretty picture was taken up by Torquemada and his first puzzle in *The Observer* (No. 37) illustrates the 'feelers' which the Sunday paper was putting out to its readers. Subsequent puzzles featured a marionette, 'all the world's a stage', 'Mrs Porter and her daughter' and other intriguing themes. Notice how many of the clues offer something a little more challenging than a straight definition (with a misleading context in the very first clue). No. 38 shows an early example of a Bible crossword from the *Sunday Companion* of 1 May 1926.

No. 39 is a concise crossword from *The Independent*, which imitates the *Daily Telegraph*'s quick crossword (complete with pun). No. 40 takes us back again to the early days of *The Telegraph* with a full version of the puzzle promised on p.23.

No. 41 was my first published cryptic crossword from the *Radio Times* in 1964, and I offer apologies to solvers who weren't watching

TV in those days. Clue scrutineers should be warned that I hadn't yet discovered Ximenes.

We turn now to *The Times*. No. 42 is from a final of the Crossword Championship. It took me four times as long as John Sykes to finish No. 42 on the train from Oxford to London. No. 43 is one of my own puzzles.

Unlike *The Times*, the *Guardian* discloses the names (or at any rate pseudonyms) of its setters. The most Ximenean of these is Alec Robins, who masquerades as Custos. Alec Robins's output has been high in quantity and quality—and not just for the *Guardian* (No. 44). On alternate months he is 'Everyman' of the *Observer*. In that capacity he helped Ximenes write his book about crosswords before writing one of his own (see p.297). We shall also meet him later as Zander (No. 69). The other half of Everyman is Miss Dorothy Taylor, who used to enter Ximenes competitions under the pseudonym of her sister-in-law, Mrs B. Lewis (hence the name of Inspector Morse's sergeant). No. 45 is one of her puzzles.

According to *The Guinness Book of Records*, the world's most prolific setter is Roger F. Squires. To *Guardian* solvers he is known as Rufus, but he sets puzzles for many papers and periodicals, including the *Financial Times* (No. 46). No. 47 is also from the *Financial Times*. It is by Quark, who is Eric Burge, an experienced setter and a successful clue-writer in Azed competitions. He also sets for the *Guardian* as Quasar. Perhaps the most popular *Guardian* setter is Araucaria (John Graham) who shows great flair in his puzzles but who is by no means a strict Ximenean in his cluemanship (No. 48).

Prospective setters may find it difficult to place their puzzles in the London dailies, but until a few years ago the *Birmingham Evening Mail* welcomed all comers. One of my own puzzles appears here as No. 49. My pseudonym 'Duck' comes from Donald Duck, in line with my philosophy that ultimately crosswords should be fun rather than inquisitorial.

One of my favourite puzzles as a teenager was The Skeleton in the *Sunday Express* (No. 50). It is a particularly interesting puzzle for anyone wanting some early lessons in how a grid can be constructed.

Nos. 51, 52, 53 and 54 are all puzzles of mine published by Quality Magazines, first with *Quiz Digest*, then with *Tough Puzzles*.

Our final blocked puzzle is from Afrit's *Armchair Crosswords*, the book which began with the famous Injunction. No. 55 looks old-fashioned to us now, in terms of both the diagram and the clues. Afrit was too early to be Ximenean, but was Ximenes himself a Ximenean? You will soon be able to judge that for yourselves!

We now move from blocks to bars. No. 56 is a plain from the very early days of Ximenes (his No. 27 from the forties). I have chosen it partly because of the clue at 16 down which won W. K. M. Slimming's first prize. A lovely idea, but would it be mean to suggest that an adjective was here being defined as a noun? Sir William has won first prizes with Azed too and is still entering the competitions. But what of the clues by the master in this puzzle? If 'Tennyson was not Tennysonian' nor was Ximenes Ximenean—in those early days at any rate. By modern standards rather less than 50% of the clues pass muster. In my view, though, this serves only to emphasize the achievements of Ximenes in formulating the rules and raising the standards.

Nos. 57, 58 and 59 were all published on 27 October 1991—in *The Independent on Sunday*, *The Sunday Times* and *The Observer*, respectively. The first two are by the same crossword setter, Richard Whitelegg, under his two different pseudonyms Beelzebub and Mephisto. (Mephisto is in fact Mephisto II—Mephisto I, Richard Kilner, died in 1973.)

Mephisto's exact contemporary at Cambridge, Jonathan Crowther, was responsible for the third puzzle, *The Observer*'s Azed. I completed No. 57 in exactly 30 minutes without *Chambers* and No. 58 took me the same time, though I used *Chambers* and *Back-Words* for the last two clues I solved. Azed took me 45 minutes without *Chambers*, but when I checked against the dictionary I found that I had one wrong. Of the three Azed is usually the hardest, consistently using rarer words and a wider range of clue types.

Nos. 60 and 61 are two of my puzzles from a magazine of the 1970s called *Games and Puzzles*. Its crossword editor Don Putnam broke new ground in crossword journalism and there is nothing like it now in the magazine displays, alas.

The Independent's Saturday magazine offers a special advanced puzzle every week. The puzzles tend to be much easier than those of *The Listener* and have therefore filled a gap in the market. No. 62 is one of my own efforts; No. 63 is by Phi, who is Paul Henderson, one of a generation of talented clue-writers and crossword setters to emerge in the 1980s.

For the next two puzzles we cross the Atlantic. No. 64 is by Stephen Sondheim, better known for his musicals. Sondheim used to solve *The Listener* crossword with Leonard Bernstein while they worked on *West Side Story*, and he did much as a setter to further the cryptic crossword in America in the sixties. This narrative type of puzzle was probably invented by Torquemada. No. 65 is the 'Puzzler' from *The Atlantic Monthly* for November 1989. Each month Emily Cox and Henry Rathvon produce a fine crossword. This one is on a par with a typical *Independent* magazine puzzle.

Stephen Sondheim is one of about fifty 'top crossworders' who receive a crossword each Christmas from Apex (the setter of No. 66). 'A Puzzle Each Christmas' has been circulating for 20 years, but the name Apex comes from 'Ape X(imenes)', something which Eric Chalkley began to do when he bought Ximenes' book. Apex also sets *Guardian* and Listener puzzles. One member of Apex's band is Michael Freeman, who contributed puzzles to *The Listener* and has his own monthly puzzle in the *New Statesman* (No. 67). Salamanca, as he is known, is a particularly inventive setter, but like Araucaria he worries orthodox Ximeneans.

The Listener crossword began unpromisingly on 2 April 1930 with a 'musical crossword'. One clue was 'Last three letters of Christian name of a great composer'. The answer (without notes) was IAN—I wonder who the setter had in mind? Mr I. Cresswell of 40 Hamilton Road, Colchester, provided the only all-correct solution but he didn't get a prize. The first pseudonymous setter appears to have been Doggerel, but the running was soon taken up by Proton (A. McIntyre) and Afrit. Before the Second World War prizes were often given to all winners, but the setters of a pre-Ximenean era confessed in print that they could not always gauge the appropriate level of difficulty.

Afrit's first 'Printer's Devilry' was first published on 2 June 1937 (No. 68). Some breaks came at the end of words; unrelated pairs of words are to be inserted; the checking is not as good as it looks because of unclued letter pairs; and there are numerous references to literature. Despite these difficulties there were 30 correct entries. Can you solve the puzzle? I couldn't, but reading the solution was interesting! During the War, *The Listener* introduced an easier (and rather poor) puzzle every other week; Afrit (none too pleased) dropped out but re-emerged after the War.

Thanks largely to the work of Ximenes, *Listener* puzzles have become more even in standard and difficulty. Only three prizes are given each week, and the number of correct entries is in the hundreds. The number of competitors has doubled since the puzzle migrated to *The Times*, and entries for the easier puzzles are close to a thousand. Nos. 69–75 are examples of *Listener* puzzles. Zander is Alec Robins (whom we have already met); Hen is Vince Henderson; Virgilius is Brian Greer, who also sets for *The Times*.

No. 73 by Mass (Harold Massingham) reminds us that crosswords need not be 'square', in any sense of the word. Look out in the *Listener* puzzle for all sorts of shapes, including hexagons. Mass also sets for *The Independent* and *The Spectator*.

No. 74 is undoubtedly the hardest puzzle I have managed to

complete. Published in *The Listener* to celebrate the Queen's Silver Jubilee, it provided me with over 20 hours of alternate frustration and enjoyment. It is three-dimensional, and I suggest you make a box. Leiruza (A. E. Hughes) has produced a number of puzzles involving knight's moves. No. 75 by Law is also a difficult puzzle but great fun. The champion *Listener* solver in 1989, who won the Solver Silver Salver, thought it the best puzzle that year and accordingly awarded Ross Lawther the 'Ascot Gold Cup' at the annual Listener Setters' dinner. (Though donated by the setter Ascot, it is not made of gold, nor is it a cup!)

And so, finally, to Ximenes and Azed. Nos. 76–78 are three Ximenes specials. His No. 1000 appears to be the first letters latent puzzle and No. 1200 marked the end of the Ximenes era. It is now over 20 years since Ximenes died, but his final puzzle is much closer to the modern Azed puzzle than it is to the plain puzzle we looked at earlier. That is a mark of Derrick Macnutt's great achievement, an achievement which I celebrated in a special puzzle ten years after his death (No. 79).

Azed has brought his own style to crosswords with new clue types and even stricter rules. But being stricter about the rules does not mean being a killjoy and in the three specials here (Nos. 80–82) we see a witty and playful spirit at work. In 1977 Azed's solvers contributed to *The Azed Book of Crosswords* (now sadly out of print). Nos. 83 and 84 formed a tribute to Azed by myself and Bristol office colleague Merlin (Richard Palmer). One or two of the clues do look dated, and the value of the top prize has risen to £30. My friendship with Merlin goes on, though. Azed too goes on, and so does the enjoyment of crossword puzzles. Long may that be so.

CROSSWORD No. 36

From *The Word Square Puzzle Book* (1924)

HORIZONTAL

1–14 Pertaining to the Church
12–17 The young of cows
18–23 Wild sheep of Nepaul
22–24 Refuse (noun)
25–27 Low marshy land
26–31 Unfriendly disposition
32–37 An intimate acquaintance
38–41 A kind of vermin
47–48 One of the bovine genus
54–56 An expression of affirmation
57–59 A girl's name
60–62 Part of the verb 'to be'
66–68 Nothing
69–72 A common beverage
73–76 To cause to fall
77–79 A snare
83–85 A kind of tree
87–91 Pertaining to the law
92–95 A heavenly body
95–97 A strong-smelling plant
100–103 A valley
105–109 An appointed meeting
110–115 To select
116–120 The top room of a house
122–127 To impress
128–133 A kind of poetic foot
140–142 To go astray
143–151 A section of the Government
152–154 Diminutive of Henry
155–157 Part of a clergyman's address
158–160 A loud sound
159–166 Guiltless
167–168 Latin for 'and'
171–172 An obsolete pronoun
173–179 A one-horned animal
182–184 Opposed to no
186–191 An ambassador
190–192 A beverage
196–200 A sailing vessel used for pleasure
200–212 Having four seeds
205–209 Frog spawn

VERTICAL

1–122 To set free
2–55 To convey
3–100 Cut or hewn
5–36 An age
7–24 A pronoun
11–25 The title of Kipling's famous poem
12–75 An edible grain
15–107 Affected by visions
16–64 An element
17–133 Having feelings in common with another
37–70 Accomplished
49–74 Dread or veneration
55–135 Compliant
57–69 A Jewish month
64–183 To revive
89–125 A pledge
90–126 In the manner of (in music)
92–116 A spring of mineral water
94–118 Practical skill
109–195 Sensible to slight touches
110–196 Austerity
124–172 To obey
134–196 Truth
135–171 A colour
137–182 A pronoun of plural number
143–200 A full-grown person
144–187 To partake of food
146–189 An ancient native prince of Peru
148–191 A square measure
165–207 The back of the neck
166–208 Produced by the lachrymal gland
179–206 A card game

CROSSWORD No. 36

1	2	3	4	5	6	7	8	9	10	11	12	13	14	15	16	17
18	19	20	21	22	23	24	■	■	■	25	26	27	28	29	30	31
32	33	34	35	36	37	■	■	■	■	■	38	39	40	41	42	43
44	45	46	■	■	47	48	■	■	49	50	■	■	51	52	53
54	55	56	■	57	58	59	■	■	60	61	62	■	63	64	65
66	67	68	■	69	70	71	72	■	73	74	75	76	■	77	78	79
80	81	82	■	■	■	■	■	■	■	■	■	■	■	83	84	85
86	87	88	89	90	91	■	■	■	■	■	92	93	94	95	96	97
98	99	100	101	102	103	■	■	■	■	■	104	105	106	107	108	109
110	111	112	113	114	115	■	■	■	■	■	116	117	118	119	120	121
122	123	124	125	126	127	■	■	■	■	■	128	129	130	131	132	133
134	135	136	■	■	■	■	■	■	■	■	■	■	■	137	138	139
140	141	142	■	143	144	145	146	147	148	149	150	151	■	152	153	154
155	156	157	■	158	159	160	161	162	163	164	165	166	■	167	168	169
170	171	172	■	173	174	175	176	177	178	179	180	181	■	182	183	184
185	■	■	■	186	187	188	189	190	191	192	193	194	■	■	■	195
196	197	198	199	200	201	202	203	204	205	206	207	208	209	210	211	212

Crossword: I.—Feelers by Torquemada from the *Observer* (1926)

ACROSS

1 Point was
7 Crux of 'Wrong Box'
14 A poulpe
15 61 across was
16 Adamsonia digitata
17 Cape in Tripoli
18 Greek fire prefix
19 Allow
20 Preposition
22 British Dominion (init.)
24 Plaything
25 Poet of husbandry (init.)
27 Worth half heels
29 In reference to
31 Very, very hard
32 N.B.
36 Infinitive of 43
38 Right-hand (abbrev.)
39 Interjection
40 Jewish ruin
41 Frenzy
44 This in tongue of 5
46 Saves suitor expense
47 Little in 32
48 Wrote 'Bury Fair' (init.)
49 My sons were sons of Belial
51 Depart
53 Before steamers
54 Sudden
56 Card game
59 We shatter sleep
61 Fabulous voyager (pop. spelling)
64 An Archbishop of York
65 Recovers
66 1578 Spanish book on drugs was this
67 Lie close . . . in tins

DOWN

1 Jemima's father
2 Higher than king (anagram)
3 Halt
4 Tristram's uncle
5 Thin in Bordeaux
6 Best of three games
8 Should not indulge in 37s
9 Inquisitive
10 Vetch
11 Arab chief
12 Excludes some 20s
13 Stage paper
17 Livingstone and Stanley did
20 An invertebrate
21 Seville Nights
23 A constellation
25 Contains a widow
26 I doubt it
28 Suited to anserine converse
30 63 is
33 Half a farewell
34 Citation makes me a sale
35 Evening when good
36 Prefix of duality
37 Unready part of speech
42 Diary of 53
43 Part of 36 across
45 Downy Roman . . . female
49 Break out
50 Flows into Danube
52 Am olefiant
54 Island of Schleswig
55 Brothers of business
57 More than one one
58 With 37 on the way
59 Defeated Zerah
60 On London trams
61 Hundredth of yen
62 Kinds of money desirable
63 Dose without circle

CROSSWORD No. 37

CROSSWORD No. 38

'No Man can Serve Two Masters' from *The Sunday Companion* (1925)

ACROSS
1 One of the Apostles
6 Where Ahab went (I Kings xviii.)
12 Two
13 Conjunction
14 Of (Fr.)
15 Part of fish
17 Spoke to our Lord (Mark xii.)
19 A group of scientific rules
21 Recline
22 Males
23 Lieutenant (Abbrev.)
25 Wickedness
26 Took a chair
28 Point of the compass
29 Matchings
32 Cries of fear
34 Flying creature
35 The raising of taxes
37 Cover
39 The definite article
42 Supposing
44 Cowshed
45 Used by bricklayers
47 Royal Institute (Abbrev.)
48 To soil
50 Where Samson dwelt (Judg. xv.)
52 A wilderness (Gen. xxi.)
54 Town in Somerset [!]
55 Brought by Mary (Mark xvi.)
57 Thrown about
58 Bottom part of a ship
60 Small pocket case
61 Asset
63 Harm
66 Those who hone
67 Parentless boy or girl
68 In front of the door
69 Increase
71 Method of cooking
72 As well as

DOWN
1 Raincoat (Abbrev.)
2 Dries thoroughly
3 Prefix meaning three
4 Using certain garden tool
5 Irish
7 Enemy of Saul (I Sam. xiv.)
8 Wife of Haman (Esther v.)
9 Period
10 Ages
11 Nickname for lion
12 Religious song
16 Occasional winter occurrence
18 Without seeing
20 Twisted by age
24 Small label
25 Form of address
27 Do up
28 Above us
30 Small bird
31 Slope of hill or mountain
32 Father of Enos (Gen. v.)
33 First woman (Gen. iii.)
36 Small bits of straw
38 Rage
40 A mountain (Num. xx.)
41 The leper (Matt. xxvi.)
43 Move by breeze
44 Undergrowth
46 The scribe (2 Sam. viii.)
47 Unusual
49 Father of Bezaleel (Exod. xxxi.)
51 Town in Mesopotamia, besieged in the War (reversed)
53 Required
54 Heavy blows
56 Mount given to Esau (Deut. ii.)
57 Seen in the sky
59 Plural of 23 across (Abbrev.)
60 Poem (reversed)
61 Talk to
62 Method or rule
64 Cast out by Zebul (Judg. ix.)
65 Finishes
68 Written folios (Abbrev.)
70 Perform

CROSSWORD No. 38

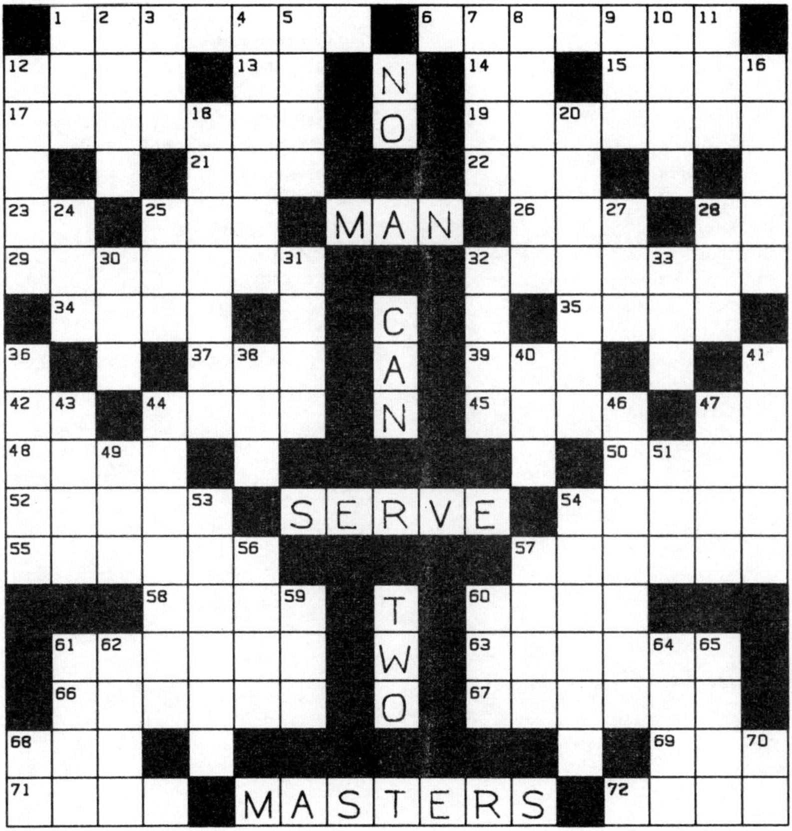
NO
MAN
CAN
SERVE
TWO
MASTERS

CROSSWORD No. 39

Concise by Quixote from *The Independent*

ACROSS

1 Parrot's name (5)
4 OT book (6)
9 Towed vehicle (7)
10 Keepsake (5)
11 Require (4)
12 Confidential (7)
13 Insect (3)
14 Asterisk (4)
16 Conceal (4)
18 Drunkard (3)
20 Embankment (7)
21 Blemish (4)
24 Tree (5)
25 Salad plant (7)
26 Ridicule (6)
27 Spy (5)

DOWN

1 Obvious (6)
2 Depart (5)
3 US university (4)
5 Undiluted (8)
6 The Netherlands (7)
7 Projectile (6)
8 Rubbish (5)
13 Short rest (8)
15 Storm (7)
17 Investigates (6)
18 Manner (5)
19 Silver (6)
22 Lacking polish (5)
23 Covered walk (4)

CROSSWORD No. 39

CROSSWORD No. 40

Daily Telegraph, 17 March 1928

ACROSS

1 International courtship repatched
10 In a bigger age colossal; the frozen tundra yields his fossil
11 However you take it this is stimulating
12 Confesses
13 With regard to this the nods usually precede the winks
14 These may suggest fun in the anagram of 12 across
17 Adoration travels with this cry
18 'Lip riot' (anag.)
19 As to manner, casual
22 May suggest 23 down, or an orator whose speciality is quantity rather than quality
24 A coming woman
25 A champion who did not burn his boats, but bartered them
26 Girl's name
29 Darkness and insulation characterise it
30 Use it before going to see that hair-raising play Dracula (hyphen)
31 These are inimical to continuity

DOWN

2 Nutritive seeds
3 A blind pilot
4 A lady from Shakespeare
5 An occasion when big ears are welcome
6 Made by those who favour a motion
7 A favourite in popular films
8 Descriptive of a plausible fellow (hyphen)
9 Whereat things of beauty are made up (hyphen)
15 What cooks need to do
16 Metallic adjective for a cheap loud-speaker
20 The sort of hope that seldom reaches a consummation
21 A useful thing to present to the importunate (two words)
22 'Show rip' (anag.)
23 A rising concern that presents many difficulties for the directors
27 More frequently leaves a church than enters it
28 Bird

CROSSWORD No. 40

CROSSWORD No. 41

Radio Times Crossword by D. F. Manley (1964)

ACROSS

1 Doctor refuses to work for TV series (10)
6 Writer distinctly lacking in warmth (4)
10 Animal in a most eerie context (5)
11 Comedian puts Scottish mountain before New York eminence (5,4)
12 What's my line? I must be absorbed by a measuring device (6)
13 Holidays for two opposites, Gilbert and Sullivan? (7)
15 Right back to 10 – putrid! (6)
16 It's on in wild parts of Canada: a gigantic reptile (8)
19 Lamb sees, oddly enough, how to start a meeting (8)
21 We should return to make a song about a household job (6)
24 Bird box leads to quarrel (7)
26 A trail suited to the Lone Ranger (6)
28 Notices by-product is unfit for TV or radio (9)
29 Livid singer with 5. (Tricky? Not altogether) (5)
30 Famous gallery in the States (4)
31 Lawyer gives drink to mother and child (5,5)

DOWN

1 Not associated with the Rolling Stones (4)
2 Poets rate these as dramatic musical performances (9)
3 Work for the home? (7)
4 & 20. Merry lot bore being tortured for actor (6,6)
5 Recognise Ron? He is moved to become a comedian (3,5)
7 Carmichael turns to the navy in Scotland (5)
8 Novelist has long way to travel for TV series (5,5)
9 Most of my rod has strange powers (6)
14 'My Word!' A really outstanding writer is needed for this (5,5)
17 Northern issue can lead to hindrances (9)
18 Note the soft whistle employed by a glass maker (8)
20 See 4
22 Listener who has read about drink (7)
23 Quiet hen in the field perhaps (6)
25 As before, radio is something well worth having (5)
27 Actor born in America is V.I.P. in Scotland (4)

CROSSWORD No. 41

CROSSWORD No. 42

The Times Crossword Puzzle No. 16,869

This puzzle was solved in the record time of 4½ minutes by Dr John Sykes, the 1985 champion, at the national final of the Collins Dictionaries Times Crossword Championship.

ACROSS

1 Producer of stage lighting for Pyramus and Thisbe (3,2,3,4)
9 High-flier having ended a brilliant career (9)
10 Stump from which some orators may speak (5)
11 Appoint as minister, or Hamlet as prince, say? (6)
12 Swimmer shows way to press forward (8)
13 Once called audibly the utmost degree (6)
15 Basil was over her Lorenzo's head (8)
18 Bird—that which is seen round Scotland's isle (8)
19 Wind instrument for communication commonly (6)
21 Ironclad might one surmise? Not this vessel (4-4)
23 Man, say, taken in by doctor is caused to go wrong (6)
26 Find out what's in the clear, naturally (5)
27 Putting a beer in it craftily could make him drunk (9)
28 But as its monarch Alexander went unrecorded (6,6)

DOWN

1 A short distance in light aircraft – prototype Jumbo (7)
2 No neo-Edwardian was so famous (5)
3 The age in which Kipling wrote (9)
4 The appearance, it's said, of one who may succeed (4)
5 Played majestically in Hollywood the West's also taking in the South (8)
6 Bid perhaps for grappling iron (5)
7 Salad's just what the old king ordered (4-4)
8 Matchless poetess involved in 11 (6)
14 Muscovite in a one-goal result proves hostile (8)
16 Hazardous game for the serpent of old Nile (9)
17 Where fools are blissfully ignorant and the birds are gorgeous (8)
18 Street Browning visited going round in this headgear? (6)
20 Titian beauty number one in the Kremlin? (7)
22 Buddhist priest put together black continental cricket team (5)
24 A jungle climber's name inter alia perhaps (5)
25 Run fast or hide (4)

CROSSWORD No. 42

CROSSWORD No. 43

By Don Manley (unattributed and edited by Crossword Editor) from *The Times*

ACROSS

1 Irrational fear may be seen in sinister pout (12)
9 Sea-going cutter? (9)
10 Female left-winger accepted by soccer authority (5)
11 Use some beef for this (6)
12 Strong supporter (8)
13 Hell can bring this! (6)
15 Having political divisions—the fashion in Panama perhaps? (8)
18 Where to have a pint after Choral Evensong naturally? (8)
19 American beauty queen is a married woman (6)
21 Their strange period establishing historical tradition (8)
23 Creepy-crawly goes back in the bath on return? (6)
26 Letters selected initially as a source of enlightenment (5)
27 Greek character, girl, is received by royal personage (9)
28 Remark about Post Office beginning to slip is not daft (6,6)

DOWN

1 Pay out to retain us—or deal thus with payment if broke? (7)
2 Top of prison twice used for demonstration! (5)
3 Bird touching bread put out on street (9)
4 Tour to rush along, missing nothing (4)
5 Islander will get brown going around Haiti possibly (8)
6 Dyke builder has left refuse (5)
7 Colours afresh material with bad stain (8)
8 Business alliance allowed Rex and Bill to get turnover (6)
14 Start of summer leading to nudity or revealing wear (8)
16 Read out story with quiet ending (9)
17 Jacks start to cheer their leading vessel (8)
18 Let fags do their worst? It's fashionable to get *healthy*! (6)
20 Little people should be shut up—right little devils! (7)
22 Trunk can come out of roots (5)
24 One who deduces God's existence from the swirling tides? (5)
25 What's in Palm Sunday's collection for distribution on Maundy Thursday? (4)

CROSSWORD No. 43

CROSSWORD No. 44

Guardian Crossword No. 15,000
Literal Transplants by Custos (20 February 1978)

The answer to each Across clue must have one of its letters removed before entry in the diagram. In each case the excised letter should be written instead alongside the word's clue. When this operation is completed the 26 transplanted letters, when read in clue order and added to 8 Down, will make an appropriate headline.

Definitions in these clues refer to the full, unmutilated answers (number of letters given in brackets); subsidiary parts lead to the mutilated forms to be entered in the diagrams. The first clue of each pair refers to diagram A, the second to diagram B.

Each of the Down clues is really two normal clues printed side by side, never overlapping, one leading to the answer in diagram A and the other to that in diagram B. The division is not necessarily marked by punctuation, and either A or B clue may come first.

ACROSS

5 Nobleman, top-drawer, I found among ruins (7)
Boring love I'd rejected in backward group (7)

6 Attendant, having pinched £2, gets sack (7)
Sends back mother after being captured by Communists (7)

9 Exams, including English, are severe trials (7)
Tolerated first of kids in family (7)

10 Fixer needs ceremony, one that conceals his true nature (9)
Unadulterated back-pedalling by heavyweights leads to outbursts (9)

11 Bankruptcy for the band (5)
A religious representation, a favourite one (5)

12 English clothing with a ring of dots around the edge (11)
What sounds like costly and better type of headgear (11)

13 At length in favour of having area left in backyard (12)
Plastic pressed so to become a diner's utensil (7-5)

18 Strait-laced in the end, blushing about it, given a sharp rebuke (11)
Why let a mob run riot? It's reprehensible (11)

21 A four-wheeled carriage that's cast in precious stone (5)
£100 is about right for the waiters' collection of tips (5)

22 Foreign girl has to write name when receiving a ring in one (9)
An undertaker, I'm in cart after a mix-up (9)

23 Servant, one who hurries about excitedly (7)
Doubles partners, perhaps, met running about court (7)

24 Putting things precisely? That's tremendous (7)
Live within confines of southern railway, in sedate fashion (7)

25 Separate company suffers setback in disreputable resort (7)
Felt hats, for when going about the East (7)

DOWN

1 Recommended getting a pleader to pass inside by means of a minister (8;8)

2 Laced stuff with which teachers' leader gets children drunk – see, dead drunk (6;6)

3 Long after the plane-trip makes frivolous petitions about having searches (8;8)

CROSSWORD No. 44 – Diagram A.

4 Fellow with skill made up a hymn tune, in the morning, after start of bardic festival (6;6)

5 Doctor, getting right on to a sovereign's deadly wound, carrying Edward round vessel (6;6)

7 Poem, produced by child with toil, still in existence, to be included in next anthology (6;6)

8 Being fuddled with claret, extolling a medium during a heat wave (11;3,8)

14 Watched William's diving ducks – watches Thomas getting duck caught by the legs (3-5;8)

15 Our sot, tipsy, holding party in the open air, solemnly poured out wine, gaining freedom, losing 'er (8;8)

16 Smack during a quarrel is hardly the sound of a frolic among Civil Service office workers (6;6)

17 Refuse, causing a disturbance, to follow closely master's principles (6;6)

19 Right joint to be constantly annoying a girl who needs help when grabbed by chaps (6;6)

20 Brewing tea, try indefatigably to jabber rubbish that diverts brides (6;6)

CROSSWORD No. 44
The clues are repeated here for convenience

ACROSS
5 Nobleman, top-drawer, I found among ruins (7)
Boring love I'd rejected in backward group (7)
6 Attendant, having pinched £2, gets sack (7)
Sends back mother after being captured by Communists (7)
9 Exams, including English, are severe trials (7)
Tolerated first of kids in family (7)
10 Fixer needs ceremony, one that conceals his true nature (9)
Unadulterated back-pedalling by heavyweights leads to outbursts (9)
11 Bankruptcy for the band (5)
A religious representation, a favourite one (5)
12 English clothing with a ring of dots around the edge (11)
What sounds like costly and better type of headgear (11)
13 At length in favour of having area left in backyard (12)
Plastic pressed so to become a diner's utensil (7-5)
18 Strait-laced in the end, blushing about it, given a sharp rebuke (11)
Why let a mob run riot? It's reprehensible (11)
21 A four-wheeled carriage that's cast in precious stone (5)
£100 is about right for the waiters' collection of tips (5)
22 Foreign girl has to write name when receiving a ring in one (9)
An undertaker, I'm in cart after a mix-up (9)
23 Servant, one who hurries about excitedly (7)
Doubles partners, perhaps, met running about court (7)
24 Putting things precisely? That's tremendous (7)

Live within confines of southern railway, in sedate fashion (7)
25 Separate company suffers setback in disreputable resort (7)
Felt hats, for when going about the East (7)

DOWN
1 Recommended getting a pleader to pass inside by means of a minister (8;8)
2 Laced stuff with which teachers' leader gets children drunk – see, dead drunk (6;6)
3 Long after the plane-trip makes frivolous petitions about having searches (8;8)
4 Fellow with skill made up a hymn tune, in the morning, after start of bardic festival (6;6)
5 Doctor, getting right on to a sovereign's deadly wound, carrying Edward round vessel (6;6)
7 Poem, produced by child with toil, still in existence, to be included in next anthology (6;6)
8 Being fuddled with claret, extolling a medium during a heat wave (11;3,8)
14 Watched William's diving ducks – watches Thomas getting duck caught by the legs (3-5;8)
15 Our sot, tipsy, holding party in the open air, solemnly poured out wine, gaining freedom, losing 'er (8;8)
16 Smack during a quarrel is hardly the sound of a frolic among Civil Service office workers (6;6)
17 Refuse, causing a disturbance, to follow closely master's principles (6;6)
19 Right joint to be constantly annoying a girl who needs help when grabbed by chaps (6;6)
20 Brewing tea, try indefatigably to jabber rubbish that diverts brides (6;6)

CROSSWORD No. 44 – Diagram B.

CROSSWORD No. 45

Observer Everyman

ACROSS

1 River's sudden dash (4)
3 Elude me not—in short—I'm part of the clockwork (10)
9 A lot of paper's about before noon (4)
10 Owner of the land given away with a packet of cigarettes? (10)
12 Take back what you said about a pamphlet (7)
13 Scowls for those that shine? (7)
14 What a kiss did for Sleeping Beauty was a revelation (6,3,4)
17 High flown Greek ode—you won't be surprised if you have it (13)
21 Chorus? Don't! (7)
23 Street in a capital without a bit of litter—it's all in here (7)
24 Rocks in the Channel make tea in France almost superfluous (3,7)
25 A big blow for a girl, ending of romance (4)
26 Sadie's back and chaps get in the way, pestering (10)
27 A theologian's tots (4)

DOWN

1 Night on the heath over, one may expect some developments here (8)
2 Best fare cooked with love for Sunday lunch? (5,4)
4 Extend term of imprisonment (7)
5 Virginia's turned an awful green—Nemesis? (7)
6 Students of household management and cheap fare (7,5)
7 Invest 500 in the Revenue (Revolution's off) (5)
8 The endless run of a songbird (6)
11 Petermen pose no threat to bathers (4-8)
15 Piece of furniture for the team managers (9)
16 Why one gets small portions from the girl in the canteen? (8)
18 The realm of working domestics (7)
19 This veg is no longer fresh, dear boy (3,4)
20 Child that's been in the water—right in, the imp (6)
22 Father, always the liberator (5)

CROSSWORD No. 45

CROSSWORD No. 46

By Roger Squires from *Financial Times*

ACROSS

1 They involve a shift in one's beliefs (6)
4 Insisted upon or abandoned? (4,4)
9 Penthouse let on a new arrangement (4-2)
10 Pretty useless object? (8)
11 Allow the Spanish poison to be brought back (6)
12 I'm off food and water (8)
13 This hat is out of date (3)
14 Put out in West winds (6)
17 One side of Glasgow (7)
21 Information a girl found in Switzerland (6)
25 The best-known surviving creature? (3)
26 Any crest may indicate it (8)
27 They grip and hold on in the last resort (6)
28 Ointment said to be used by the Royal Family (8)
29 He is or could be a shopkeeper (6)
30 Political favours? (8)
31 Stable companion? (6)

DOWN

1 It sounds highly unnatural (8)
2 Very frightened, I take a short rest before I can reorganise (2,1,5)
3 He expects people to put up with him (8)
5 Where you may find a sailor on the way (6)
6 Rising payment for the artist (6)
7 Key batsman? (6)
8 Growing anger? (6)
12 When people may collect in the streets (4-3)
15 The German uprising is serious (3)
16 A work unit (3)
18 Begin to fix a fight (3,5)
19 A lemon is strangely sweet (8)
20 TV's pop group? (4,4)
22 A bend in the road (6)
23 Climbs and balances (6)
24 Company guard (6)
25 First form (6)

CROSSWORD No. 46

CROSSWORD No. 47
By Quark from *Financial Times*

ACROSS

1 It's always sharp but can be shaken (7)
5 Brook's bird? (7)
9 A novelist to study, we hear (5)
10 As sheet-worker I go on the attack (9)
11 Fashionable although bound to be wet (2,3,4)
12 Arsenic layer is rather grey (5)
13 Give view round tree (5)
15 To raise collection get change in position (9)
18 Dress gone—taken to the cleaners, lost? (9)
19 Sequence seen on the road (5)
21 I, fool, getting torn paper (5)
23 Stop, pal—the game is up! (9)
25 Indicative of the firm that's shaky? (9)
26 Looks in, it is said, for an award (5)
27 Compiler going back on transactions in river? That's outrageous (7)
28 Petition in town centre attracts many (7)

DOWN

1 Got in trouble with river endlessly whirling (7)
2 Narrow escape? Close it! (4,5)
3 Iceberg sticking up, partly revealing bird (5)
4 Traffic hold-up on the way to the factory? (9)
5 Collection of twigs seen in clearing (5)
6 Might be encountered in The Old Curiosity Shop (4-1-4)
7 Scattered shale can be bind (5)
8 Train followers (7)
14 Try to keep balance dancing on some ice (9)
16 One who's likely to get lines (9)
17 The city pitch is among a number providing fruit (9)
18 Emphasise in French warning about end of EEC (7)
20 Heater wire could be iron (7)
22 Allowed in certain public items (5)
23 Invent one away in an island (5)
24 Not working? Take up subject to change (not English) (5)

CROSSWORD No. 47

CROSSWORD No. 48

Alphabetical Jigsaw by Araucaria (*Guardian*)

Method: Solve the clues and fit in the solutions wherever they will go.

A bell that rang elusively in part (7)

B ship on the wrong river gets more smart (8)

C bond where churchmen to a junction come (6)

D instrument left out of celli – drum? (8)

E the Dark Lady, topless, is way out (6)

F woodwork tool when worry was about (7)

G like an old tree sculptured by Legrand (7)

H first of all invading famished land (7)

I should bring interest at Mass as priests (11)

J girl – yes (Ger.) – catch terriers (men, not beasts) (7)

K sounding wanted, after may be rolled (7)

L in security, state bird of old (8)

M major route which City's fans (say) enter (4,4)

N false clue is innate – group round a centre (8)

O act too much: where's re-mi-fa in tune? (6)

P's only round about the rug too soon (11)

Q leave when obligations have been paid (4)

R music's ear returns without what's laid (6)

S dog or bitch? Dog's tailless, split in six (6)

T nethermost, ate piece the heat to fix (10)

U house with rows in sunset, not the Pope! (10)

V – by the left! – contains some drink or dope (4)

W vole: hence Watson's dad's docked slips (5-3)

X Persian king who punished waves with whips (6)

Y in Colne Valley, place he madly wrecked (7)

Z oxide, red, is citizen's effect (7)

CROSSWORD No. 48

CROSSWORD No. 49

Birmingham Mail Special by Duck, 1 March 1982

ACROSS

1 One working out the taxes makes masses sore but not me (8)

6, 11, 24 Dn, 28: I have got jug at home – heed our rollicking. (Dai may sing this) (5,2,1,4,5,7)

10 Awful spite shown by the French in communication (7)

11 See 6 Across

12 Tooth? Not sweet rejecting bit of treacle (5)

13 Club having records on? Then it's sure tricky to talk! (9)

14 Timid chap, person pestered with kids? (3,5)

16 A witty saying about something very small (4)

20 One's 'green', vying? This may be in evidence (4)

21 Daniel's no wound leaving a - - - - - - - -! (5,3)

24 Pet has gone back to the street, girl! That's absolutely right! (4,5)

25 Lager would make this composer drunk (5)

27 Aged men tremble when mate is near (3-4)

28 See 6 Across

29 Appointed meeting to put good man to the test? (5)

30 Walk to Northern Territory? It's sounding harsh (8)

DOWN

2, 15 Dad's said 'Vanity!', spoiling this time of celebration (5,6,3)

3 Former wife, frightful rioter, creating a scene outside (8)

4 Sporting course – sea comes up – waver round (8)

5 Negligent concerning a girl (6)

6 Dwarf without foot on part of sundial (6)

7 Received from ancestors, it is put in abode (9)

8 Escape from eastern lord, end of servitude (5)

9 Oxford college where they'll celebrate tonight? (8)

15 See 2 Down

17 This country? My anchor is fixed here (8)

18 Bird's evening booze? (8)

19 Silly men, beginning to embrace, she had entangled (8)

22 Narrow passage of water without bends, we hear (6)

23 For a painter irritating experience has entity (6)

24 See 6 Across

26 Presented information about four in Ancient Rome (5)

CROSSWORD No. 49

CROSSWORD No. 50

Sunday Express Skeleton

In the Skeleton Crossword the black squares and clue numbers have to be filled in as well as the words. Four black squares and four clue numbers have been inserted to give you a start. The black squares form a symmetrical pattern; the top half matches the bottom half and the two sides correspond. So you can fill in 12 more squares at once to correspond with those given.

ACROSS

1 Bible man with very little time to take a snack
4 Act oddly in providing food for one of the tribes
9 Money man able to achieve a flying turn
11 Last post dispatched by someone seeking business
12 Carry gently a short distance past Heathrow terminal
13 Embarrassed grandee in a passion
15 Means of making notes or backing a horse
16 Show it's wrong to be back in a depression
17 Your lot won't admit it's different inside
20 Nag a newcomer
22 Feeling it's a long way round Mile End
23 Real inciter of mischief going straight
24 Make further use of personal mobility
25 Islander organising a quiet upheaval beyond the city limits

DOWN

1 It might be longer if Tom got elevated on hot air
2 If not in the water one might give you sauce
3 It indicates the number approved for inclusion
5 The man who finds a way to move with difficulty
6 People afloat sounded pleased with themselves
7 Chalky having got it in the neck as a songster
8 Jack and Alan worried about trade union having eight members
9 When food comes up mostly fat he goes in for takeaways
10 Can it be right to find a thriller writer pedestrian?
13 It's the last thing one hopes to gain
14 Several light out when there's no drink
18 Praise what was formerly a different lot
19 Girl in a state looking after the kids
21 Being so taxing it's a departure from frivolity
22 Light-headed? Not a bad description

CROSSWORD No. 50

CROSSWORD No. 51

Misdirected Letters by Duck from *Quiz Digest*

A letter which should have appeared once in the answer to 5 across has turned up in the answer to 1 down (no other similar letter appears in 1 down). The same mistake has occurred in the answers to 7 across and 2 down, and so on. The subsidiary indications in the clues (*eg* anagrams) and the numbers in brackets refer to the mutilated forms to be entered in the grid; definitions are normal. When you have completed the crossword, you will find that the misdirected letters, taken in order, spell out an appropriate three-word message.

ACROSS

5 Clown, disgustingly idle beast (8)
7 Charm shown by backward-looking sultanate, primitive civilisation (6)
9 Russian exchange has leader of diplomats upset (7)
10 Marshal on far side of hill in old-style combat (6)
11 Bird with gloomy look evident around Early English church (6-3)
13 What makes crime soar disastrously (4)
14 Ugly woman's house somewhere in Surrey (6)
16 Piece of rag in wrong position (6)
18 Smooth beat (4)
19 Exceptional saint, inwardly so keen he is (9)
22 Enslave heart madly with hint of love (6)
23 Sheep with a twitch that's sudden (7)
25 One to expel a boy (6)
26 Fleet Street area rumour – leader in *Express* is obscure (8)

DOWN

1 Sounds of pain from gunners caught up in battle (6)
2 Something extra good in Paris to exploit (6)
3 B-brightened up – but not well (4)
4 Trade Union basis for action may undermine nation . . . (8)
6 . . . Give money perpetually to terminate dispute? (6)
7 Let Athens get adapted for Olympic contestants? (9)
8 Fabulous creature at sea intended to embrace marines (7)
12 Manager joining firm is chap who may get waxy (9)
14 In the country sit in bar getting drunk (8)
15 Racing vehicle with some pinking? OK. A retuning is needed (2-5)
17 Unusual herons somewhere near water (6)
20 Agitating Miss Proll's right let down (6)
21 Finally forgot a quote – must be unsaid (6)
24 Sound of animal in desolate area (4)

CROSSWORD No. 51

CROSSWORD No. 52

Numerical Sequence by Duck from *Quiz Digest*

Some of the answers are harder than others! *Chambers 20th Century [English] Dictionary* could be useful.

ACROSS
1 3 (7)
5 Get big belly around with 'piggy' food that's on board (7)
9 Setter's gone wrong – tries again (7)
10 Sees the stars perhaps making visits (5,2)
11 Badly burnt, have become hazel-coloured (3-5)
12 7 (6)
14 Evilly influenced, a crude nurse needs to be reformed (5,1,5)
17 Smashing hotel (Hotel West) provides everything (3,5,3)
20 2 (6)
21 Bob not at home, having to go round supermarket – the way to get ice-cream in tubs? (5,3)
23 10 (7)
24 5 (7)
25 Oak, *eg*, chopped by a boy? It's criminal (7)
26 This mending makes Ming everlasting (7)

DOWN
1 9 (8)
2 Soft laxity like this is something that sounds commonplace (8)
3 Insecure, lacking heart – right? Pay me for security (7)
4 Unconstrained gate – it's favourable for progress (4,6)
5 1 (4)
6 Get no healing from an amateur? (7)
7 Insist upon having a bit of hair sticking up (6)
8 8 (5)
13 6 (10)
15 4 (8)
16 Good man speaks, speaks hesitatingly (8)
17 Germans munch a lot, we hear (7)
18 An older, decrepit man (7)
19 Start of university term, it seems, is to get modernised (6)
20 Travel to spot – see one expected to come? (5)
22 Some god, I (Norse) (4)

CROSSWORD No. 52

CROSSWORD No. 53

Theme and Variations by Duck from *Quiz Digest*

The four unclued theme words have something in common, and each has two variations. The four pairs of variations are related to their theme words in various ways, but both members of a pair are related to their theme word in the same way.

Theme word A: 27 across **Variations:** 12 across, 5 down
Theme word B: 3 down **Variations:** 19 down, 30 down
Theme word C: 13 across **Variations:** 20 across, 15 down
Theme word D: 16 down **Variations:** 26 across, 6 down

ACROSS

1 Greeting – it needs musical instrument (6)
4 Thrashes bat, slams spin (8)
9 Reprieve or annoy again? (7)
11 Can noisy? Then get lubricant, wrapping (7)
14 Shallow judgment only half formed (4)
17 Formal record touching the heart of the matter with hesitation (8)
18 Bit of wood to advance slowly? (5)
22 A sharp blow comes back, then a high ball comes back in a curve (8)
28 Wind in most of summer month (4)
31 Escaping number I rescue going west (7)
32 S American city has rest disturbed – by them? (7)
33 Road most messy? Use these coming home (8)
34 Fish Katharine's brought aboard (6)

DOWN

1 One making great effort – *eg* Peter on the water (7)
2 Left with a sharp pain, permanent (7)
7 Black substance the man had acted like a balm (7)
8 It's not heard to be golden (7)
10 One more for the team (6)
20 PS. Nudes are dreadful – keep out of office for a while (7)
21 Head of celery and eggs served up – a party hors d'oeuvre (7)
23 Let up on becoming rich (7)
24 Painters in dire straits (7)
25 Earth maybe putting energy initially into vegetable (6)
29 Business is steady (4)

CROSSWORD No. 53

CROSSWORD No. 54

Instruments by Duck from *Tough Puzzles*

Seven of the across clues are normal, but their answers must be transformed before entry in the grid. The remaining across clues have normal definitions, but their subsidiary indications refer to the form in which they are to be entered in the grid, that is, with one letter omitted. These letters, taken in order, give the name of the man desirous of the transformations to the other across answers. Solvers must decide to which type any particular clue refers. Down clues are normal.

ACROSS

1 Gravity to pitch into the trough of the sea one returning aboard
3 Being one of those called to decide damage?
9 After crash sends around box (black)
10 Bed – a bit of underwear needed by Virginia. A warm relaxing place? (2 words)
11 Instrument cut Italian flower first
12 Resolve but do show hesitation
14 A year's end, relaxing without energy, informal
16 Being without confidence should be praised somehow
17 Dignity of cardinal leading to bloody enmity
18 When most sent out various distributions
21 Infantry regiment – back half of it retreats
22 Brave appeal with exceptional pride
26 I supposedly get good results in the field or I sprint – versatile!
27 Uproarious noise – record by wiggling Rod
28 Artist steams angrily
29 Restrain river

DOWN

1 To produce drink mix two parts of lemon juice (no ice) with drop of port (5)
2 Thieves caught in country – egg-stealers? (5)
3 Ship's captain with father on the golf course (7)
4 She tells tales – cute senora, rambling (10)
5 German oil? (4)
6 Sailor's behind (5)
7 A little boy tucking into cereal like a cow? (8)
8 Dismisses bank workers (8)
13 Colleagues with zero assets, ruined – American agency brought in (10)
14 Telling your grandmother . . . ? (8)
15 Neighbourhood with endless sin and weapons (8)
19 Refuse to employ Marxist philosopher (7)
20 Rebel big just below the waist? (5)
23 Marks, singular cricketer (5)
24 Fine comic (5)
25 100 square metres – that's one (4)

CROSSWORD No. 54

CROSSWORD No. 55

From *Armchair Crosswords* by Afrit (1949)

ACROSS

1 Givest tips, from which the caddies receive what's coming to them (8)

10 You know your A.B.C.? Then the bet's off and you'll have to write this in as one letter (5)

11 A view which you may enjoy bare-headed, or in your hat (8)

12 Only a hundred left? It must be divided in two then (5)

13 The telegram you send to your wife, perhaps, when she's away. Quite mad, of course! (4)

14 Describes what you will recognise in a twinkling, making the rest all look silly (7)

16 It's no good trying to make this more difficult. There's nothing to see except air (6)

18 You'll have to put back a lot more than a pound whether you pay it or not (4)

20 A bit more strenuous than golf: a course of it would straighten that slice (9)

22 You need this to get a bite with, though the fish won't be large (9)

24 No one can say it's a clear case even if they're up your sleeve (4)

26 He gives me pain, as Simple Simon might have said (6)

27 A. had something on, and it's all helped (7)

30 Keeps the home fires burning? Get that idea out of your head! (4)

32 Whoever gets slain won't find it as hard as these (5)

33 This is obstinately difficult, but then it's half Irish (8)

34 A fisherman might lose one if it were shorter, but it's a disgrace to lose it altogether (5)

35 The whole of it is only part of it, so there must be a bally contradiction in it (8)

DOWN

2 Tax-collectors do, and you can't say it isn't right (5)

3 A policewoman, no doubt; anyway, she takes a nine (5)

4 He did a lot of speaking in public, but Brother Aldous has caught him up and gone on longer (6)

5 When he's good he's very, very good; but it's the very devil holding a married man in Paris! (9)

6 What brings you to town? Oh, the market shows an upward trend (4)

7 Remember that it isn't only youth that may follow hounds, and you'll guess it, however well it's wrapped up (7)

8 If internal combustion must be taken on spec. as a particular remedy (8)

9 There's a tangle at first, but the hair is all right afterwards. If you can't guess it now, you'll be on to it before morning (8)

15 Since the money-box is broken, replace it with a cheerful air (4)

17 It has long been a popular form of collecting, but not altogether lately (9)

18 It's plain at half the price, but what don't you care about it? (8)

19 In the same way, you won't have to suffer fools gladly (8)

21 See which way the cat jumps, and then you can exercise it (4)

23 Glides away, making you turn pale (7)

25 If we anticipate evil, sure enough it's in the ship's biscuit (6)

28 The result of employing too many cooks. It brings your heart into your mouth (5)

29 If an artist ever wants a pound, he can raise it with ease (5)

31 Gives an imitation of split peas (4)

CROSSWORD No. 55

CROSSWORD No. 56

By Ximenes from *The Observer*

ACROSS

1 Scene of a council—a rotten fiasco (6)
6 Had a long range, though out of breath (6)
11 Does this Prince? Ask 'ens wot's 'ad it! (6)
12 'Dope' Riley took this risk (5)
13 Mad Chloe gets spasms of overcrowding (8)
14 Philip keeps them brushed back (4)
15 It sounds as if it went to the head of *Le Malade Imaginaire* (9)
18 Australian brushman's Xmas dinner, luv? (7)
19 She loved one of whom there's some talk (6)
20 One of the 28: a 'cunning old' dog? (6)
22 Nogs of it are mixed (and with it) (6)
25 Hamlet grudged a penny for this bomb (6)
27 One of these agricultural implements won fame in the War (7)
29 I'm a rum plant myself, but my eponym's son's is even madder! (9)
31 Crop that will nearly make you mad (4)
32 Lord of Antioch gives Muse a dud cheque (8)
33 Hoard, a German submarine drama? (5)
34 The popinjay's jesting seems illegal (6)
35 It's no good saying that this acid can't be helped in the Bible (6)
36 Ira, the Victorian rowing coach! (6)

DOWN

1 For water on the knee try minced carrot (6)
2 Thrilling for the very young! (5)
3 Provided Hebrews with plenty of cabs (4)
4 *Bêche-de-mer* is mostly boring (7)
5 Stanza, put in Canada by Mr Weller? (6)
6 A windjammer starts this strife (6)
7 German tutor, a little French at heart (9)
8 All but the bun is held before it (8)
9 Dark blues take it out of fun for Lent (6)
10 Outsiders don't give the truth in answer (6)
16 Not the course a bull takes, to the discomfiture of a man in red! (9)
17 Cockney non-chemist's epithet for the skin of a living cow? (8)
21 Well known mound, etc., in Algeria (7)
22 (2 words) Make a mess of the purist (6)
23 The very image of a limbless wire (6)
24 Look at the colour of the poor child! (6)
25 Expresses contempt for tall hats (6)
26 Kipling says you are more so, Madam! (6)
28 Well equipped to take Romans for a ride! (5)
30 The Artful Dodger's mail-post (4)

CROSSWORD No. 56

CROSSWORD No. 57

By Beelzebub from *The Independent on Sunday*

ACROSS

1 Find another berth before entering ancient harbour up north (6)
8 To steal about pound is robbery! (4)
11 In trouble then, everybody in debt, they say, would be in slavery (10)
12 What's crazy about having a go? (4)
13 Form practice no longer is to work out amount (6)
14 Romany drinking bowl lets ice fall out (4)
15 Metal enclosure for bullock could be poison (5)
16 In outrageous code you have to detect spirited tyranny (12)
20 High cloud runs between Channel Islands and country further west (6)
22 Alarm caused by a bloomer going round bend (6)
24 Flounders, say, have the room at sea—for floundering! (12)
25 What's new in distinctive character of frogs and toads? (5)
27 With heavy knife, how far do Chinese go to get staves from it? (4)
29 I'd come for treatment from him! (6)
30 Burning sun, till no longer seen (4)
31 It could make square bashing a long treat (10)
32 Dagger of kings is here (4)
33 Isolated length is atop cathedral (6)

DOWN

1 They are left in air and used for shooting (7)
2 Employer's present during course— nervy if a student finally leaves (12)
3 Dark area of shiner in part's roughly concealed by drunk (8)
4 Cunning's working for a Greek magistrate (6)
5 Scot, say, accepted as species (4)
6 The Spanish tufts, old fashioned clotted hair style (8)
7 Fleeing debtors would, having left in appropriate guise (4)
8 Do Irishmen say it to ask for occasional Scotch? (7)
9 Wanting different cut a girl has range to be fit for farmers? (12)
10 Little space after scouring out of glacial valley (4)
17 He's God's gift to love with activity in that place (8)
18 Embroidery material showing a Frenchman holding head (8)
19 Endless hunt round Romania that is resulting in doubts (7)
21 Majestic mound in Arabia needing external support (7)
23 Flying lemur's surprised cry sucking in worm! (6)
25 Running thus, a donkey may drop tail? (4)
26 Caught breaking in at one? There'll be official proceedings! (4)
28 Grandfather's at all Scottish lochs without reactions locally? (4)

CROSSWORD No. 57

CROSSWORD No. 58
By Mephisto from *The Sunday Times*

ACROSS

2 Soccer team standing in wide net is holding upright (11)

10 I have to follow railroad (American)—it's difficult to catch! (7)

12 A pass in India mostly provided for foreign commander (4)

13 Groove circling very large round window (6)

14 Day we don't look forward to? The wrong time for Spenser! (6)

15 Private sport Frenchmen throw themselves into (5)

18 Those swimming with oil may be bony fish (8)

19 A sound we hear creates irritation (6)

20 Nut-cracking's dated—and ignorant? (6)

21 Time of day for local to welcome in politician, humble, Scottish (6)

22 I rush round a Roman province (6)

24 Dead man's bloomer—getting sold heap in crash! (8)

28 Lichen that's not extinct in America (5)

30 Put over by rodents, you have to scrape it off (6)

31 Mac's disgust with rye concoction of yellowish colour (6)

32 What do French have in mind? Swamping English in fish! (4)

33 Simple compound accommodates men with room supply (7)

34 Ma's off wine that's dry, valued and reserved for holy use (11)

DOWN

1 Forward run favourite has to restrict (4)

2 Withdrawn attitude, a look characterised by head (9)

3 Mountain sheep—number mass on height after climbing (6)

4 Desert plants make me most happy—sun required! (12)

5 Glacier snow moves over in a straight line like this (4)

6 There's energy in no sail deployed with uniform angles (8)

7 You'd see stars once hit when this shell explodes (12)

8 Old painter is shorter when he stands up (4)

9 Pulse raised I kept being upset, affected (8)

11 Frenchman in green get-up (4)

16 One who is caught in act should be set free (9)

17 A mineral I found in British Columbia is like igneous rock (8)

18 Gibbon playing by hole has a little time inside (8)

23 Language sound not once restricted in volume (6)

25 Frenchman getting under the German's skin (4)

26 In keener winds this has forced bird upwards (4)

27 A countryman loves to dress in brown (4)

29 Old tune always has second note at the end (4)

CROSSWORD No. 58

CROSSWORD No. 59

By Azed from *The Observer*

ACROSS

1 Grass-like sea plant—see one beside shingles (7)
6 Bars not closing in short supply (5)
10 One that's quick to seize drink, getting head stuck in (9)
11 Archers' slot, hit for radio audience? (4)
12 His partner was playing around on court disgracefully (7)
13 Team of racers runs, that is going after gold or silver disc (6)
16 The French in Britain returning one 5 francs in old money (5)
17 Fashion of yesteryear is cracking fit (6)
19 A quickie with nuts—it's refreshing for submariners (9)
21 Cheese—one to get those arms and legs moving? (9)
24 Drop of rain cheers back palm trees (6)
26 Suggesting squirrel fur, I'll have to change clothing (5)
29 What happens when all have scratched the object? (6)
30 Crack assistant for nereid (7)
31 Waste water: take some of it for hot bath (4)
32 I'm flanked by pages and feel train being jerked (9)
33 Was outstanding name in Oxford, possibly (5)
34 Clergyman displaying power to connect (7)

DOWN

1 Extract of benzine, by-product that kills fungus and insects (5)
2 Natural paraffin, Reichenbach's first, one found in sticky ooze, etc. (9)
3 Completion involves working out of clue—an age (7)
4 Strong drink—one over the eight and AZ's reeling! (6)
5 Well mounted, careers wildly round? Possibly (9)
6 Child having to beg after seconds (5)
7 Task: do one in arithmetic class? (6)
8 Uranium feeding power plant (4)
9 Italian town flogged Tiepolos leaving Italy (7)
14 Ruddy horse coming up under barrier—duck (9)
15 What's anadyomene (Greek, rising) in a sun*set*, silly? (9)
18 Group, so stuck up, that girl's in (7)
20 Not much of a song, awfully trite, in Carmen? (7)
22 What's this writer in store? We dole out the measures (6)
23 'Egg-cells in the female archetype', a melodic cadence (6)
25 Ship's end—hear rocks—no see this? (5)
27 Now, a yeti is different . . . isn't a—! (5)
28 Powerful launch—essential for Ninja tosh (4)

CROSSWORD No. 59

CROSSWORD No. 60

Next-door Neighbours by Duck from *Games and Puzzles*

Clues are normal but each solution is to be coded in one of two ways – either by taking the next letters in the alphabet or by taking the ones before (A follows Z). Thus FAG is entered as either GBH or EZF, and EZF could also be the code for DYE (the other possibility being CXD). Half the words are 'coded forwards' and half 'coded backwards'. Solvers must decide which code applies to each clue. *Chambers* is recommended.

ACROSS

1 Alloy in strange coin is all right (10)
9 Uranium in geological formation produces grin (5)
11 See Rolls-Royce – the ultimate in flashy transportation (5)
12 Ridge in part of Sussex – around Hassocks primarily (5)
13 Drags back for a pause? (5)
14 Missionary's old coin – catch (4)
15 Strain to express regret, we hear (3)
17 Brute issuing expression of disgust, getting a pair (5)
19 Poor house – one with a rodent (5)
22 Song about a valley (3)
23 Gin – homely way of getting Jock high (4)
24 Shoot chap in Devon? (5)
26 French vineyard and container for wine (5)
28 I'll have chanted about going to court (5)
29 Signal from British Prime Minister going West (5)
30 Salt – I'd eat it on bit of ham minced up (10)

DOWN

1 Laze around? One's immersed in rum and lemon, claret (10)
2 Go well together, get a local victory (5)
3 Hot old ale could make you spin round (4)
4 Plant, yellow one, given to child (5)
5 Brood of a nuthatch? No thank you (3)
6 Old backgammon? Wait to roll (5)
7 Gin, Alice? No, that's awful, it makes you numb (10)
8 Tribal woman with endless croak (5)
10 Bob's neck, something short and fat (5)
16 Kick old crank (5)
18 Everything's fine with a religious animal (5)
20 Part 1 of Shakespeare, volume given to relation (5)
21 See awful rot about an old city (5)
22 Batting? Illingworth's out – this weather doesn't help batsmen (5)
25 Tungsten embedded in another metal, something very similar (4)
27 Take for example Mr Maudling? (3)

CROSSWORD No. 60

CROSSWORD No. 61

Empty Pockets by Duck from *Games and Puzzles*

Each solution must have a word omitted before it is entered in the diagram. The missing words have something in common.

Both the definition *and* the subsidiary indication refer to the unmutilated solution.

ACROSS

1 O, a dunce will need it somehow! (9)
4 Jane? Inwardly English and very good, is outwardly not at all attractive (7)
7 Learner in art I mus' work – to become this? (10)
9 Heroic woman opposing subversive army activity (6)
10 Hampshire water, not fresh, provided by old spring (6)
11 Apparently I, bound by an ancient vow, will be most fortunate (8)
12 One lunatic somersaulting in a convulsive fit and going around naked? (8)
15 Crop to grind etc. when cut (6)
16 Marches past as red revolutionary (7)
18 Cooking apples out on the table as a matter of course (9)
19 Seemingly remove a barrier for protection (7)
20 Disparages exercises we hear (7)

DOWN

1 It's sensible having the top flat it seems (11)
2 Plain yellow record book with name entered in (8)
3 Ransack hotel's inside – in Scandinavia somewhere (7)
4 Condemned lover created by Continental writer – not half frightened (9)
5 Dazzlingly live deans e.g. gave gospel message (11)
6 Despatched about a hundred tree-trunks, dry through – sources of sweet smell (12)
8 Young member of family, girl gobbling short dinner, getting ill (10)
13 Commanding fairy in pain after initial application of iodine (8)
14 Harsh-sounding singer? Yes and no! (6)
17 Location with top class inside? (6)

CROSSWORD No. 61

CROSSWORD No. 62
Blankety Blank by Duck from *The Independent Magazine*

In one part of the television game *Blankety Blank*, contestants are asked to complete a phrase. For example, in 'Long ———' the blank could be 'boat', 'shot' or 'trousers' (among many other possibilities). The scoreboard then shows three answers given 50, 100 and 150 points. In the grid below, two keywords have been used (that is, the equivalents of 'long' above), each of which has three answers. Each answer is to be prefixed by its score so as to form a new word which is then entered on the grid.

ACROSS
1 Keyword (5)
5 Flier must go beyond field with tree (7)
11 What sounds like fast Aussie vehicle? It's centuries old and noted to move slowly! (9)
12 Bill leads superior chaps with quickness of perception (6)
13 Weasel one found hidden in bracken (5)
15 Sol you finally mix with me, right? (7)
16 Paint claim by painter in Yellow Pages! (7)
17 34 ac ——— (5)
20 Like a bird that's heard in the river (6)
22 Tree in Colombia surrounded by Indians (6)
25 1ac ——— (5)
27 Nature's unruly wind (7, hyphenated)
28 Sire she upset bristled (7)
30 The rector will have no pagan god set up (5)
31 A gypsy man does 'ave smells (6)
32 Simpleton at home with no money (8)
33 Tent is fixed to end of guy – tightness required (7)
34 Keyword (5)

DOWN
1 Support Indian district having shortfall in the country (6)
2 1ac ——— (4)
3 Instrument Mabel played in company (7)
4 What sounds like folded line is made by dagger (6)
6 Governor is entertainer welcoming in member (7)
7 What I must give in all-out effort is wild (5)
8 Toxic soup – soon I may collapse (9)
9 Silver about on seabed? (7)
10 1ac ——— (5)
14 A nice, pure unbridled hedonism is what I'm after (9)
18 Girl in Ireland John upset (7)
19 Overtake worker walking to the right (7)
21 Where earliest Christians were opposed to nothing connected with church (7)
23 Wheeled carriage in northern town (6)
24 Etna's exploding round the south – see a flame on it? (6)
25 34ac ——— (5)
26 Scores nothing according to report (5)
29 34ac ——— (4)

CROSSWORD No. 62

CROSSWORD No. 63

Treasure Hunt by Phi from *The Independent Magazine*

The grid is a treasure map: north is at the top, and the treasure is marked in the usual way. Letter clashes between Across and Down answers in some squares (and only these) are to be considered directions. Starting at the clash in the top row and moving thence from clash to clash will reveal which of the possible sites conceals the treasure. Solvers should shade this square. One spelling (of a word not in *Chambers* 1988) is historically accurate; one proper noun appears only in an etymology.

ACROSS

1 With a bit of fructose added, this dish is prepared from bland nuts! (12, hyphenated)
10 One went off course, dropping velocity, and came back (8)
13 Source of wine knocked back by female, say, going round about (5)
14 Train former journalists (7)
15 Firm's current days for business (5)
16 Scots to predict the outcome? Odds are not right (4)
17 Tackled the garden – the man would have nothing planted in (4)
19 The cloth getting cut in circles (7)
21 It contains original features of Elian style, for instance (5)
22 Woody will appear round a disreputable house (5)
24 Noted plunger has 2,000 on the spot in one part of contest (7)
26 Spurs, say, needed for harnessed horses? (4)
27 Mournful cry is the last you get from happy bird (4)
29 Provide weapons as before – clumsy marine drops one (5)
30 Sport workshop the French subject to regulations (7)
33 Statesman, say, getting vote – one in 10 (5)
34 Old Scots rulers study music and literature, say (8)
35 Bit of kit needed in playing as in Centre Court, ultimately? (12, hyphenated)

DOWN

1 Announcement of wedding for girl in Bahamas (5)
2 Former husband clearly embraced by mysterious nude, with no alibi? (11)
3 Return, taking away fruit harvest (4)
4 Movie on TV service held up – only end of movie's respectable, on reflection (8)
5 One abandons theatre floors – you'll see me in the gods! (4)
6 Part of farm shelter housing a pig (7)
7 Love's revolutionary when one's embraced a nymph (5)
8 Use SRN to redefine these? (6)
9 Terminology from computing method one rejected, repeated in symbol mostly (7)
11 Put in other words, let's narrate in a new way (11)
12 British, with hesitation, to become part of US fraternity? (4)
18 No meal is ground from this (8)
19 Birdie? Introduction of curtailed round permitted it (7, hyphenated)
20 Left in marks showing gaps in popular wines (7)
23 Siren: knockout bit of naughtiness, morally loose internally (6)
25 Everything I'm capable of is curtailed by witchcraft (4)
26 'Raise skill' on the spot for this answer! (5)
28 Minimum delay that one's involved in (5)
31 Door-keeper shuts out hard drug addict (4)
32 Report shows barristers getting £1,000 (4)

CROSSWORD No. 63

Murder Mystery by Stephen Sondheim from the *New York Magazine*

'I **40A**(3) we're **39D**(3) here,' said the Inspector. He was standing in the jungle-like **1D**(12) of the **6D**(9) of the late Sir Leonard Feisthill, **19A**(4) while adviser to the Secret Service Department of **11D**(12) and setter of the weekly crosswords in its house organ, *The Secret Service* **3D**(6). He was speaking to Lucius I. Feisthill, the deceased's nephew, Dr. Nathanael Parmenter, his medical adviser, and **37A**(3) LaFollette, his secretary: 'Last week we had a **18A**(3) that Sir Leonard was about to denounce someone close to him for selling state secrets to the **33D**(5). His **35A**(6) was to publish the traitor's name – in **21A**(4), perhaps – as a warning to the betrayer to cease his nefarious activities. But it looks as if he was **13A**(6) at his own game, for here he lies, **2D**(4) in the back. I suggest we step into the study, where the victim's flight from the murderer began, to **40A**(3) if his desk will **44A**(5) us further clues.' None of the suspects dared **5D**(4) the suggestion and they **39D**(3) followed him, walking carefully around Sir Leonard's **1A**(7).

The walls of the study were lined with books on classical antiquities, Sir Leonard's only reading **7D**(6). (Hidden behind some of them was his famous collection of pornographic one-**20D**(7).) Among the **38A**(6) furnishings (Sir Leonard was a devotee of the decorative **37D**(4) and **25D**(7) on nothing) was a large African desk, acquired in the **26A**(5). On it were a glass of **30A**(3), his well-thumbed copy of the **45A**(7), his rusty typewriter, a thin **16A**(7) of ferric **12A**(5) all over it, and the crossword reprinted on this page, which was to be published the following week. The only other **8D**(4) was an unfinished pencilled work-sheet of Clues for it, as follows:

> Gun Bogart might have used in 'Born to Say No'
> Stare and see parts of the mosaic!
> Alternative finish for a Biblical witch? Quite the reverse!
> Call for help gets nothing for fair.
> Plan in retrospect to help if you put on weight.

'A four-letter, five-letter, six-letter, seven-letter and an eight-letter word,' murmured the Inspector, no **29D**(6) at puzzles himself. 'Odd . . . well, no **7D**(6).' In the **42A**(6) room, **39D**(3) that could be heard was a ladylike **22D**(4) from **37A**(3) and the rasp of a **43A**(5). The Inspector lit his pipe and suddenly turned.

'Miss LaFollette, Sir Leonard had a reputation for being quite a **41A**(3). How well did you know him?'

'Quite well,' the **32D**(5) replied. 'We first met **34A**(3) years ago at one of those literary **36D**(4). **10D**(6) summer it was, I remember, the trees all gold – '

'Her favorite color,' sneered Lucius, trying to **7A**(5) her innocent tone.

'In your **23A**(3), you **9D**(8)!' she screamed – inaccurately, for Lucius was by no means stupid.

CROSSWORD No. 64

'**15A**(6) on,' the Inspector cautioned.

'**37A**(3) is right,' the Doctor put in with his characteristic Vermont **28A**(5). 'I was treating **27D**(6) for a ruptured **31A**(4) at the time – he had chronic trouble with his back.'

'But not with his head,' mused the Inspector. 'Sir Leonard was a man who **4D**(7) himself quickly to any situation and I'm convinced that somewhere in this puzzle is an indication of the murderer's identity, made perhaps even in his presence but too subtle for him to **40A**(3) and therefore destroy.' He gave the puzzle and Clues a moment's study, then whistled softly in realization. 'Now I **40A**(3),' he said, and promptly arrested one of the people in the room.

Whom did he arrest, and what was Sir Leonard's method of accusation?

CROSSWORD No. 65
By Emily Cox and Henry Rathvon
(The Puzzler from the *Atlantic Monthly*)

Cryptic Menu: The listing below, which seems to present a dinner menu (with a number of cryptic recipes), actually comprises the 18 Across clues to this puzzle. The clues are strung together in no special order; solvers may locate the answers in the diagram with the help of the Downs, which are normal. Answers include one proper noun; the first Across answer clued in the menu is a two-word phrase.

ACROSS

Turkey Dinner
Choice piece wrapped in nutritious grain roll with a stuffing

Chicken-Seafood Supper
Meat-filled loaf done on a barbecue's top, with sole and shellfish

Heavenly Stewed Prunes
A large (nine-crate) mixture with fruit tops smothered in mace seasoning

Fish Sandwiches
Uncooked, flipped with chicken article

Spanish Hero
Tart Spanish corn pieces and asparagus pieces go together with cooked eel & rat

Desserts
Gelled tripe from the East, brown outside, with mixed nuts, hand-shelled, placed around parsley or sage

Iced Treat
Fruit drinks containing cored pulp, stirred

Strudel
Flaky little piece with egg in it (top-grade)

DOWN

1 Singers brought up one drab bag (8)
2 What spies on cult use endlessly (6)
3 With one penny, English soprano gets towels (5)
4 Have faith headed by ancient god, once in a while (6)
5 Send car off with jumpers? (7)
6 Food serving overwhelms a sense of taste (6)
7 Grammatical forms in place atop Russian range (7)
8 Soldier invades nearby—that's reasonable (7)
9 Dry borders of seashore (4)
10 Music for nine lacking ultimate zip (4)
11 Twisted pretzels with salt (but no pepper) and drinks (8)
12 Crafty person gets a red stain out (7)
13 Central government supporter failed SAT—it's true (7)
14 Wearing tails, he tries again (7)
15 Flying jet, ace has stuff thrown out (6)
16 Join the heartless cat coming back (6) (2 words)
17 Container for suds (about a thousand) (6)
18 State greeting between two oceans (4)
19 Support victory with a shout of praise for a woman (5)
20 Republican coming in used to be fighting (4)

CROSSWORD No. 65

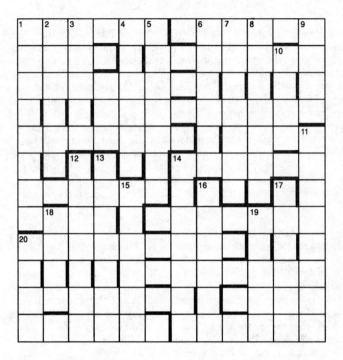

CROSSWORD No. 66

University Challenge by Apex from *Games and Puzzles*

Clues are either Definition and Letter Mixture or Printer's Devilry. Solvers must discover which is which. DLM clues each contain a definition (one word or more) and a mixture of the letters (beginning with the beginning or ending with the end of a word in the clue) of the required word. Example: 'Why has the sea-going captain upset the Question-master?'; Answer: GASCOIGNE (SEA-GOING C . . .). Printer's Devilry (PD), each clue is a passage from which the printer has removed a hidden answer, closing the gap, taking liberties sometimes with punctuation and spacing, but not disturbing the order of the remaining letters. Example: 'Is the question "Mice?" asked the Principal of Somerville.' Answer: ASTERN ('Is the Question-master nice?' asked the Principal of Somerville.) Each passage when complete makes sense. At the end of an exciting contest the Chairman, who had asked all the questions without batting an eyelid, added up the scores (two points each PD, one point each DLM) and announced that a replay would be necessary.

ACROSSBRIDGE

1 How does Euripides encourage the writer of tragedies? (9)

10 Why does a bride have tows after a wedding? (7)

11 Why is the poem a goer in the front row? (5)

12 Who relinquished the kilt to teach Scots a lesson? (4)

14 Which racehorse always bolted when the stabs were opened? (6)

15 How often did Lely visit the buxom beauties of Hampton Court? (6)

18 When did the kangaroo get a footing in Australia? (7)

19 Why did the malignant sprite keep ill-treating the Water Babies? (6)

20 Do all footballers report swear in contrasting colours? (6)

21 Why shouldn't the Cobble rub standard rubbers on? (6)

23 Which dramatic critic said 'This wreath is best!'? (6)

25 In which month were the seven veils chosen for dancing? (7)

28 Which Indian asked if he could have the chapter because he was full up? (6)

29 Who swam out every morning to collect alms in Scotland? (6)

30 What will all the idle hands do in a dispute? (4)

31 Which gambler always entered for a set never won? (5)

32 Why did the kind-hearted wardress lather dinner? (7)

33 Which dramatist in Eire is updating the plays of George Bernard Shaw? (9)

DOWNBRIDGE

1 Why has poet most of the Tories against him? (5)

2 Who outwitted the Red Villain in Lear's Book of Nonsense? (6)

3 Which TV Publicity Agent said 'Tow or tar wood below you!'? (9)

4 Which of the beneficiaries of a will said 'Is the Mall yours?'? (6)

5 Who was the most threatening of all Guy Fawkes' confederates? (4)

6 Who accused the strange Mr. Otis of poisoning his daughter? (8)

7 Why did the reputable firm give the biggest raise? (6)

8 Which well-known flirt gazed and winked at the poet laureate? (10)

9 Would Ophelia have loved ads like Hamlet? (6)

13 Which General gave his brave horse wine after every battle? (10)

CROSSWORD No. 66

16 Why does inferior cheese put some rats off? (9)

17 Why are the top pieces of a lantern light always obscured? (8)

21 What should one use to prevent worming over a garden? (6)

22 Why is the bruiser at fun facing everyone? (6)

23 Do you know that ass trying his luck on Mastermind? (6)

24 How does a revolving index help one to read a dial? (6)

26 Who relaxes with Margery on the see-saw? (5)

27 At what time did the mound own the clock? (4)

CROSSWORD No. 67

Automania by Salamanca from *New Statesman*

Three types of clue are encountered: i) Who For; punning or definitive hints are given as to suitable owners – e.g. dog-lover (ROVER): ii) Used Cars; clues treat answers in their subsidiary forms as though they are locked inside a car (total length indicated) while defining the real answer only: iii) Scrap; each clue contains a definition of one or more words and a hidden jumble of the answer, the answer in each case being entered with an extra letter to make another real word, the extra letter being the 'bonnet' of one of the cars used in ii, the remains of that car also to be found as a hidden jumble in the clue.

WHO FOR

1Ac A boulevardier (8)
1D The DIY golfer? (8)
3 An astronomer (4)
5 A Covenanter (7)
7Ac A glutton? (4)
9 A Caribbean? (6)
10 A grass (4)
22 A geologist (8)
23 The forgetful (5)
24Ac The drinker/driver (6)
24D A simpleton (2 words, 7)
31Ac A circus performer (6)
32Ac The drinker/driver (6)
32D An old-fashioned girl (4)
33 A sportsman (4)
39 A fighter ace (8)

USED CARS

7D Ghostly old English learner drivers with big bird in road smash (12)
8 Flying one got cut, ovine perhaps, of deer (15)
12 Author to live secure mostly (8)
14 Well-built small dog's brown, a wild hound, see? (14)
16 Devil grasped by head lama after gold deer (10)
17 Girl showing pain mostly is aged, decrepit (11)
18 Fail to hold what's threadlike one time (8)
19 Praise specially huge lump of wood, i.e., as I chopped (12)
21 Lord in court has game in hand perhaps (8)
25Ac Bird season for turning coalman out (11)

26Ac Tree: one's to spot one in mud (9)
27 Burgundy eleven study (7)
31D Pal flew in patterned flight (8)
35 Learner to choose one different role (8)
38 Have an advantage, being gowned in e.g. dress (9)

SCRAP

2 Driving made pleasant at this school (3)
4 Going to pass, I'd use signal correctly (3)
6 Drove excitedly and once gave a yell (4)
11 Pressed, pedal would go down to the bottom without a hindrance (4)
13 Local man that carries blood to save noble (4)
15 Tool vital for measurement of axle load (3)
20 Driver, one going over six acres (3)
25D Made engine rods go smoothly inside lorry (5)
26D Good drivers are ones that listen and look (4)
28 Tangle caused by the Rolls crashing initially (3)
29 Birds fare badly on these roads (4)
30 Avoid bad language, do! (3)
34 Employ lorries up in Bolton (3)
36 Many chaps taking the final test now (4)
37 A battered Beetle stuck in a trench (4)

CROSSWORD No. 67

CROSSWORD No. 68

Printer's Devilry by Afrit from *The Listener* 1937

The lights are complete words which were originally 'hidden' in the clues. It is to be presumed that the compositor, seeing that certain consecutive letters spelt a word or words, removed them and closed up the gap, sometimes taking a further liberty with the spacing and punctuation, but not altering the order of the letters. There is only one break in each clue, and the lights show the omitted letters in their original order.

ACROSS

(1) See 26D. **(4, 7D)** ' "Surely", said I, "surely that is something at my wine!" ' **(7, 13D, 42D)** Some numbers in Swinburne nest at Ely, kindly friend. **(11)** ' "Pooh!" trilled a linnet, and each dew-note had a lilt'. **(12, 10)** An article of faith is not merely an opinion bet. **(16)** 'Ah, wasteful woman, she that may on her own self sown price!' **(18)** 'The grey sea and the long band, the yellow half-moon large and low'. **(22, 14, 36D)** 'Something . . . moved a poet to prophecies – a pinch o' guarded dust'. **(24, 39D)** In robore fasces. **(25)** Asters go out, cricket comes in. **(27)** 'Here tone is music's own, like those of morning birds.' **(28)** 'My laver flags, and what are its wages?' **(30)** The party when parting had heard the curlew's knell. **(32, 21D)** The bad land is little but dear. **(34)** In olden days two fat people on one leg called for no remark. **(38)** 'The cliffs of England stand glimmering, and vain the tranquil bay'. **(41)** How shall poet's soul stand rapt when 'throughout the music of the suns is in her soul at once!' **(43)** See 31D. **(44)** Being a fashionable damozel, the stars in her hair were seven. **(45)** The concourse lulled to sudden silence awed my speech. **(47)** See 31D. **(48)** See 46D. **(49, 17D)** 'Shepherds feed their flocks by shallow river falls, melodious birds sing madrigals'.

DOWN

(1) 'Nor amid these triumphs dost thou scorn the humble glow-worms to adorn'. **(3, 35)** 'The dense hard passage is blind and stifled that crawls by a turn to climb'. **(4)** Errors oft in the stilly night break your slumbers. **(6, 2)** May the big never distinguish many merchantmen! **(7)** See 4A. **(8)** Some were here, some there, and the rest where? **(9, 19)** 'A good boy am I' makes Jack Horner's pie to *my* mind. **(13)** See 7A. **(14)** 'Will there be children in their hall for ever and for ever?' **(15)** 'Nor will occasion want nor shall wed with dangerous expedition to invade Heaven'. **(17)** See 49A. **(20)** Ascend we now, find foot-holds, cling to the rocks above. **(21)** See 32A. **(23, 29)** 'And that smile like sunshine (shall) dart into ma heart'. **(26, 1A, 5)** 'And not bows: only when daylight comes, comes in the light'. **(27, 33)** 'O the eternal sky, full of light and of dignity!' **(31, 47A, 43A)** 'Fatigued he sinks into some pleasant lair of wavy grass, an air and gentle tale of love'. **(36)** See 22A. **(37)** A nod or a beck, a quip or youthful jollity – which do you prefer? **(39)** See 24A. **(40)** 'Let a Lord once own the happy lines, how it brightens!' **(42)** See 7A. **(46, 48A)** Aspirer 'with slow but stately pace kept on his course.'

CROSSWORD No. 68

CROSSWORD No. 69

Justyn Print by Zander from *The Listener*

Each clue in italics is the imaginary title of a new book by an unknown author. Solvers are asked to deduce the authors' names from the broad hints given by their titles: e.g., if one such title was *The Broken Window* (3,5), the author's name might be EVA BRICK. Apart from several proper names, all words are in *Chambers 20th Century [English] Dictionary*. The unchecked letters of the authors' names make up the following new book title: UP HILLS, BY AL PING.

ACROSS

1 See 50
5 Tax associated with square vessels (4)
9 It goes to a Scotswoman's head a great deal, we hear (5)
13, 36A *Drake's Hammock* (5,8)
15 Breath-sweetener offered by a child, round, swallowed by copper (6)
17 A drama out East, with one after a wild ox (4)
18 Source of a varnish that takes a heavy knife to impair (5)
19, 55 *The Sprawling Metropolis* (5,6)
20 A cake-decorator in a quick-service restaurant (4)
21, 37 *Left In Suspense* (5,6)
23 This act is wicked and spiteful (7)
25 See 28
28, 25 *News From De Southland* (6,2,5)
31 Fatty tumour caused by taking marijuana into the mouth (8)
34 Gift with built-in resistance element (5)
35 It's a day's work to check vessel coming into Strait (5)
36 See 13
37 See 21
39 Frontal surfaces appear to be reflected around the upper end (7)
41 One who's late can cross this river – or can he? That's questionable (7)
47 Suit having the tail in front is a bore (5)
50, 1A *Getting A Move On* (4,5)
52 Old-fashioned case from which to obtain quiet drink (5)
53 Quintet, having a crude violin, becomes indistinct (5)
54, 30 *De Bestest Band What Am* (4,9)
55 See 19
56 See 52D
57 Advance payment about right for a beastly home (5)
58 Earth dug out and thrown up reveals rejected English child (4)
59 Holy building at Mecca, a double one, attended by leaders of bedouin Arabs (5)

DOWN

1 Payment in old shillings and pence diminished in Milton's time (6)
2, 42 *Tudor Banquet* (9,5)
3 Bitter drug that forms oxygen in drinks (5)
4 Margaret rings one with a lasso (5)
5 See 47D
6 Type of fibre cloth, usually striped, laid on Mac's drive (5)
7 See 9D
8 Beetle caused endless panic, landing on a baby's head (6)
9, 7 *Stay Where You Are* (4,4)
10 Funny hat, one originating in an Asian country (4)
11 A Glaswegian buys, and —— up, by the sound of it? (5)
12 Hector achieving peaks of heroism under fiercest fighting (4)
14 Type of cereal that gives one endlessly passionate ardour (3)
16 Defensive apparatus fitted with spikes around battered portal (7)
22 See 38
23 Bond drops in for a cheering drink (3)
24 A month to live – start to tremble, getting het up about it (6)
26 Weel supplied wi' bawbees, I'll lodge in the better room (4)
27 Energy, having for basis a power emanating from the supreme deity (3)

CROSSWORD No. 69

29 Small flock of sheep you've to convey round river (4)
30 See 54A
32 Enraged, losing normal composure (7)
33 Stale cattle fodder, almost entirely (3)
36 A letter that's got lost without the end being lost (3)
38, 22 *Continental Breakfast* (6,6)
40 Find an easterner, used to the high life, with an unusual turn of phrase (6)
42 See 2
43 Malingerer is sullen, being without work ultimately (5)

44 Musical pipe accompanying English tale of yore (5)
45 Group of African peoples that has no beggars (5)
46 Mother in trouble looks up the serpent-witch (5)
47, 5D *Teenage Party* (4,5)
48 It's nitrogen in the Strait that makes the Scots yawn (4)
49 Frenzied shout given by woman embracing love (4)
51 Mixed fruit I lug all over the shop (4)
52, 56 *Incognito* (3,2,3)

CROSSWORD No. 70

Heart Transplants by Duck and Hen from *The Listener*

Each answer must be given a new heart: the word that would naturally belong at the heart of another answer. Each clue contains (in any order) a definition of the 'pre-transplant' answer, a subsidiary indication of the 'pre-transplant' answer and a one-word definition of the new heart. *Chambers 20th Century [English] Dictionary* is recommended. Ignore one accent.

ACROSS

1 Cavalcade quite miserable round Scottish city boundary? (7)
6 Copper had news of explosive beside a road (5)
10 Bed one pal improvised, part of horse shelter (9)
12 One with pain curtailed thanks god (4)
13 Coin box, one in Italian city (5)
14 Whale? Money, we hear – no small amount – applaud! (8)
16 Corn, peel and suet cooked round plaice (12)
19 River tide that floods, swamping matter (limonite) (6)
21 Hard worker has not aged (4)
22 Vessel – note it by Channel Islands reversing (4)
23 Grandiloquent, reactionary judge imprisoning man shows excessive feeling (6)
24 Lu has my apron on, home protection (12)
28 Going round valley a little kid came to coin (8)
30 American place of massacre – in a short time, look – nothing! (5)
31 Site to be changed if this place is squalid (4)
32 Street in almost complete collapse, business centre before simplicity (9)
33 Spike sneering bitterly, blue about heartless exposure (5)
34 River with dye, see, spoiling fish, tree (7)

DOWN

1 Stay motionless? Old tablets set up twitch (5)
2 One at far post, waving to us, coming in vestment (9)
3 A foreign flower contest, old-womanish (5)
4 Ol' voter converted, a Conservative swinging round to the left course (12)
5 Party racket in bed-sitter or tenement (4)
6 Story-books – this chapter's all about joint rulers (12)
7 Evil Sarah harbouring anger when upset in a row (8)
8 English drinking cup's short gold letters (4)
9 Removes chemical product from animals, street being messed up with lead and sulphur (7)
11 Stain on one good man, judge maybe (6)
15 Court submission about to interrupt the accused's plea (9)
17 Superior trooper running wild – one driving out native fellow? (8)
18 Oxalis is sure to upset innards finally – they give out (7)
20 Engineers standing still begin to rest (6)
25 Look around – a learner beat man on his own territory (5)
26 In criticism revolutionary student hammers governor (5)
27 Chair, bottomless yielding one, exists (4)
29 Sloth? Get out of bed, rebel! (4)

CROSSWORD No. 70

CROSSWORD No. 71

Hydra by Duck from *The Listener*

The 11 unclued lights are words which have something in common and which have been processed in a similar way. *Chambers 20th Century [English] Dictionary* is recommended.

ACROSS

11 People giving a refund for old collars? (8)
12 Strong chap sets one on edge (5)
13 Soon like a member of the Lords? (5)
15 A mostly sharp fruit (4)
16 We've some priceless oil! (4)
20 The EEC's confused about Germany's word to describe more than one German female (8)
23 Fails to justify unfilled tummies (6)
27 The man (lay worker) to get blunt (8)
29 Fillets, A1, eaten with excitement (7)
32 Onset of fever leads to a hospital note (3)
33 One-time flighty girl's engagement is fun (3)
38 Row about what's right? Judge required (5)
39 Simpletons, leaderless lot (6)
40 Bird hot with love? (8)
47 Wench shows desire bringing a touch of sexiness to the fore (4)
49 Swearword from the pastoral Henry (4)
50 To kick old copper's heartless crime (5)
51 Priest, a help for alcoholic chap (5)
52 One making a loan to leading character of Cowper? (8)

DOWN

1 Bird in California has sense to grab revenue (7)
2 Half peruse morning papers? (4)
3 Relation *not* 13, doddery (4)
4 Such primarily may have troughs (5)
5 Rough point in throat (4)
6 'Ellenic poet's dry measure (4)
7 Plant needing heat for brew (4)
8 Born in endless poverty (3)
9 Card game has fool taken in by wager (6)
14 Style of building, in short, is roguish (4)
17 To heal in oldentimes hand would conceal bit of old plant (8)
22 Cad's to hide as before (4)
23 Liz's letter to the Hebrews (4)
25 Socialist sets upset leaders of National Executive initially (6)
26 Discarded stakes – could be used around north for plants (4)
28 Rag sort of bandage triply wrapping one (4)
30 Indispositions caused by drinks we hear (4)
31 Instrument not half abused (4)
35 Plant with flower cracking a road up (7)
36 Australian beast in prison we hear (6)
37 Grass, rank when decomposed (4)
41 Worm wriggling round earth's surface may be seen on lawn (5)
42 More than one such guild could be gripping (4)
43 Cart may turn up here (4)
44 Goat-antelope – with head hung down it might appear to be a deer (4)
45 Boozy party for English after victory (4)
46 One wants the reverse of non-sweet sweets (4)
48 Kick and drag audibly (3)

CROSSWORD No. 71

CROSSWORD No. 72

Mixed Doubles by Virgilius from *The Listener*

Each clue has two possible solutions, thus each pair of clues yields four answers. Solvers must work out where these go – it is decided alphabetically where each one appears.

ACROSS

1 Usually nothing can be seen in this – but negro's in view/Transport flier from here – it gives harassed flier help, going round (8)

6 Sort of suit North or South might lead for this island?/Do some scratching in sporrans, perhaps – remove quarters outside and it's left over (4)

9 Give clear bit of encouragement – you might have it on horse/As done in Scotland, produce a bit of witch-craft, parking in sea-tangle (4)

10 Not concluded yet, and put into view – without use of crook?/Dancing walk produced by one who's staggered (4)

11 Completed – a bit of paper work (it precedes the start of tippling)/One attracted by male swan, almost kept under control (3)

12 Rum else Madeira or Curacao is, left at end of bottle/Name for girl, is this? Look back in Biblical legend for answer (4)

15 Eel's first (and second) in Italian fishing-place – it's little use as wages these days/I display vacancy, with an extreme of eccentricity – mouth's opening here (4)

16 Article with a point – are women left this?/A result of manipulating enough of electorate? That might shock you (3)

18 Rod may be used for me, or Kipling's master/Mature, at end of life, moved to one side in Cumbernauld (4)

20 River in which Oxford college's dumped last of hock? Just the opposite/I'm true royal chap – prince for a Russian community (4)

21 Used for observations rarely (third letter made plural)/Inert material – use this, also, as lights' contents, perhaps (4)

22 Faults in red items uncommonly required/Walter wanting fifth part upset, it's clear – I go into sea near Dover (8)

DOWN

1 Sort of neat, to shape course for fish/Spot an edge, last put inside in a fairly bad condition (8)

2 Small part of old language, literally a vowel/River making appearance at centre of Firenze (4)

3 Female I watched (out West) and I associated with sexiness?/Up country in S.A., dispatch first letter in practice (3)

4 Girl's married name to a certain extent/What rivers may come from, though poet's lost source of brook (4)

5 I uphold what's been laid down – e.g. it's all in order/Tapered wood holding pole when in action – got from wine casks? (8)

7 It's associated with an unusual girl/Result of instinctive impulses in South-East part? (4)

8 Easy, in a way, for party after end of debating/Device for catching side in piece at end of boot (4)

13 Behaves amorously – see a bit of England (South)/Ultimate of sites originally, soon inaccessible since in Scottified environment (4)

14 Not working with energy, one takes set without last letter/Seen in noble regalia, in different version of 'Lear' (4)

CROSSWORD No. 72

15 Not favourable weather required to start producing ore under regulations/Musical female (4)

17 Designed to give sharpness in argument – you'll observe only second to change/Don's last English North-East river (4)

19 Bit of food we passed up? Not a great amount in proportion/Some suitable region to plough (in accepted English long given up) (3)

CROSSWORD No. 73

I-Spy by Mass from *The Listener*

Twenty-four letters of the alphabet occur round the outer circle, each one being diametrically opposite itself (e.g. R at 3 and 27; or Q at 15 and 39; etc.). In one case, the letter is initial to a radial answer entered normally from rim to pupil; in the opposing case it is the first letter of a jumble of an answer, e.g. QEVIUR from QUIVER (or QCITAU from ACQUIT). Two radials are proper names and one a Latin plural not in *Chambers*.

The second circle from the rim contains eight thematic words of six letters each, reading clockwise.

The fourth circle from the rim, reading clockwise, contains five words of an expression continued by those letters which have been *misprinted* in the twenty-four clues leading to *normal* entries. In half these clues the misprint affects the definition part; in the others it affects the subsidiary indications. The remaining clues for answers to be jumbled are conventional.

RADIALS (6)

1 Try sex for a change: it'll grate on Jones
2 Monastic place for cats: Father divided by cost
3 Woolly gelding, sow and most of stock
4 Double German craving?
5 Extract from ballad in old, old Castalian tongue
6 Like a swine dropping new penny in a phenol
7 Toothy construction mounted above round cote
8 Caught US General consuming endless oil
9 Who once deceived is ardent, we hear, with the Queen
10 Sword and plates are kept here, it's said
11 One unformed barrow for Jock getting right
12 Scottish king's evil pointless yarn
13 Worker chiselled on the inside, tilted antique
14 Guess old type's making a will
15 Wood man in distance in drizzle
16 Greet return of copper packing-ring
17 Deity has power with horrific clipped head
18 Spine of arch is forked elaborately
19 A smile *can* be seen in a visor
20 Turning dotty about me with pithy sayings
21 Greek priest swallows heartless lay humour rarely
22 One who stands in record breaking attendance
23 Domes of antiquity quite round in appearance – almost
24 Coax lo'ed one into kinky lace
25 Annoying losing face to an unknown, belching
26 Personal likeness for eastern t-trifle with bit of yoghurt
27 Like Panama, dry as pea-stalks
28 Bruce up first, to sustain
29 One hard at it, (and, for Spooner, what he's unlikely to do!)
30 A Red header in play – or back-heeling
31 Look, register's backed and bound clumsily!
32 Roil, ring and shake
33 Wild zebra crushing Eastern farrier against wild beasts
34 She's out of breath (after blasting a lot?)
35 Arabic bird, shapely in manner of chest

CROSSWORD No. 73

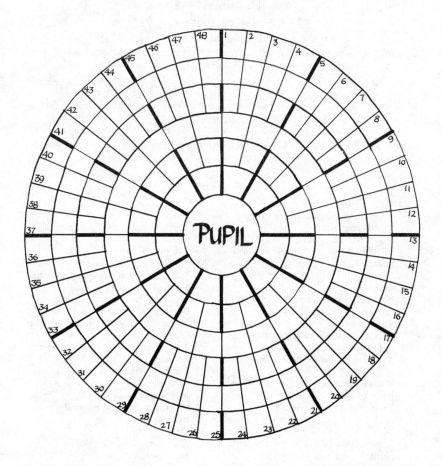

36 Gets to register end of dyspepsia
37 A metallic monoxide counter unknown with tantalum
38 Deity, in wood, burned as tray exploded
39 Injure, snare recoiling like weasel
40 Goddess, with a palm, king suits
41 Cope with American notable Centaur
42 Kicks and struts around North

43 They're ruts: one limps round one
44 Spirits must have gravity, landlords
45 Dissembler returns concession whole
46 Luke has disorderly rooms with entrance to tombs
47 Rectifiers for features of shells
48 More than one rubs e.g. glass boss, edge of lens

CROSSWORD No. 74
A double harness by Leiruza
All the Queen's horses from *The Listener*, 1977

The diagram represents an opened-out cube around which two knights, starting at 1–1, make independent closed tours, each knight visiting each square once only, conveniently missing the date. The moves of each knight give 180 degree symmetry to the halves of each side of the cube, and an identical pattern to each pair of *opposite* sides, consecutively spelling its respective clue answers, stopping one move from the start. The five 3-letter words in each circuit are to be entered as written. Thirty letters and eight moves common to each tour have been entered, further to assist the solver. *Chambers 20th Century [English] Dictionary* is recommended, except for two proper names, viz. clues 23– & –21.

CLUES

1– Hawk's rein attached to Eastern church candlestick (5)
2– Scot scratches back in prison (4)
3– Wind socks as told, using separate threads (7)
4– Rarely rode up North to attack, we hear (4)
5– Nothing taken from native bottle returned for medicine (4)
6– Rash firm (4)
7– Type of ringworm caught in the forest in Eastern parts (5)
8– A shark to rub the wrong way, Noel! (5)
9– GET
10– What the accoutred knight did, when late? (6)
11– Trap some tame shrew (4)
12– AGE
13– DEY
14– Viewer takes in first newsletter with old-fashioned grin (5)
15– Local food supplied by meat shops (4)
16– ERR
17– To be inconstant can stir up anger (5)
18– French sketch is ruined without first and last numbers (7)
19– One day's work, in Scotland, to get a saint's mausoleum? (5)
20– Spenser's temper is a hindrance (5)
21– Cheater comes back a month short over bet! (5)
22– Tidy kine (4)
23– A portrait painter solely, but not very good (4)
24– It is pure shame to cover with wax (7)
25– Malay boat comes to different end from a Dutch one (4)
26– SUE

–1 In France I deliver a blunt javelin (5)
–2 Fixes the price of brandies and soda (4)
–3 RED
–4 The brat to catch one in (4)
–5 Spenser's hair was hearsay! (5)
–6 Sporting combination of brass and wood, of course (4)
–7 EAU
–8 Even if stale, beer gets no soaks back (5)
–9 Stable to a degree, was fitted with drains (5)
–10 This vessel has speed when there's nothing in it (4)
–11 Some transient Shakespearian offspring (4)
–12 Meaningless kink (4)
–13 Short violent blow naturally causes traumas (7)
–14 DEE
–15 High note or *not* – a note! (4)
–16 An abyss has no sun going over to truly speak of (4)
–17 Reckon the term of life from tree (4)
–18 Without song, French zany son shows over-excitement (6)
–19 Sandarac tree around about here? Or a little behind? (6)
–20 Take in, for example, Solomon's common NCO (5)
–21 It's hard to be in this German district (5)
–22 Was this impudent person once very clever? (4)
–23 The Bard's carrion eater in an earthy environment (4)
–24 Sallow skin (4)
–25 Head back and double in Paris (4)
–26 Artists' frame pointed South towards the East (6)

CROSSWORD No. 74

27– Malay boat has new prow getting lakeside salt (4)

28– Sounds like the bunny-girl part of the joint! (6)

29– On the sheltered side although the heart's not in it (4)

30– Get the vinegar on the way back, otherwise I must go in (5)

31– Foot's last product is said to scare! (4)

32– Perhaps the zip required to trap a Turkish bobby (7)

–27 Loki's daughter freezes screw-propellers (7)

–28 GAS

–29 Tangles with Swedish money (4)

–30 For blackcurrants and the like, car is best thrown away (5)

–31 With no returned sale, evaluates old cellar (5)

–32 I *must* be absorbed by Dane to condescend to take in Shakespeare (5)

–33 GAY

CROSSWORD No. 75

A Three-Pipe Problem by Law from *The Listener*

The grid represents the floor of a room with peculiar plumbing. Three pipes, α, β and γ, enter at the top and leave at the bottom, but the routes they take are circuitous, to say the least, and it is not known which outlet corresponds to each inlet.

Each square contains two sections of pipe joining the midpoints of its sides, in one of three configurations:

1 ⊞   2 ◹   3 ◺

(N.B. In configuration 1 one section passes above the other—they do not meet.) The 24 re-entrant sections around the outside ensure an uninterrupted flow.

The alphabet has been divided into three groups, one corresponding to each configuration, and one letter is to be entered in each square in such a way that a) the appropriate pipe configuration is below each letter, and b) each of the three pipes traces out a series of words from inlet to outlet (note that the re-entrant sections have no letters). The starting squares of these words are given, numbered in the top left, top right and bottom left corners for pipes α, β and γ respectively.

Three types of clue have been used, the type for any particular word being determined by the group to which its initial letter belongs. Words with initial letters in group 1 have normal clues; those with initial letters in group 2 have definition-and-letter-mixture (DLM) clues, each of which contains a definition and a mixture of the word's letters, beginning and/or ending at a word-break; while those with initial letters in group 3 have clues with a misprint of one letter in the definition part. Each letter of the alphabet appears as the initial letter of an answer at least once: thus the letter-groups may be determined and the path of each pipe traced.

It will be seen that the final clue for each pipe is not given. The correct letters in the misprint clues, taken in the order in which they are presented, spell out an exceptional clue, which can be read as either normal, DLM or misprint, and so leads to three answers as required—though which corresponds to which pipe is to be determined.

For clarity, the internal pipe sections need not be shown on the completed diagram, but the solver is asked to identify the outlets corresponding to inlets α, β and γ by lettering them appropriately.

Two apostrophes are to be ignored, and punctuation may be misleading. *Chambers English Dictionary* (1988) is recommended.

PIPE α *(numbers in top left corners)*

1 Spenserian casket material, seen in use a little (4)
2 Give up fur: money is the real essential, ultimately (4)
3 Mede, frozen, miswrites timeless edict (4)
4 Pitiful Scot – locally, he has not many round about – it's acceptable (5)
5 The poor thing's lost – 'Come here, Daisy' (4)
6 A blind child must certainly wear a bib (5)
7 Quiet of old, uninterrupted by noise (5)
8 Scottish child's coy: dress is back to front, right? (4)
9 Compound found in tap water needs removing – wads might do (6)
10 Audibly apprehend large amounts of wit (4)
11 Ghana's where this officer's found – crazy one breaks rule on return (7)
12 I adjudge Spenser's in a bad mood (6)
13 Henry's gold, extremely luxurious togs (5)
14 Colloquially, *thou*'s certainly acceptable (*thou* for *thee*) (5)
15 Being tense inwardly (3)
16 Map of Slavonia shows us Sweden in Iran – confused? (7)
17 Actor dressed as cowboy for rodeo scene (4)
18 Endlessly arrogant old fool leaves dregs of mail (7)
19 Ian's door is shut, yet not locked (4)
20 An old dish, but as bonny as they come (5)
21 Take in backward idiot in game (4)
22 (6)

CROSSWORD No. 75

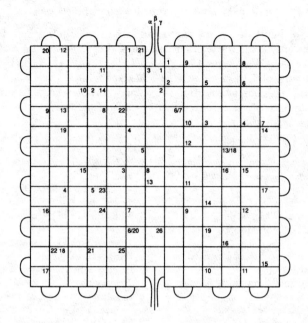

PIPE β (*numbers in top right corners*)

1 Particle which may be formed by lots of electrons with one beside (3)
2 Fixed up uncle – married without him in the country! (6)
3 Began to be ruthless (4)
4 Carpet material causes flirt to become ten times as bad, initially (8)
5 A theologian returns to the East with books of mythology (4)
6 Embroider a tale with cunning and resourcefulness (4)
7 Evil spirit is not to be believed (4)
8 Subdue a West Indian Negro that's escaped (5)
9 Spade, perhaps, used to excavate coal in the early stages (3)
10 It takes three men to plant a tree (4)
11 Be careful with the garland – it's fragile (3)
12 Dry sherry's 60% I see! (5)
13 Horticulturist initially requires one local germen (3)
14 Settee in unoccupied building has insignificant person on it (5)
15 Do you dislike plums? I don't! (4)
16 Open country exposed to the elements (3)
17 Carry the books home, finally (4)
18 Queer bloke displaying ornament (8)
19 Holy man's put out in slammer (7)
20 See me somersault in the river – I may be old, but I'm free! (5)
21 Scots, shorn of southern latitude, with initial antagonism to English (4)
22 Old leap – note – into a creek (5)
23 Part of crab will open slightly (5)
24 Cloth covering for racket in common use (7)
25 Local stone cap set awry before (5)
26 (6)

PIPE γ (*numbers in bottom left corners*)

1 Old coin creates a buzz of interest (3)
2 Heavenly model, driven by dogs, hid from detestable, headless weird (6)
3 Squirrel's nest found in the farmyard (4)
4 Rilke enters the fold in Aberdeen (4)
5 Slow disdain in Perth evinced by tailless lizard (5)
6 Sh! Music's ending (3)
7 Glees about backward fools on the outside (6)
8 You must quickly escape – a soldier is coming (5)
9 The crowd pressed forward with threatening and rude gestures (5)
10 It's a very *rara avis* that will dress *after* dinner! (5)
11 Become thin by not eating fat (4)
12 Run and ring noisily of old (4)
13 Mick, though ancient, causes giant's head to drop (4)
14 Seeds, skimming, risk confusion with roots of other plants (6)
15 Gay part of life spent in laughter? Just the reverse! (7)
16 (6)

CROSSWORD No. 76

On The Wagon by Ximenes from the *Observer*

Ximenes (in Lent) invites solvers to join him in substituting soft drinks for hard in the answers to the ten italicised clues; thus *ransacked* might appear as RANCOCOAED, *lauwine* as LAUWATER, *Martinique* as VICHYQUE. The definition parts of these clues, and the bracketed numbers at the end of them, refer to the original words; but subsidiary portions, such as anagrams, reference to parts of words, etc., refer to their 'softened' forms which are to be entered in the diagram.

ACROSS

2 *Buttercup: see same among a tangle of vegetation, pale, about beginnings of Oct. and May* (7,5)

9 Badly off, without a start – that's dreary in Glasgow (5)

10 Total battle produces a call to surrender (7)

13 Products of the soil, mixed, are stored here (4)

15 Sweat goes through it, to make a careful study (4)

16 *Very good reversed Indian pillar, all of a piece – a memorial* (10)

17 That hurts! Stop! That hurts just the same (That's like what may come out at the dentist's) (8)

18 Ill-founded pleas will do (5)

19 *It's a marauder: fight back in the confusion* (8)

20 *Ingenuous and a novice? Quite the reverse: I wake people up* (5)

24 Small vehicle, in a restrictive space, may sting you (5)

28 Revolutionary gripped by Irishman or marauder (8)

29 *Ten injured – keeping cool – makes car move on* (6)

31 Tear open one bank of the Tiber of old (4)

32 The old port must be made to go round (4)

33 Opposing Territorials between Genoa and Milan (7)

34 A few drams helpful for forgetting fevah when full of the warm south? (5)

35 *M.D. wanted: you'll find M.D. alone here, harassed* (6)

DOWN

1 *Rolly couple here, rocking wildly – I'll sell tracts* (10)

2 *'U' old ruffian, ancient bird, with grasp of the turf* (6)

3 Stuffs the last of the infantrymen in trenches (6)

4 Take a quick look up and down in Princes St (4)

5 Having a bend – here's a thing to drink out of (6)

6 In Latin you and I have grasped the reverse of badly Cicero & Co. (6)

7 Leaves that could well be moist (5)

8 A mere number, a corporal: his name's not given (6)

11 *Secretary's job – the pay-rate's absolutely rotten* (11)

12 To make a searching enquiry about a fuddled toper is an employer's right (8)

14 Let's have an aid to calculating – I almost get bogged in sexagesimal arithmetic (8)

21 She's one to relax – she often spoils children (6)

22 A 'U' Frenchman is seen in skill over love (6)

23 Matthew Arnold's watery husband of a human bride has to flirt with one (6)

25 Deserved attention and study – get it up (6)

26 *To choose, in brief, glorification of principle* (6)

27 Unjustifiable delays keep one in longer (5)

30 Label bag, inside, last stop before Waterloo (4)

CROSSWORD No. 76

CROSSWORD No. 77

Letters Latent by Ximenes (No. 1000)

Someone somewhere claims (as Ximenes couldn't dare to when this series started) to know of '——. . . .——'. Each of the two blanks represents 4 words (18 letters); the dots represent 4 other words in the middle of the quotation which are disregarded here as irrelevant. The 36 relevant letters in turn should really occur (in some cases more than once) in the 36 answers to be entered in the diagram, the first in **1 ac.**, the second in **6 ac.**, and so on successively in the right order up to the last letter, which should occur in **30 dn.** But these letters must all be omitted, wherever they should occur, when the answers are entered. Definitions in the clues refer to the full, unmutilated words; subsidiary indications, e.g. anagrams, references to parts, etc., refer to the mutilated forms to be entered in the diagram. Numbers in brackets show the full lengths of unmutilated words.

17 is a compound word in Webster, not in Chambers; **20** is the Greek form, given in Chambers as a derivation, of a Latinised word; one answer is a prefix.

ACROSS

1 Rough-tongued red revolutionary about in Feb. (8)
6 Expand old railway – augment, perhaps, as before (7)
10 Sid got wild, gripping club, stubborn as before (13)
12 Greek money down – a quid short: the unit system (8)
13 Groans, tetchy, losing heart, inclined to grumble (7)
14 Returning east likewise was sweet (5)
15 Pop singer – wrong transactions curtailed (7)
16 Snakes like consuming a satisfying finish (9)
17 Ties can, when broken, make a law void (8)
23 They cause variations: choosed – that's wrong (9)
24 Ornamental vessel, incorrectly centred (8)
26 Premier returning in state, waterlogged (6)
28 Squabbles shortly following in certain conditions (5)
29 Concentrated, with a distinct aroma, we hear (7)
31 Beauty queens? They always get left (8)
32 It helps the crystal-gazer to see heroics, love, gold in a cache returned (12)
33 Eskimo conjurer in strange occultism (8)
34 Bird gets half dose of the cat with severity (7)

DOWN

1 Clasps in grief – O, O, O, O, O . . . . (6)
2 A bribe – dollars, apparently (9)
3 Officer gets commendation, derived from calculus? (6)
4 Relay high spot – hare all over the place (9)
5 Salt – it's multiplied by one pinch of Jock's (8)
6 I'm hippy: off with constable's headpiece (7)
7 Ruddy Scots dove up a tree – or Scots cuckoo (7)
8 (2 words) We're in slapstick – dress up, act madly (11)
9 The man overcomes trouble without any guidance (8)
11 Filmy green plant – fibres rent all to pieces (11)
18 Heere's the best of luck, little birds (8)

CROSSWORD No. 77

19 Unmechanized cultivator, pipe with prominent ridge (8)
20 With no S.A. wild youth, uppish, harbours mites (8)
21 Powerful car – girl unwell inside (8)
22 Something orthorhombic, even including a monkey (9)
25 This introduces something hairy, waving a torch (6)
27 Big city wise, one hears, about rising purpose (6)
30 Sharp rebuff – certainly not, little sir (5)

CROSSWORD No. 78

Legsin Cricotas by Ximenes (No. 1200 in the *Observer*, 1972)

Today's puzzle, the last to be composed by Ximenes before his death, marks the end of an era. The brilliance of its diagram composition and the ingenuity of its clues combine to show the compiler at his most inspired.

The 21 initial letters of the words ACROSS, when correctly shuffled, form a 3-word Single Acrostic appropriate to the number of today's puzzle. Every word is in *Chambers 20th Century [English] Dictionary*.

ACROSS

1,23 (3 words) HQ makes dolt err, scoring duck (18)

5 Jovial chap – tipsy veteran by end of bar (8)

11 Is one, a sticker, sent back? That's divine (7)

12 Bill O'Reilly's last two: he has to sweat (5)

13 Club has last of tail in, and there's a spot (5)

15 A player catches Hill – it's the Guv'nor (6)

16 No-ball? Accuse then – hand over for penalty (9)

17 Old province puts one in the air, wildly (7)

18 Eat away part of the wicket, chaps (4)

22 One in a tour shows Mac in a good light (7)

23 See 1 across (13)

25 Overseas hero, X, produces a screamer (7)

29 A Surrey batsman back: once went in first (4)

31 Opening, stumped in Fifty club's reverse (7)

33 Ray going after club's feminine supporter (9)

34 Ere a collapse, returning, might miss stump (6)

35 Am run out, take off pads (5)

37 Gil—— bowled fast: observe wreckage (5)

38 Rest bat here very badly (7)

39 We look fine in the middle – pegs ne'er upset (8)

40 Ray's batting – it's sticky (5)

DOWN

1 We amuse – a lot of cricket among the trees (9)

2 Flighty opener's caught in gully, 50 (6)

3 Youngster put up in order – pulse noticeable (3)

4 Made a test 100 – was worth weight in gold? (6)

5 Slow – encourage to go for low catch? (7)

6 Tourist gets six – one right over the hill (6)

7 Spinning – rubbish: a century about one (8)

8 See 'im in a knock that's uppish – it's usual (5)

9 Boundary up – batting when he's round's fast (8)

10 Hendry out – he's out – it's under a ton (4)

14 With a brilliant pair set up, playin' in (9)

19 These diggers are tidy craftily led players (9)

20 Old game trio on a tour (8)

21 I am what's wanted in a bad spot, a cutter (8)

24 More than one third man at Perth? Without hesitation, that's stupid (7)

26 Men from overseas: slip in silly miss (6)

27 He who gets out is down on maker of appeal (6)

28 Ray taken in by shooters – long, hard test (6)

30 Saw an Indian cutter in maturity (5)

32 Lure towards short leg (4)

36 Dinna rin – bear up as before (3)

CROSSWORD No. 78

CROSSWORD No. 79

Tribute by Duck from *Crossword*

The clues are of two types: **1 Letters Latent** (L). From the answer to each clue one letter must be omitted wherever it occurs in the word before entry in the diagram. Definitions in the clues refer to full, unmutilated answers; subsidiary indications refer to the mutilated forms to be entered in the diagram. Numbers in brackets show the full lengths of unmutilated words. **2 Misprints** (M). Half of these clues contain a misprint of one letter only in each, occurring always in the definition part of the clue: their answers are to appear in the diagram correctly spelt. The remaining clues are correctly spelt: all their answers are to appear in the diagram with a misprint of one letter only in each. No unchecked letter in the diagram is to be misprinted; each letter appearing where two words cross is to appear as required by the correct form of at least one of the words to which it belongs. All indications, such as anagrams, etc, in clues lead to the correct forms of words required, not to misprinted forms.

The diagonals 1–37 and 10–36 spell an appropriate message.

ACROSS

L 3 He engraves lines around about piece of wood and ridge (11)

M 11 Diplomat's concluding words (5)

M 13 Caste once, to cease without god (6)

M 14 Bit of overstrain has mother closing exhausted eye (8)

L 16 Observe number – put it in! (7)

M 17 Secluded old offices set back (6)

L 19 Returning to look for tall plants (5)

L 20 Lent goes out with ultimate in jollity immediately after (6)

M 21 Filthy spectacle taking man aback initially (7)

M 23 Butler taking care over connection on drain? (7)

M 25 Hands cut off – is severe reproof putting disciple off? (5)

L 28 Fine, dry (5)

L 31 Most Excellent name that is recollected by solvers primarily? (7)

M 32 Jock's building-site shows his building material perhaps round about (6)

M 33 Geller? Trick has endlessly mysterious power (8)

M 34 A holy Frenchman, it seems, rare as before (6)

M 35 Suppress not completely novel idea (5)

M 36 Being sure offer a prominent position (10)

DOWN

M 1 Dan-Air is company flying a particular class of planes (10)

M 2 The old wonder at the present-day morass? (6)

M 4 Scientist's answer to 'What'll make the world go round?' perhaps! (6)

M 5 Song about e.g. sergeant in place of massacre (7)

M 6 Find new cork for liqueur half gone (5)

M 7 Resin in a source of gold (6)

M 8 Words from blown up cads? (8)

M 9 Volume discharged from Severn exceptional in eagres (5)

L 12 Woody tissue – what could be 'elmy'? (5)

CROSSWORD No. 79

L 15 Unusual screen around this French church, grotesque projection (11)

M 18 See this A1 performer producing rats? (8)

M 22 It's odd getting upset over a shower? Pestilence as before (7)

M 24 Succeed in getting pike fried (outside Scotland) (6)

M 26 Become wearisome aboard ships (6)

M 27 English snipe to get away safely (6)

M 28 Show excess feeding in the motel (5)

L 29 One scrapes – yen to get endlessly austere? (6)

L 30 Fibre, one sow turned up (5)

CROSSWORD No. 80

Noah's Ark by Azed from *The Observer*

The 26 Across lights are all creatures (20 animals, 5 birds and a fish), each beginning with a different letter of the alphabet. They are clued two by two, each double clue being an anagram of the two creatures to be entered in the relevant row. Down clues are normal, but the answers are to be entered in jumbled form (in one case reversed). The three unchecked letters in the down lights, from bottom left to top right, spell, as befits, another animal. *Chambers 20th Century [English] Dictionary* is recommended.

ACROSS

1 and 7 Jays clench bun (7,6)
12 and 13 Rush up our axis (4,9)
15 and 16 Octoroon pact (5,7)
17 and 20 A warm R.A. cobalt (10,3)
21 and 24 Make ale as well (8,5)
27 and 30 Half an ugly fey (6,7)
32 and 33 Our Welsh ogre (6,6)
35 and 38 O, million merge (7,6)
40 and 42 Ah! Vice scandal (5,8)
45 and 47 Zebra-hide oven (3,10)
49 and 51 Aliquot delta (7,5)
53 and 54 No foreign chum (9,4)
55 and 56 Always disable (6,7)

DOWN

1 Stays in bounds (5)
2 Middle of the boat on the river? Could be (3)
3 Give up including Latin in worship (4)
4 Views expressed by the church in organized fast (6)
5 Wild and woolly one inhabiting mountain range (5)
6 Dance is almost over (3)
8 Lack nothing needed to manufacture this disguise (5)
9 Refined corporal, say, a remarkable thing in Edinburgh (4)
10 North French cable-bar (6)
11 Moves unsteadily – it's a tropical disease (4)
14 Old clothes, inclined to sag (5)
18 Battle-axes pound twice, cleaving twice (5)
19 Expert Aussie shearers, going like the clappers? (7)

22 Endless stretch of land? No, precisely measured (3)
23 Sunday's this even when Ida comes in (4)
25 Almost everything in moderation – the sign of a saint (4)
26 It may form part of manure agriculturally (4)
27 Squint? Put head in this – it's used for tests (4)
28 The attraction of beer and of getting up before noon (4)
29 Glacial snow still rises (4)
31 Freeman of old King Cole possibly (5)
34 Infernal goddess in Swedish Elysium (3)
36 It shelters some skiers caught holding drag (6)
37 Delicious food for good behaviour, we hear (5)
39. M. Antony's wife, 56, embraced by rising changeling (6)
41 Was patient – same where patients should be (5)
43 Contemptible types, sly Scotsmen, take one in (5)
44 Silver, a length of worsted? That's cock-eyed (5)
45 Mexican ruler, dead, one superior to leaders of Aztecs (4)
46 To frighten away, fire guns endlessly (4)
48 A flooded dale – that's pleasant to the ear (4)
50 Gull, making old belly rise (3)
52 Bewitch upset Nigerian (3)

CROSSWORD No. 80

248

CROSSWORD No. 81

Spoonerisms by Azed from *The Observer*

Half the across and half the down clues lead in their definition parts to Spoonerisms of the correct answers to be entered. Subsidiary indications in these clues lead to the correct answers themselves. In the remaining clues the definition parts have been distorted by one Spoonerism per clue. Subsidiary indications in these clues likewise lead to the correct answers.

NB: Spoonerisms may be either consonantal (e.g. MENHADEN/HEN MAIDEN) or vocalic (e.g. BUNTING/BIN TONGUE), and may be accompanied by changes in punctuation.

Every word is in Chambers 20th Century [English] Dictionary, except 8 (in O.E.D.) and one archaism.

ACROSS

1 Tetchy king – what you might call 'sticky' round about (5)
5 Pigs from the fast, head following bottom (7)
11 'Here Priam perished' – with which chorus-leader harmed cheerers? (9)
12 Crown king one held in palm (5)
13 Almost give up, concealed inside straw (a tip-off) (6)
14 Sparing backchat, left workers to go to bed (8)
16 Nail to turn round gorse bark (8)
17 Belt a Scot? Confront one rudely (6)
18 Wave out breast, perhaps; I'll turn holding it (5)
20 Scrambled egg or bright produce (5)
23 Desert food – it's wallop one imbibed (6)
25 Sounds like best crew get to meal faster of old (8)
27 Fighting bout – it's great getting hand in (8)
29 Medley gets a toe twinkling round – not the thing for one wanting slow number (6)
30 Maud Barker married Eric, Conservative turned Liberal (5)
31 Hide head: hides once in difficulties (9)
32 World out as haste set edge spinning (7)
33 Deflector of signs at me, more lustful losing head (5)

DOWN

1 Genuine ice-cream lingers – count nuts (12)
2 Plan in main a way to row initially (7)
3 J.B.'s sound of distress when beheaded (4)
4 Winging steed first in National on purpose (6)
5 Dog tail appendage (tree family) (6)
6 Paddy cut Enrico in pieces (6)
7 Lop parts of teg, long hung in street upside-down (6)
8 Bottom raised, tidy round pillowcase (8)
9 Ne'er rice irrigation rears (5)
10 Spaded roughly, long engrossed, not well – a sovereign spade money (12)
15 Peeps excitedly round stroke of luck – period property location (8)
19 Issue perverse fit assurance with formality (7)
21 Call 'Smash' for Jews first in Golan, climbing division (6)
22 It's torn to make sables, maybe, happiness with a soft inside (6)
23 Ate a little? Quite full round end of Lent (6)
24 Stop English river from right to left on map (6)
26 Take what has been let off wine, one rustic drink (5)
28 In dormer phase rest out (4)

CROSSWORD No. 81

CROSSWORD No. 82

Here is Wisdom (Azed No. 666 in *The Observer*)

To mark the number of the puzzle (see *Revelation* xiii, 18), Azed this week offers a beastly competition. Each of the 23 asterisked clues leads to an answer which contains in consecutive letters the name of or word for an animal. On entry in the diagram the animals are to be omitted. In an asterisked clue the definition refers to the full answer, whose length is shown by the number in brackets; subsidiary indications refer to the answer entered in the diagram (rarely a real word). The clue also contains a consecutive jumble or reversal of the letters of the omitted animal. Remaining clues are normal. All full answers and animals are in *Chambers 20th Century [English] Dictionary*, 1983 Edition, except two geographical names (one of them appearing in the definition for its derivative), and the adjectival form at 2 (in *Collins English Dictionary*).

ACROSS

*1 Power of mesmerist, one in amalgamation of items (15, 2 words)

*8 Who often has named entrances, cunning turns? (9)

*11 Brood of pheasants, not old, twelve (8)

*12 Family of trees, and apparently bushes: name one fringing river (11)

13 Divine spear brandished in rituals (7)

*14 Coat for walking (double-breasted), intricate weave (9)

16 Certain whitefish die, netted by nippers in US (8)

*17 Start of reading must be in simple story (9)

*20 Unfinished gloss, what one in cast goes by? (9)

21 Pope, one in American city (6)

22 Tomboy (och aye!) at home fairly made to swallow loose lip (6)

*25 What's dead, murdered, gone, curtailed, gathered? (8)

27 Soak, dry inside, cut off (6)

29 I crash badly: as before cuts, bangs, etc (8)

*32 Frenzied shout, call to rise (7)

33 Hydrocarbon responsible for a fair amount of interpenetration (7)

*34 Remove tail of bear: task anticipated (11)

*35 Vital asset that idiot's left mostly frozen (6)

*36 Dismal backward cranial sutures (7)

37 Actor struggling with task – what to stand round in? (9)

DOWN

*1 Purple, old, suffering harm at inn (9)

2 I take lead in batting after knocking up 100, blissful (8)

*3 They're meant to encourage laying – get the point? (8)

*4 One sneaking AB receiving shelter? (10)

*5 Maintains existence having grabbed privy watch-towers (9)

*6 Society caps duck, creature with more leg than body (9)

7 Samba dancing round band circling percussion instruments (8)

8 Cow having to stagger round was hobbled (9)

*9 Vagrant fixed course on Bangalore finally (8)

10 Non-verbal mode of expression, one lemans contrived (7)

CROSSWORD No. 82

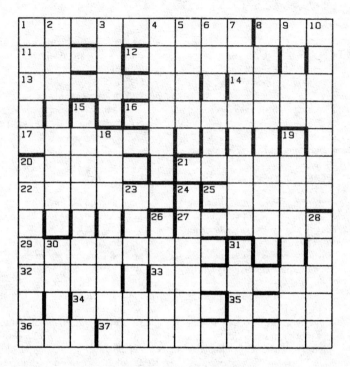

*15 Right wing splitting out is oddly
    traditional (12)

*18 Passing name in temper I mis-
    spelt (11)

19 See in one such as Heraclitus
    what's loosely symbolic (8)

20 Superbrain? Mine endured round
    middle of Dec. (7)

23 Coin, one going quickly in gamb-
    ling game (6)

*24 Those responsible for grouping
    roster disastrously (9)

26 Papilionaceous trees, bushy, not
    lacking leaves? (5)

28 Concern following the Northern
    migration (5)

*30 Jakarta brew, narcotic, I swal-
    lowed (7)

*31 Mangle's replacement raised cloth
    in ridges (9)

CROSSWORD No. 83

Book-ends I by Duck from *The Azed Book of Crosswords*, 1975

ACROSS

1 Put in exalted position after you've got foremost of clues (3)

3 Loud 'oliday resort, a low down place (5)

5 I've a long day – little kid's swallowed acids (7)

11 See 48 across

12 Beat me and lump will appear terribly (6)

13 A sling specially prepared, did David wait for this? (6)

16 What you may have found in some rye-bags (4)

17 Start of snoring by inconsiderate person? Give a jolt (4)

19, 22 down. Author's output gets purely nominal reward – worth £3.50 at most (4,5)

20 Have a little look round part of fortification (4)

23 A definite amount obtained by collector of money in street (5)

24 A planet without radioactive material. There's some vegetation (5)

29 Hitherto could include head of ale, bit of spume (5)

32 Fur is more exciting for 'Arry (5)

33 Prince, one beset by wickedness, is to succeed (7)

34 An old poem to repeat (5)

36 After year's end gives extra, cares as of old (5)

37 Exceptionally odd Sabbath craze – being gripped by it you'll have uttered defiant noises endlessly (4,9)

38 Almost the only one to be a greedy type? (5)

41 Withered dean organised – could you call it 'evensong'? . . . (8)

42 . . . Inquire about strange rites and symbol mentioned in the rubric (8)

45 Refuse malt – it's sharp and deadly (6)

46 Old fashions – square hats (6)

48, 11, 49. Frenzied soul (canon) is anti-porn – zeal produces rewards (6,11,6)

49 See 48

50 Queen conveniently beheaded – an Elizabethan slaying (5)

51 Society has anguish; it used to glitter (5)

DOWN

1 I gather in material from the seam, having taken up short dress (4)

2 My position produces ill-feeling we hear (4)

3 Old deceiver very much in evidence around London college (6)

4 What *was* wooden and used for defence in field – or what *is* . . . ? (6)

6 Flower cut for love (3)

7 See 25 down

8 Improper international gathering? (6)

9 See 25 down

10 Fabulous contender gets record score broken (9)

12 Inconsistent rubbish in lyric (7)

14 Player of Derby Co. team in unexposed position (7)

15 We serve refreshments – spirits but not gin initially (5)

18 Beastly homes constructed by e.g. sober men of Kent (5)

19 What nasty tribes may turn out to be? (6)

21 Father almost 2 metres? That's not English, common speech is required (6)

22 See 19 across

24 In brief very old and devious (4)

25, 9 down and 7 down. To a great extent, my cover being tatty must get repaired on the outside – oddly enough a nice, appropriate description for Azed's book (4,6,9)

CROSSWORD No. 83

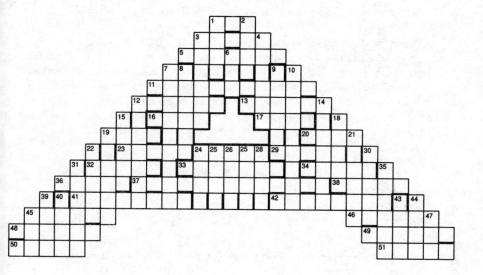

26 Stag night? Get a round in – and whoopee! (4)

27 Name remains – in Bath especially (4)

28 Jock's to stop fellow without hesitation (4)

30 I scored with unusually long shot (5)

31 You want to get to the heart? Meal is to be cooked (6)

35 Risk a bit of fun? That would be unusual for them (6)

39 Lottery selector misses one out. Pine as before (4)

40 One who used to persecute Jock's very being (4)

43 Solver's error e.g. may be noted hereon (4)

44 Compiler's taken up my name – see me on his stickers (4)

45 Inmate of zoo, I and my kin are sung about (3)

47 Tiny sum of money for a qualified nurse (3)

CROSSWORD No. 84

Book-ends II by Merlin from *The Azed Book of Crosswords*, 1975

The three theme-words form a group. The variations on each theme-word are related to their theme-word in the same way but this way is different for each theme-word. The variations on A are two pairs of words. The eleven remaining across clues each contain a definition (of one or more words) and a mixture of the letters, either beginning at the start of a word or ending at the end of a word. The down clues are normal. All words are in *Chambers* except for a scientist (given under his Christian name) and a familiar geographical name.

THEME-WORDS
A 34 across; variations 15 and 16, 25 and 28 across
B 6 across; variations 1, 12 across
C 2 down; variations 18 down, 22 across

ACROSS

13 Played without care, being leg before wicket (7)
14 Run out trying to back up, not grounding the bat (4)
17 Retired hurt after a battery of three bouncers (4)
18 Caught off a ball moving away, not keeping the bat straight (5)
19 Bowled: this bowler, if erratic, is a really fast one (5)
21 Hit wicket! Don't be hard on him – I observed many stars do that (5)
23 Obstruction! A brazen act! I hold no truck with it (4)
32 Handled the ball! Must offer the skipper an olive branch – an ale or two (4)
33 Hit the ball twice – run to the pavilion in shame (7)
35 Stumped – what you get anticipating a delivery that may yet alter course (7)
36 Not out – this youngster is an example to the others (4)

DOWN

1 Prince and the class he might join if bewitched (4)
3 Age makes a chap do as Old Father William (4)

4 Sound made by washing-machine? Put a pair of tee-shirts in this and see what they become (4)
5 Vessel contains mostly gas (4)
7 One with funny lumps? I have rash (9)
8 Old mounds containing iron show some volcanic activity (8)
9 Heartless con-man is more impressive (6)
10 Polish comedian (5)
11 Radio with a cat's whisker, maybe (4)
19 Bean, see, in pile rising, with Jack on top (9)
20 Two things put on trifle may be put in crackers (8)
22 Take in output of quarry on railway – clockwork model (6)
23 'Ey! What 'ave we 'ere? Close to a Dollar (5)
24 Corrupt pound has uncertain weight (4)
26 The Times shows English-ness? (4)
27 Bird, small breed swallowing bit of daddy-long-legs (4)
29 Like the sea in Sunderland (4)
30 Decrees followed by Romans (4)
31 It's handy for pottery with middle bit missing (4)

255

CROSSWORD No. 84

Solutions, Notes and Commentary

Solutions are provided in diagrammatic form. This makes reference to any particular solution relatively easy and facilitates the separate provision of notes. For most of the early puzzles complete notes are provided, but not all the clues are explained for some of the harder puzzles already published. In such cases the solution notes are usually those already published. The provision of notes on all clues would be extremely space-consuming and for a solver tackling (say) puzzle No. 79 understanding the clues is likely to be the least of his worries!

There are alternative ways of providing crossword notes—e.g. (car + pet)/(car-pet) and (I in man)/(ma-I-n). No attempt has been made to enforce a complete editorial consistency, but the meaning in each note should be evident.

In addition to the notes I have taken the opportunity to comment on aspects of some of the puzzles.

Don Lemon's Puzzle No. 6

Caleb Plummer; Betsey Trotwood; David Copperfield; Sairey Gamp; Nicholas Nickleby; Tilly Slowboy; Nancy Sykes; Sam Weller; Florence Dombey; Dick Swiveller; Oliver Twist; Barnaby Rudge.

(But wasn't Nancy called 'Sikes'?)

Don Lemon's Puzzle No. 200

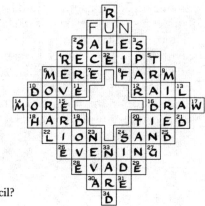

TOSS
RAINBOW
ARMADILLO
DRUMMER
ERRAND
WICK
INFLAMMATION
NEGRO
DEBT

Don Lemon's Puzzle No. 541

COWSLIP

1

Not too demanding, but do *you* understand 9 down? *I* don't!

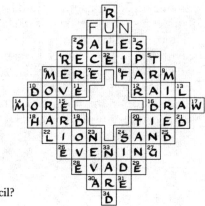

2

Did *you* use pencil?

3

4

Note how this diagram has the same pattern when given a 90° (quarter) turn as well as when given a half turn. This is an optional extra that can give a diagram a particularly pleasing appearance.

5

Are you getting bored with EGO, EGG and ERG?

6

Not for the first time we meet SET. Unlike EGO, though, this word has many meanings—in fact, more meanings than any other three-lettered word in the English language.

7

The setter of this puzzle used the *Reader's Digest Encyclopedic Dictionary* and the *Dell Crossword Dictionary*

8

9

Across: 6. double definition; 12. cryptic definition (an 'er word').

Down: 2. cryptic definition; 4. cryptic definition; 5. reference to sugar (Tate and Lyle); 7. flower=river (a common 'er word'); 9. upright type used in printing; 14. not really!

10

Anagram indicators:

Across: 1. newly; 5. form of; 6. it could be; 8. translated into; 10. to upset; 12. destroyed; 13. redeveloped.

Down: 1. unruly; 2. may become; 3. possibly; 4. diverted; 7. swinging; 9. weird; 11. odd.

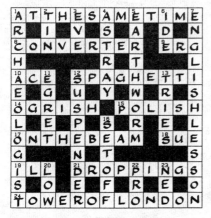

11

Across: 8. reference to rugby; 19. I will = I'll; 21. out is a common AI.

Down: 1. AI: get excited; 4. AI: could deviate; 7. cryptic definition; 22. pro = professional.

12

Across: 1. lad in May; 4. side in as; 8. 2 meanings; 9. anagram; 10. red actors; 14. gran + den (verb in the straight reading, but noun in the cryptic reading) + trance; 16. range in Oman; 20. The ban; 21. drawer reversed; 22. anagram; 23. anagram.

Down: 1. 2 meanings; 2. tool reversed; 3. sir in deed; 5. anagram; 6. Di's + count (adjective in the straight reading, but noun in the cryptic reading); 7. desserts reversed; 11. mined reversed; 12. anagram; 13. cad avers; 15. 2 meanings (note double meaning of doubles, which may mislead); 17. 2 meanings; 18. Edam reversed; 19. anagram.

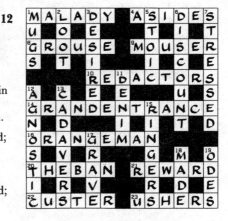

13

Across: 1. sounds like heart; 3. lisped sound of sinkers; 8. hidden; 9. anagram; 10. anagram; 14. glanced decapitated (i.e. losing g)=lanced; 15. anagram; 17. a+bun+dance; 20. rep+rises; 21. drop h from hedge; 22. lit+I+gate; 23. tasks minus t.

Down: 1. nest in holy; 2. rum in ant (Were you looking for a word meaning 'booze' inside a word meaning 'worker'? Bad luck!); 4. heroine minus final e; 5. anagram of 'and gave it' ('out' being the anagram indicator); 6. hidden; 7. wets reversed; 11. anagram; 12. anagram; 13. ever in lets; 16. hidden; 18. pastoral minus past; 19. Sprat when heartless (i.e. without r) = spat.

14

Across: 1. f+east; 4. t+rifle; 9. ten in Anna; 10. pie in SS; 11. RA+RE; 13. S+ketch+ER; 14. Dr+agony minus y; 17. be+a+St.+s (first letter of slay); 19. pass+ages; 21. V+era; 25. W in sing; 26. anagram; 27. hidden; 28. even+t (last letter of August).

Down: 1. L in fair; 2. a+C+tor; 3. tend (10d in old money); 5. anagram; 6. L in fights; 7. censures without head (first letter)=ensures; 8. M(=2×500)+Ark; 12. AI+R; 13. NUS (National Union of Students) reversed; 14. EP (extended play record) in dosed; 15. sail in a SS; 16. range in OS (outsize); 17. bus is almost bust; 18. hidden; 20. 2 meanings (Sir Anthony Eden); 22. I in Eyre (Jane); 23. AB+out; 24. hidden.

15

Across: 1. ring+sound of rode; 5. hidden; 9. anag. of collapse minus O; 10. men in tort; 11. e+a+pint+he'd in lark; 13. anag.; 14. RE course (religious education); 15. 'ome+let+te(a); 18. legat(e)+o; 21. brave+New World; 23. war+rant; 24. rev. of art+an+is; 25. hidden, rev.; 26. p+resided.

Down: 1. re+solution (message to solvers!); 2. again, rev.+RA; 3. anag. of 'hate made rip' in rage; 4. Ag+lets; 6. spread+one+swings; 7. Chubby C.; 8. 'etty; 10. the ses(sion); 12. 2 mngs.; 15. s+tree+t; 17. hidden, rev.; 19. a+era+Ted; 20. anag.; 22. taws (rev.).

16

Across: 1. 2 mngs.; 5. az in hard; 9. anag.; 10. cat's+pa+w; 11. anag.; 12. hidden; 13.2 mngs./cryptic defn.; 16. right+r+ever+end & lit.; 20. 2 mngs.; 21. anag. in Oaks; 23. dud+anag.; 24. May+Pole; 25. err in shy; 26. L in (in Kings).

Down: 1. spa in car; 2. Ava+I+led; 3. rings up+there in bar; 4. timer, rev.; 6. anag. & lit. (Sir Martin Ryle was the Astronomer Royal when the puzzle was published); 7. A+p-plies; 8. do+wagers; 10. C+oracle; 14. lied+own; 15. (ed+I) rev. in press; 17. anag.; 18. O in dragon; 19. ass-ess; 22. Tim+on.

17

Across: 1. la+MB; 4. init. letters;
10. (do+later) in is; 11. hidden;
12. anag. in cake+a+way;
13. sal(t)+via; 14. (a+son) in reed;
16. anag.; 18. O in baths; 21. anag.
(semi & lit.); 23. L in bind;
24. concern+ed; 25. res(t) in digs;
26. L+Ely.

Down: 2. a Ken in (a+wing);
3. br.+ewer; 4. anag.; 5. sound of
cast; 6. (win(dow)+anag.) in Strand;
7. anag.; 8. discus(s); 9. social+
standing; 15. anag.; 16. (r)ich+a+bod;
17. AB+ducts; 19. trad in SS; 20. NN
in feel; 22. G in ride.

18

Across: 1. imp+anag.; 5. hidden;
9. minim+ally; 10. ill in Va.; 11. T+O
in Ron; 12. hack+sound of 'need';
14. Cryptic definition (tarry, vb., ref.
Ancient Mariner); 17. cryptic definition;
21. brill+I+ant; 23. a+vert;
24. Lear+n.; 25. anag.; 26. 2 meanings;
27. pant+her.

Down: 1. in+mate; 2. 2 meanings;
3. anag.; 4. anag.; 5. P+ay; 6. Ave. in
RN; 7. Hal+c+yon; 8. stand+a+Rd.;
13. anag.; 15. F in relation; 16. 2
meanings; 18. anag. & lit.; 19. 'posh'
sound of 'cheater'; 20. sound of 'stair';
22. hidden; 25. sound of 'queue' & lit.

19

Across: 7. hidden; 9. (ea.+Po) in TT;
10. rig+el; 11. initial letters (n,g,e,s) in
anag.; 12. 2 meanings;
15. nog+o+o+d; 16. R in sting (ref.
Hilaire Belloc's poem); 18. (act+er) in
biologist; 20. 2 meanings; 22. r in ague;
24. p+later; 25. anag. minus I.

Down: 1. P in terrain; 2. 2 meanings;
3. peri+sh!; 4. gats, rev; 5. n+Au+
seating; 6. bore+as; 8. anag.; 13. GI in
locality; 14. 2 meanings; 17. anag.;
18. roll in by; 19. 2 meanings;
21. do+RA; 23. grim(e).

20

Across: 7. anag.; 10. 'amper+sand;
11. anag.; 12. MA+con; 13. anag.+t;
14. RAF+fle(w); 16. pun+c.+Hy;
17. 2 mngs.; 19. S+camp; 21. 2 mngs.
(Oliver T.); 22. Poe+taster; 23. 2 mngs.

Down: 1. EC in balm; 2. hidden;
3. anag.; 4. ad in show; 5. pa+anag.
of'inn got'; 6. ER (East Riding),
rev.+vert (ER now fading from use);
8. anag.; 9. 2 mngs.; 15. fals(e)+Taff;
16. P+recedes; 17. S+E+toff;
18. imp+TU (rev.)+e; 19. scar+AB;
20. 2 mngs.

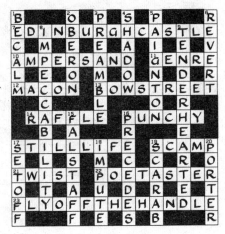

21

Across: 1. des+pot+i/c; 9. alar+mist;
10. hidden; 11. anag.; 13. 2 meanings;
14. orc in exist; 15. o in anag.; 16. ham+
pers(onal); 20. anag.; 22. anag.+1; 23.
Po+anag.+anag.; 25. Is.+Is.; 26. don in
anag.; 27. anag.+ant.

Down: 2. p in anag. & lit.; 3. anag.;
4. anag. in anag. & lit.; 5. 2 meanings;
6. lava+B.O.; 7. I'm in LA; 8. TU in
states; 12. anag.; 15. trap+pi+St.+lit.;
17. Au+spices; 18. anag.; 19. anag.+ch.;
21. Essen(C)e; 24. war+D.

22

Across: 1. anag.; 7. gasp+ar.; 8. no.+
well; 9. all+anag.; 11. man+kind;
13. 2 meanings (see 8 across);
15. o+men; 21. anag.; 22. Bible
quotation; 23. ma+tin; 24. 2 meanings;
25. 2 meanings; 28. 2 meanings;
29. 2 meanings.

Down: 1. hidden; 2. anag. (not & lit. of
course!); 3. hidden; 4. in+N; 5. (r)ed
win(e); 6. anag.; 10. Ur+n; 12. Kin(g);
14. anag.; 16. anag.+pal; 17. s in comic;
18. past+oral; 19. anag.+très; 20. anag.
incl. M; 26. MA+y (ref. Peter May,
cricketer); 27. OS, rev+p.

23

Across: 1. a-r-gem-one; 7. nu'll;
8. As-ar; 10. h in anag. & lit. (1st prize
in Crossword Club comp. for author);
12. e-I-ld; 13. pom-E; 16. hidden;
17. s-one & lit.; 18. gei(s)t; 19. i.e. ten
dance.

Down: 1. anag. minus U; 2. hidden,
rev.; 3. anag. incl. E & lit. (1st prize in
Azed comp. for author); 4. MA-ser.;
5. n-a-il; 6. anag.; 9. s-MIT-ten;
11. men-ed; 14. ob-O-e; 15. init.
letters.

24

Across: 1. anag. incl. MM;
7. bo(rev.)-late; 8. 2 mngs.; 9. stic(k),
rev.; 11. ut-is; 12. sound of Thames
(Jumblies – E. Lear); 15. 'ared;
16. sound of barred; 17. g-H-AZ-al
(36 clues in normal AZ puzzle);
18. ent-end-er.

Down: 1. anag.; 2. tale(rev.)-ER;
3. ro(b)in; 4. I-blis(s) (semi & lit.);
5. t-a-it; 6. mes-s-Ido-R; 10. tit-ree;
11. ur-ban; 13. m-eat & lit.; 14. L in
dab, rev.

25

Across: 1. comp. anag. & lit.;
5. (r)asp(ing); 8. move s of sort;
10. f for p in painting; 11. alt. letters;
12. move d of drape; 17. a t for IV in
oblivion; 18. interchange n and w of
nowt; 19. comp. anag. & lit.; 20. move
s of sting.

Down: 1. alt. letters; 2. comp. anag. &
lit.; 3. move s of tipples; 4. alt. letters;
6. interchange t and s of tens; 7. ag for o
in Poe; 9. i.e. Miss Ion if positively
charged; 12. interchange o and r of
orcs; 13. a but; 14. comp. anag. & lit.;
15. comp. anag. & lit.; 16. comp. anag.
& lit.

26

Across: 1. la-c.-col-it-H; 10. a-lum;
11. moor-band; 12. anag. minus OK;
13. lov-a-g-e; 14. b-ore-r; 17. f-E-Dora;
19. bar-rico(chet); 20. hidden;
22. (D)ante; 24. RA(rev.)-moire;
26. a bat or; 29. be(gg)ing; 30. anag.;
31. a-L-lending; 32. O in anag. incl. C;
33. ac-TA; 34. p-re-hen-sor(t).

Down: 1. lab×2; 2. anag. of a l an
'ors(e) & lit.; 3. culvert-ailed; 4. hidden;
5. 10 do form; 6. T-rib-ES;
7. ma-C-rob-I-otics; 8. 2 mngs;
9. RADA, rev.; 15. alt. letters;
16. scar-I'd-a-e; 18. do-OK;
21. or-vieto (anag.); 23. B-ogno
(anag.)-R & lit. (ref. George V);
25. hidden; 27. bel-ch; 28. m-a-n-S-e &
lit.; 29. 2 mngs.

L	A	C	C	O	L	I	T	H	M	O	A
A	L	U	M	M	O	O	R	B	A	N	D
B	S	L	M	A	N	D	I	O	C	C	A
L	O	V	A	G	E	O	B	O	R	E	R
A	R	E	T	H	S	F	E	D	O	R	A
B	A	R	R	I	C	O	S	O	B	O	L
A	N	T	E	B	A	R	M	O	I	R	E
A	B	A	T	O	R	M	M	K	O	V	N
B	E	I	N	G	I	M	A	N	T	I	S
A	L	L	E	N	D	I	N	G	I	E	E
I	C	E	B	O	A	T	S	A	C	T	A
L	H	D	P	R	E	H	E	N	S	O	R

27

Across: 1. be/t (. . . best art); 5. Tes/s
(. . . test, a lesson . . .); 6. G/ot (Giro
not . . .); 7. t/own (. . . tree down).

Down: 1. 'er/e (. . . players tire?);
2. street-bu/s (. . . street, but a rest is
impossible . . .); 3. Cat/s (Cataloes . . .);
4. T/ies (Trendies dress . . .).

28

Misprinted words and notes:

Across: 1. sippet (sip-pet); 7. wagon
(te-leg-a); 8. income (2 mngs);
9. voodoo (v-oo-do-o); 10. light
(anag.); 11. leases (anag. minus SS).

Down: 1. Coin (St.-Iver); 2. Mean
(den-OT-e); 3. plural (p-l-Ural);
4. people (Pe-Op.-le); 5. Egmont
(e.g.-Mon(E)t); 6. claws (t-a-L-ons).

S	D	P	P	E	T
T	E	L	E	G	A
I	N	C	O	M	L
V	O	R	D	O	O
E	T	A	L	O	N
R	E	L	E	T	S

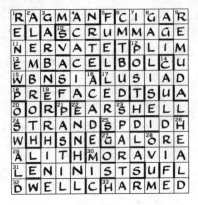

R	A	G	M	A	N	F	C	I	G	A	R
E	L	A	S	C	R	U	M	M	A	G	E
N	E	R	V	A	T	E	T	P	L	I	M
E	M	B	A	C	E	L	B	O	L	C	U
W	B	N	S	I	A	L	U	S	I	A	D
P	R	E	F	A	C	E	D	T	S	U	A
O	O	R	P	E	A	R	S	H	E	L	L
S	T	R	A	N	D	S	P	D	I	D	H
W	H	H	S	N	E	G	A	L	O	R	E
A	L	I	T	H	M	O	R	A	V	I	A
L	E	N	I	N	I	S	T	S	U	F	L
D	W	E	L	L	C	H	A	R	M	E	D

29

The code word was
ZANTHOXYLUM

Across: 1. 2 mngs.; 6. rev. minus t;
10. sc.-RU-m-mage (anag.);
11. (E)nervate; 12. plim(soll);
13. anag.; 15. RESIGN (2 mngs.:
re-sign); 17. anag.; 18. p-re-face-d;
22. ear's-hell; 24. 2 mngs.;
25. WICKET (2 mngs.); 27. gal-ore
(2)*; 29. al-I-t.; 30. mora-via; 31. nine,
rev. in lists & lit.; 32. l-lewd, rev.;
33. H-armed.

Down: 1. re-ne-w; 2. ale-m.-broth;
3. garb(oil), of=made from (usually
disliked by Ximeneans as redundant
word?); 4. AC×2-I-a; 5. fu-elle-rs;
6. BEADLE (be-adle, anag.);
7. interchange t and s of impots;
8. gall-is-e; 9. mud in anag.; 14. anag. in
cafe; 16. a-cade-Mic(key), ref. Mary had
a little lamb; 19. ER-rhine; 20. rev. of
(laws in do); 21. past IL (=49,
supposedly); 22. CHATTY (c-H-atty);
23. S-part-A; 26. hea-l-d; 28. (n)ovum.

*This denotes the second word spelt ORE
listed in Chambers, a standard convention
in notes. An alternative would be ore², also
commonly used.

30

S	R	A	P
A	L	L	E
R	N	D	N
E	T	E	D

Full words and notes:

Across: 1. SCRAP (s-rap); 5. HALLE
(all-E); 6. RANDAN (RN'd-n.);
7. METED (hidden).

Down: 1. SABRE (eras, rev.);
2. RELENT (R-L-n-t); 3. ALDER
(anag.); 4. SPEND (2 mngs.)

The word made from the latent letters:
CHAMBERS.

31

The unclued lights are the names of Astronomers Royal, 'given a start' by Galileo (24A).

Across: 9. 2 mngs.; 14. M.Ali (ali(t)); 16. land-au; 18. hidden; 20. sear-is-k; 22. et al.-on-s; 24. (I lag) rev.+Leo & lit.; 25. twits with last 2 letters twisted; 26. coom-B; 28. N in anag.; 31. 3 mngs.; 33. Theta-sk(y); 37. d.-rape; 39. e-is-el-l; 40. 'arm; 41. anag.; 42. b-y(e)w-ays; 43. Earp (rev.)-tors.

Down: 1. anag.; 2. re-a-st (without=outside); 3. sting-O; 4. (m)alari(a), rev.; 6. Aga can't; 7. l-add(anag.)-ie; 8. hidden & lit.; 10. anag. & lit.; 11. un-crow-de-d; 12. anag. incl. S(=Society); 13. eye-toot-H; 15. bon-nil-y; 21. S-US-pens-E; 29. As-Kant; 30. l-eas-ow; 32. e-MB-ase; 34. anag. incl. p (soft); 35. 2 mngs.

The original puzzle omitted 'unconsciously' at 31A, and I am still slightly worried about the fairness of 4D.

32

Across: 1. anag.+t'+ant; 11. a-n-ur-ous; 12. hidden; 13. s-tr-ong; 14. SP-here; 17. Ure-ter(race); 18. ee in anag.; 19. U-rar(e)-I; 21. rev of Silas-an (*Acts of the Apostles*); 24. SA-tana-S; 25. cen. in SA; 28. comp. anag. & lit.; 30. car-lo-t; 32. anag.; 33. rev. of red-e'er; 34. 2 mngs.; 35. c-I-trine; 36. anag. in site.

Down: 1. u in spy-sad, rev.; 2. anag. of animal, tre(e),R; 4. comp. anag. & lit.; 5. (c)rone (wanting=lacking; c=common time, p. 1771*); 6. anag. in ea; 7. I'm press; 8. t-e-hee; 9. anag.; 10. sound of tears; 15. p for f in refinement; 16. Seat-Ur-tle; 20. anag. of O is not+H; 22. aspirin'; 23. SA-tires; 26. S-cup-S; 27. 2 mngs.; 29. (C)overt; 31. yet-I.

*p. 1771 refers to the page in *Chambers* (1988 edn.).

33

The notes below are those supplied by X himself. From this point on we shall not necessarily provide an analysis of every clue.

Across: 6. R. go by; 7. L. ul(na); 8. L. Delian:R.B-Ra-g-ly; 10. L. B (road); 12. L.ela(n)-net; 16. L.clam-be; 17. L.a-l-B-ion & lit.

Down: 1. L. WR+(link E) anag. & 2 mngs., by J. H. Grummitt, 1st prize; 3. R. sail; 11. L.été; 15. L. ob-oes.

```
W H O R T L E B E R R Y
R A S U R E G O B I E S
I N U L I N G U I N E A
N A I L E D B R A G L Y
K P A I R S I N S T E E
L O B O S E R E T A R D
E L A N E T D E R I D E
S O T S O I B G I L L A
C L A M B E L E G I O N
A L B I O N A R O U S E
P O L L E N K I P P E R
A P E R S E E A S I L Y
```

34

```
P U L S I D G E S H A M
A B I N N E R S P A C E
R E G A I N O A I R E R
T R A N S U M E G A N S
S M N S L D E G E S T A
P E E W E E T O L S E L
O N W A R D P R I O R Y
U S A N C E E E A F P L
T C R M C A S H M E R E
I H R A M C H E R E I N
N E E R D O W E L L S D
G I N K A N A L Y S E S
```

35

```
F L E S H T E A C H E R
R E D P O L L F L U K E
A V E R G A T H E R E D
M A R I S H C P A R D D
P N A G H S H A V I N G
O T T R E L I T E C O U
L E H M A C H I N A T E
D R E A D E D N U N O R
K A R L S R C A V E R N
A V I A R I S T U R N S
V I S T A S H E L T I E
A D H E R E D D A I S Y
```

Definition-word first, then no. of word clued, then note if needed.

Across: 1. body: (25); 5. coach: (32) (anag. & lit.); 11. bird: (18); 12. flounder: (31); 13. state: (30); 14. together: (19) (no=far from); 15. slough: (6) (E.-Lt.-Chi-(N.-A.)); 18. bit: (24); 21. mineral: (17) (p-a-tin-ate-d.); 22. intrigue: (16); 24. awful: (33); 28. hollow: (7); 29. bird-fancier: (2); 30. vases: (26); 31. view: (3); 32. pony: (5) (pony=crib); 33. stuck: (11); 34. flower: (1ac.) (3 mngs.).

Down: 1. cross: (20) (guy=flight); 2. fly-by-night: (14) (ga-there-d): by J. H. Eyre, 1st prize; 3. spray: (34) (da-is-y & lit.); 4. measures: (22ac.) (mate, tea); 6. envoy: (28) (envoy, envoi=last part); 7. split: (23); 8. storm: (21) (anag. & Te); 9. supplemented: (27); 10. rubbish: (13); 16. fairly: (8) (hurr(y)); 17. filmed: (4) (hog=arch, vb.: ads.); 19. bird: (29); 20. garment: (1dn.) (f-ramp-old); 22. salt: (15) (salt-marsh); 23. red: (22dn.); 25. lobe: (12) (3 mngs.); 26. drink: (10); 27. keen: (9).

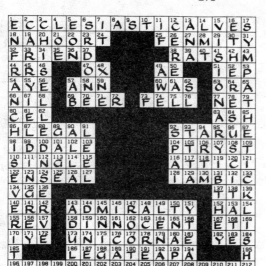

36

37

Across. 1. Yeomen of the Guard;
7. Stevenson and Osborne;
22. South Africa; 25. Thomas
Tusser; 27. cribbage; 31. pencil;
40. Hebrew; 44. French;
48. Thomas Shadwell; 66. C. de
Acosta.

Down. 2. ace; 4. Tristram Shandy;
5. French; 21. Spanish; 25. J. M.
Barrie; 33. tata; 34. licitation;
35. 'Give you good den' (Shak.);
45. Latin; 58. obiter; 63. d(o)se.

38

Truro (54 across) is of course in *Cornwall*!

39

1 and 4 across form a pun for POLYESTER.

40

Some nice attempts at cryptic definition (esp. 5 down). 3 down is outrageous: ('blind' is supposed to suggest 'without eye' and hence 'without i'; hence 'i-less' pilot = plot!). The unhelpful checking is infuriating at 25 across (if you did not understand the reference—I didn't— might you not guess 'Harry'?).

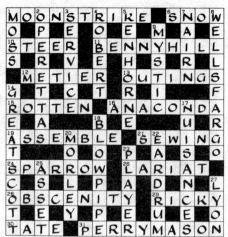

41

By Ximenean standards this is not a great puzzle, but I was (and remain!) proud of the charades at 1 across, 31 across and 8 down. RICKY (29 across) was Ricky Livid, the pop panellist in 'Round the Horne' presided over by 5 down (surely better known as Kenneth Horne).

42

A puzzle with some entertaining features but does it depend too much on the solver being well read? I confess to having guessed the answer to 8 down (correctly as it happened).

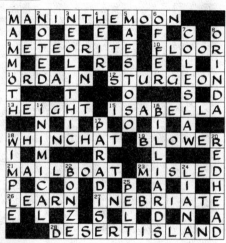

43

I have not kept a record of the editing on this puzzle but remember that 12 across was changed because two of us setters had used anag. of law in start. I was rather proud of 23 across (re-dips, rev.).

44

The transplanted letters spell out
QUINDECIMILLENARY CROSSWORD.
A model of soundness with clues that paint
interesting pictures. The meanings of some
of the double clues are bound to be a bit
stretched though because of the constraints
imposed.

Diagram A

Diagram B

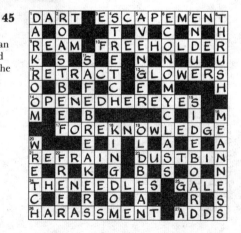

45

A fine puzzle in the Everyman tradition.
Azed has queried whether a definition can
be 'for' a subsidiary indication and would
argue that the *SI* is there for the sake of the
D—see 25 across and 15 down. Readers
may like to form their own view on this.

46

Quite a different flavour from the previous puzzle as the full notes show:

Across. 1. anag.; 4. 2 mngs; 9. anag.; 10. cryptic defn; 11. el bane (rev.); 12. fare+well; 13. cryptic defn; 14. anag.; 17. cryptic defn; 21. gen+Eva; 25. cryptic defn; 26. anag. & lit.; 27. on in anag.; 28. balm+oral; 29. anag.; 30. cryptic defn; 31. cryptic defn.

Down: 1. cryptic defn; 2. I nap+anag.; 3. cryptic defn; 5. A.B.+road; 6. reward (rev.); 7. 2 mngs; 8. 2 mngs; 12. cryptic defn; 15 das (rev.); 16. (cryptic?) defn; 18. 2 mngs; 19. anag.; 20. cryptic defn; 22. cryptic defn; 23. 2 mngs; 24. 2 mngs(?); 25. cryptic defn.

Some of the cryptic definitions are superb, but perhaps there are too many. Anagram indication is dubious in places (see p.63) and the definition not always adequate (e.g. at 28 across). Nevertheless this puzzle has much to commend it.

47

Some pleasing clues, with a touch of brilliance in the anagram indicator at 18 across. This diagram is used by many newspapers and in it ELEMENT and REARRANGE frequently occur. It is very difficult to clue the latter in any way other than rear + range.

48

Clues not entirely Ximenean (e.g. innate=in nate: see pp.64 and 130) and rather weak on meaning in places. An interesting challenge, though.

49

An example of how many clues can be linked by a common theme.

50

An entertaining puzzle but there are difficulties with parts of speech.

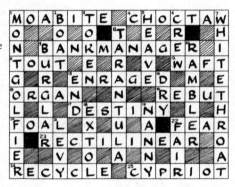

51

The message is RETURN TO SENDER. In 26 across rumour=on-dit. 20 down refers to Astrid Proll, whose 'r' is moved.

52

The answers to the numerical clues are the ten minerals, in ascending order of hardness, used in Moh's scale of hardness—hence the hint in the preamble. They are listed under the entry for 'hard' in *Chambers*.

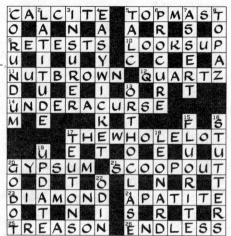

53

The themewords are from Churchill's wartime speech: BLOOD (variations: VEIN and ARTERY, blood vessels), TOIL (variations: LABOUR and WORK, synonyms), TEARS (variations: STARE and ASTER, anagrams), SWEAT (variations: SHOP and BAND, words to which it can be added).

Note the anagram indicator at 4 across (spin, an intransitive verb, not a noun). The less than helpful checking at 13 and 27 across, 15 and 16 down can be justified by the close linking of the themewords and their variations, and by the need to fit in a lot of short words.

54

Lord, make us instruments of your peace. Where there is *hatred*, let there be *love*; Where there is *injury*, let there be *pardon*; Where there is *discord*, *union*; Where there is *doubt*, *faith*; Where there is *despair*, *hope*; Where there is *darkness*, *light*; Where there is *sadness*, *joy*; for your mercy and your truth's sake. Amen
St Francis (of Assisi)

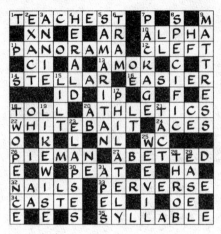

55

Few of the clues are less than 10 words long; 7 down has 20 words. Despite this prolixity Afrit often only provided a subsidiary indication for part of the answer (see e.g. 33 across—PERVERSE indeed!).

56

Some of the words are not in the 1988 *Chambers*. I have edited the notes below, based on those published in *The Observer Crossword Puzzle Book* (Penguin, 1948).

Across: 11. roup 'urt; 14. (Ph)ilip, rev.; 15. 'sham pain'; 18. Vul+turn; 19. Alex., *Brit. Gren.*; 20. Fury, *Alice*; 25. Petar-d (iii, 4); 29. Richard(son)ia; 34. wit+wal [breaking law?]; 35. anag. of holpen [many solvers entered phenyl]; 36. revivalist hymn 'Pull for the shore'.

Down: 2. =frilling [!]; 4. trepan-g; 5. Ottava (w); 6. brig-ue [Afrit and Ximenes early on would give a subsidiary indication for part of the answer]; 7. petit [another partial subsidiary indication); 8. tri-bun-al [is this an & lit., because a trial precedes a tribunal?]; 9. Hilar(it)y; 16. 1st prize by W. K. M. Slimmings; 22. anag. [is 'Make a mess of' doing double duty?]; 23. te(leg)raph; 30. Dawk(ins).

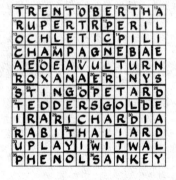

57

There were no printed notes. Perhaps the trickiest clue is 28 down: ava+lochs minus ochs!

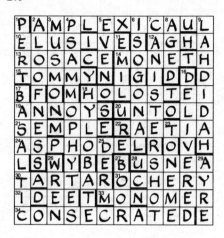

58

No notes with this one in *The Sunday Times*. 3 down (no.+m+sum, all rev.) and 2 across (XI in ample caul) were the two I found most difficult.

59

Across: 6. spars(e); 11. i.e. knock; 13. ecu+r i.e.; 16. le in GB (all rev.)+a; 21. i.e. limb-urger; 29. i.e. none go (= there are no starters); 33. n in shoe.

Down: 2. R I in anag.; 4. nine AZ anag.; 5. oh (rev.) in anag.; 8. U in arm; 9. anag. less I; 15. Gr. (rev.) in anag.; 20. anag. in AA; 23. ova in Eve; 27. comp. anag. & lit.

60

Across: 1. NICROSILAL; 9. RISUS; 11. LORRY; 12. RAPHE; 13. SELAH; 14. PAUL; 15. SYE; 17. YAHOO (O+O= pair of ducks in cricket); 19. HUTIA; 22. RIA; 23. TRAP; 24. SPRAY; 26. CRUET; 28. SUING; 29. BLEEP; 30. DITHIONATE.

Down: 1. LOLLSHRAUB; 2. AGREE; 3. PURL; 4. ORACH; 5. SIT (sitta minus ta); 6. LURCH; 7. LIGNO CAINE; 8. SQUAW; 10. SCRAG; 16. WINCE; 18. OKAPI; 20. VAUNT; 21. TRURO; 22. RAINY; 25. TWIN; 27. REG.

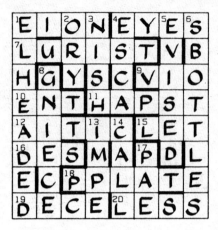

61

Missing words are all sums of money, in this order: ducat, ore, mina, rag (farthing), sol, pie, dam, mil, para, sou, fen, sen, lev, dinar, fin, franc, angel, cent, rand, rial, as, lac

Across: 4. Jane Eyre

Down: 4. Francesca da Rimini: France (Anatole)+sca(red)

62

In this puzzle 50=L, 100=C, 150=CL. Hence 2 down scores 50 for BLACK ICE. And so on.

63

Example of clash: 10 across is ANSWERED and 3 down is REAP. The S clashes with the E so the arrow points to the SE.

64

The first four clues written by Sir Leonard led to negate (ne-gat-e), tesserae (anag.), Endor (end+or) and so-so (S.O.S.+O), and the fifth was the devious indication of where to look for the murderer. It led to the word 'diagram' (aid(rev.)+gram), which told the Inspector to look not at the puzzle, but at the bars which separated the words. These bars are in the shape of Lucius I. Feisthill, whom he promptly and correctly arrested.

65

Across answers are listed in the order of their appearance on the menu.

Across: WH(ITE M)EAT; RO(A)STER; C(LAMB)AKE; OVER (double def.); A-B-ALONE; SUPERN-A-L (*prunes* anag.); NECTARINE (anag.); ACES (hidden); CO(WAR)D (*raw* rev.); A-CID; SP-EARS; RELATE (anag.); TOR-TES (rev.); SUNT-AN (*nuts* anag.); S(HERB)ET; A(PP)LES; RUSTLED (anag.); I(O)T-A.

Down: 1. CAS-TRAT-I (rev.); 2. O(n)-CUL(t)-US(e); 3. W-I-P-E-S; 4. RA-RELY; 5. DANCERS (anag.); 6. P(A)LATE; 7. PL-URALS; 8. LO(GI)CAL; 9. SERE (hidden periph.); 10. NONE(t); 11. SELTZER-S (*pretzels* anag. −*p.*+*s*); 12. A-R-TISAN (*stain* anag.); 13. STATIS-T (anag.+*T*); 14. RE(HE)ARS; 15. EJECTA (anag.); 16. T(h)E-AM UP (*puma* rev.); 17. BE(A-K)ER; 18. O-(HI)O; 19. BRA-V-A; 20. WA(R)S.

66

Clue types with word breaks for PD

Across: 1. DLM; 2. PD, tow/s; 11. PD, po/em; 12. DLM; 14. PD, stab/s; 15. DLM; 18. DLM; 19. DLM; 20. PD, re/port; 21. PD, r/ub; 23. PD, w/reath; 25. DLM; 28. PD, chap/ter; 29. DLM; 30. DLM; 31. PD, s/et; 32. PD, l/ather; 33. DLM.

Down: 1. PD, po/et; 2. DLM; 3. PD, t/ar (Harry Worth, Mike Yarwood); 4. PD, M/all; 5. DLM; 6. PD; 7. PD, ra/ise; 8. DLM; 9. PD, ad/s; 13. DLM; 16. DLM; 17. DLM; 21. PD, worm/ing; 22. PD, f/acing; 23. PD, as/s; 24. DLM; 26. DLM; 27. PD, mo/und.

67

Used cars:
7D. Elan; 8. Volvo; 12. Daf; 14. Polo;
16. Audi; 17. Dodge; 18. Fiat; 19. Ghia;
21. Honda; 25Ac. Llama; 26Ac. Saab;
27. Maxi; 31D. Ford; 35. Opel; 38. Robin.

Original report in *The Listener*: The only **68**
mistake was ALIBI at 11A, but TESTER
at 41A and IT ARID at 46D, 48A were
offered in a few cases. All three clues were
quotations—TORE at 9D ('it makes J.H.'s
pie *to* recur to one's mind') is rather
awkward, but is accepted.

Across: (4,7D) Poe, Raven. (7) To a Cat.
(11) Humbert Wolfe, The Lilac.
(16) Patmore, Angel in the House.
(18) R. Browning, Meeting at Night.
(22) Hardy, Shelley's Sky-lark.
(27) E. C. Pinkney, A Health. (28) Hood,
S. of Shirt. (38) M. Arnold, Dover Beach.
(49) Marlowe, Pass. Shepherd.

Down: (1) Marvell, Hymn to Light.
(3) Swinburne, Forsaken Garden.
(14) Tenn., Aylmer's Field. (15) Paradise
Lost. II.340. (23) Longfellow,
Maidenhead. (26) Clough, 'Say not the
struggle'. (27) Emerson, Each and All.
(31) Keats, To one long in City. (40) Pope,
Criticism. (46) Richard II, v.2.

69

Across: 5. VAT-s 9. sound of much
15. a-ch.-O in Cu 31. tea (=marijuana) in
stoma 34. bo-R-on 35. tin in St. and two
mngs 39. rev. of seem around top 47. agree
(=suit) with last letter first 53. V+a gue
58. rev. of E.-kid 59. ka-a-b(edouin)-A(rabs)
Down: 4. Ri-a-ta 6. aba-ca'
8. scar(e)-a-b(aby) 11. sound of coughs
(up) 12. initial letters 14. zea(l). 16. c. +
anag 23. cha(in) 24. be-t(remble) in rev. of
het 27. E-on. 29. t-R-ip 32. anag. and
literally 33. fee(d) 36. san(s)
43. s-(wor)k-ulk 46. rev. of ai-ma-l.

Pre-transplant answers (heart in parentheses):

Across: 1. so(war)ry; 6. h(ear)d; 10. ped(alb)one; 12. i(do)l; 13. p(ais)a; 14. ca(chal)ot; 16. pleu(rone)ctes; 19. bo(go)re; 21. h(an)t; 22. s(ai)c; 23. e(mote)s; 24. orph(anas)ylum; 28. to(tall)ed; 30. A(lam)o; 31. s(ti)e; 32. rus(tic)ity; 33. s(ark)y; 34. re(dey)es.

Down: 1. s(lee)p; 2. out(sen)try; 3. a(nil)e; 4. levo(rota)tory; 5. r(an)t; 6. hept(arch)ists; 7. se(rial)ly; 8. e(ta)s; 9. de(sal)ts; 11. (egis)t; 15. def(ere)nce; 17. up(root)er; 18. is(sue)rs; 20. re(po)se; 25. l(oca)l; 26. m(all)s; 27. s(of)a; 29. r(is)e.

70

71

The unclued answers are place-names in Thomas Hardy's novels entered with remaining letters after the first in reverse order, viz.:

Across: 1. Wintoncester; 18. Marygreen; 24. Ivell; 34. Idmouth; 36. Knollsea; 42. Tivworthy; 53. Casterbridge.

Down: 10. Shaston; 19. Trufal; 21. Dundagel; 33. Glaston.

Other notes: 52 across. ref. John Gilpin, 3 down. indirect anag.: anag. of late (naughty? see pp. 60–1).

72

Note: Allocation to the four squares is on the basis of the letters—A, B, C, D—in the top left-hand square (*where each one appears—see preamble*).

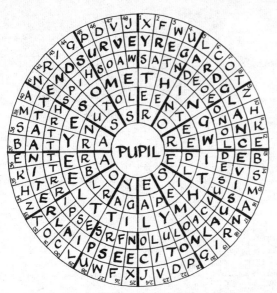

73

Title/4th circuit/corrected misprints = I-SPY/
WITH MY LITTLE EYE SOMETHIN●
BEGINNING WITH ALL BUT Q AN●
Y.

Corrected misprints/JUMBLES: 1. *bon●*
2. *eats*; 3. *sog*; 4. HUNGER; 5. *Castilian*;
6. ORCINE; 7. *note*; 8. GOTTEN;
9. GLOZER; 10. *planes*; 11. *informed*;
12. CREWEL; 13. *tinted*; 14. DEVISE;
15. *good*; 16. SALUTE; 17. VISHNU;
18. *worked*; 19. MESAIL; 20. *ditty*;
21. *tumour*; 22. DEPUTY; 23. *homes*;
24. CAJOLE; 25. YEXING; 26. EFFIG●
27. STRAWY; 28. *brace*; 29. TOILER;
30. *leader*; 31. LOLLOP; 32. *ro*ll;
33. *barrier*; 34. BERTHA; 35. ARKITE
36. *guts*; 37. BARYTA; 38. *turned*;
39. MARTEN; 40. *quits*; 41. *cape*;
42. SPURNS; 43. *nuts*; 44. GHOSTS;
45. POSSUM; 46. *duke*; 47. VALVES;
48. *ruby*.

74

Word chain 1–
JESSE; STIR;
SLEAVES;
RADE;
DRUG; FAST;
TINEA;
NURSE; get;
BELTED;
MESH; age;
dey; SNEER;
EATS; err;
RANGE;
EBAUCHE;
DARGA;
DELAY;
REVIE;
NEAT; LELY;
SINCERE;
PRAU; sue;
URAO;
RABBET;
ALEE;
ESILE;
SHOE;
ZAPTIEH.

Word chain –1
JERID;
PEGS; red;
GEIT;
HEARE;
CLUB; eau;
ALBEE;
SURED;
BOAT; SIEN;
NULL;
SUMATRA;
dee; NETE;
AVER; DATE;
FRENZY;
ARREAR;
SARGE;
HESSE;
PERT;
HYEN; SEAL;
TETE;
EASSEL;
HELICES;
gas; ORES;
RIBES;
VAUTE;
DAINE; gay.

75

Pipe outlets left to right: β, γ.
Letter groups: 1. CEFMQTVWX;
2. ABDLNPUYZ; 3. GHIJKORS.

Pipe: Seal; Sell; Iced; Waefu'; Proo;
Blain; Lound; Girr; Retene; Seas;
Jamadar; Addoom; Hauls; Kokum; Ens;
Russian; Doer; Hauberk; Yett; Bason;
Faro; Borate.

Pipe β: Ion; Clewed; Fell; Moquette; Edda;
Darn; Deev; Quash; 'Tec; Neem; Lei; Xeric;
Hun; Squat; Lump; Lee; Tote; Breloque;
Stutter; Exeme; Slae; Vaute; Pleon; Reproof;
Stean; Tartan.

Pipe γ: Zuz; Orrery; Dray; Lirk; Geck; Sic;
Scapas; Apace; Urged; Array; Bony; Rand;
Gore; Skirrs; Majesty; Rattan.
Clue spelt out by correct letters in misprint
clues: Boat returns salt—touch of sun.

76

Across: 2. bumbo-at woman (*H.M.S.
Pinafore*): m-ilk-at, w-o-m-an; 9. (p)oor;
13. anag. & lit.; 16. Graves-tone:
O.K.rev.-lat-one; 17. O-don't-O-id.;
18. anag. & lit.; 19. pil-lager: pi-llim-e;
20. la-rum: naive-a-L.; 29. en-gin-e:
ent-on-ice; 34. beaker, Keats; 35. he-ale-r:
anag.

Down: 1. col-port-eur: anag.; 2. mo-hock:
mo-sod-a; 6. tu-lli-I; 8. Nym, *Merry Wives*;
11. ste-nog-raphy: anag.; 14. stic(k);
23. ballad. *The N.*; 26. ava-tar: p-opt-ar,
par=brief, noun.

Quotation: 'A thousand raw tricks ... which
I will practise': *Merch. of V.* iii.4.end.

77

Across: 1. radulate: ult.; 6. stretch: S.R.-ech;
10. high-stomached: mace; 12. monadism:
mna-dism (a-£), down=dismal;
13. grouchy; 14. soote; 15. Sinatra: tr.;
16. anacondas; 17. disenact; 23. rheocords;
24. decanter; 26. swampy; 28. tiffs: f.;
29. centred; 31. legacies: leg-aces;
32. dichrooscope: epos-o-or-hid rev.;
33. angekkok; 34. sternly: ly(nx).

Down: 1. wrings; 2. hush-money; 3. lithic;
4. torch-race; 5. xanthate: x-an-tate;
6. sciatic: scat; 7. redwood: doo; 8. custard
pies; 9. helmless; 11. bristle-fern;
18. cheepers; 19. horse-hoe; 20. domation:
domatium: no-it-mod rev.; 21. Cadillac;
22. enstatite; ene.sai; 25. tricho-;
27. Sydney; 30. noser: sr.

78

1200=MCC=Marylebone Cricket Club

Across: 25. X=chi; 33. ray=re; 37. A.E.R. Gilligan.

79

The puzzle was published ten (X and no. of letters latent clues that omitted X) years after the death of Ximenes (X). Hence the X-shaped message: In Memoriam Derrick Macnutt. The clue types are those invented by X.

80

Down: 1. jumps; 2. oar; 3. cult; 4. fa-CE-ts; 5. urial; 6. pas(t); 8. cloak; 9. unco; 10. norman; 11. yaws; 14. togas; 18. bills; 19. ringers; 22. are(a); 23. holy; 25. halo; 26. urea; 27. (Headin)gley, cricket ground; 28. foam; 29. névé; 31. ceorl; 34. Hel; 36. chalet; 37. manna; 39. Fulvia; 41. bided; 43. toads; 44. agley; 45. (Porfirio) Diaz; 46. shoo; 48. aria; 50. mew; 52. obi.

81

Across: 1. narky, R in cany; 12. tiara, R+a in ita; 14. scant lip; 16. whin peel; 17. zone Inn; 18. SA in ego (rev.); 20. gay grow; 23. rat sap, a in strap; 27. war spell; 30. board marker (1st prize by R. A. Mostyn); 31. leather ness.

Down: 1. sterling cone, nuts=mad; 3. bay gee (g)roan; 5. cur fin; 6. ire sawn; 8. bed reared; 9. enema (rev.); 10. paddle siller, l in anag.+ill a R; 15. fee site; 19. sally gee; 23. tasted; 24. wo Test; 28. anag.

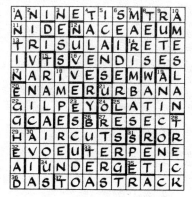

82

Across: 1. animal magnetism; 8. tradesman('s entrance); 11. noontide; 12. Pandanaceae; 14. redingote; 17. narrative; 20. stage-name; 22. anag. in gey; 25. dog-Latin; lat(e) in; 32. evocate; 34. undertaking; 35. zoetic; (ass)et ic(y); 36. lambdas.

Down: 1. amarantin; 2. I r van in in (rev.)+C; 3. nest-eggs; 4. tale-bearer; 5. barbicans; 6. sea-spider; 9. runagate; 15. tralatitious; r ala in anag.; 18. impermanent; 20. egg+e in had. ref. Observer OUP comp.; 24. assorters; 26. bu(shy)+tea; 30. Batavia; 31. spin-drier.

83

Across: 1. c-up & lit., ref. Azed comp.;
5. RNA; 16. hidden & lit.; 19,22. ref. Azed
comp.; 24. U (abbr.); 29. ye-as-t & lit.;
32. 'otter; 37. swor(e) in anag. & lit.; 42. ref.
Azed comp.; 45. 2 mngs; 48,11,49. ref.
Azed comp.

Down: 1. froc(k) rev.; 3. LSE; 6. Nil(e); 10.
Lion & Unicorn; 14. Francis Lee; 19. anag.
& lit.; 21. pa-tois(E); 24. abbr.; 25,9,7.
highly in anag. & mended; ref. Azed comp.;
27. Beau Nash; 30. Gustav Holst; 35. anag.
& lit.; 39. erne(2) (Ernie); 43. def. & lit. ref.
Azed comp.; 47. sen(SEN).

84

Themeword A: Torquemada
(variations: Adam, roquet;
amoret, quad—
anagrams)

Themeword B: Ximenes (variations:
rays, chromosome—
words prefaced by X–)

Themeword C: Azed (variations:
alpha, omega—Greek
equivalents of A and Z)

Across: 21. Tycho Brahe, astronomer.

Down: 3. a guy (rev.—i.e. standing on its
head); 4. whi(te)r; 5. argo(n); 7. I+anag. of
lumps+I've; 8. Fe in mottes; 9. nob(b)ler;
11. set+a; 19. flag+(lo in tee) rev.; 22. r.
in ore+ry; 23. (h)alloa (near Dollar in
Scotland); 26. E.ras; 27. d in toy; 31. de(l)ft.

Appendices

Appendix 1

Some common indicators for one, two or three letters

This list is by no means comprehensive, and is designed for the solver to browse through rather than refer to for specific answers. Ideally we should provide another appendix where the solver can look up 'doctor' to find DR, GP, MP, MD, MO etc., but it is beyond the scope of this book to provide a crossword dictionary. Such dictionaries do, however, exist, and I would particularly recommend those by Anne Bradford and Jeremy Howard-Williams in this respect (see Appendix 2).

* =	used mostly in advanced cryptics
† =	unsound/not liked by all Ximeneans
‡ =	not in *Chambers*, but found in other dictionaries
A	one* [not used by all setters of everyday cryptics, more common in Azed etc.]; article; adult [as once used to denote certain films]; note†; key†
AB	able-bodied seaman (*sailor, tar*)
ABE	Lincoln [Abraham]
AC	alternating current; account (*bill*)
ACC	account (*bill*)
ACE	card; champion; expert; one; pilot; service (tennis)
ACT	decree; performance
AD	in the year of our Lord (*in the modern age*); advertisement (*notice, promotion* etc.)
ADD	sum; tot
ADO	fuss
AG	silver
AGA	ruler
AGE	(long) time, mature, period
AI	first class [the letter I and the number 1 are mutually transposable in crosswords]
AID	help
AIR	appearance; display
AL	Aluminium; Alan; Albert; Capone
ALE	beer
ALL	completely; everybody; everything
ALP	mountain, peak
AM	in the morning; American

AN	one* [see A above]; article
ANT	worker [working insect]
APE	copy; primate
ARC	curve
ARM	limb; member
ART	contrivance; craft; cunning; painting; skill
AS	when
ATE	(goddess of) mischief
AU	gold, to the French
AY	yes
AZ	Azed* [most frequently in his puzzles]
B	British; black; born; bowled; book*; note†; key†; bishop‡
BA	Bachelor of Arts (bachelor, scholar, graduate etc.)
BAN	curse; outlaw; prohibition
BAR	Inn; prevent; pub; save
BE	exist; live
BEE	worker [working insect]
BIT	chewed; piece
BR	British Rail (railways); branch; brown*
BRA	female support(er); undergarment
C	100; carbon; conservative; circa (about, around, roughly etc.); caught; cold; note†; key†
CA	accountant; circa (about)
CAN	is able to (able to†); vessel etc.
CC	two hundred
CE	Church of England (church)
CH	church; child; Companion of Honour (companion)
CHA	tea
CHE	revolutionary; guerrilla [Guevara]
CHI	Greek character
CI	Channel Islands; 101
CIA	spies
CL	chlorine; 150
CO	care of; commanding officer (commander); company (firm)
COL	pass; neck
CON	study; trick
COT	bed
CR	credit
CS	Civil Service
CU	copper
D	500 (many†); (old) penny; dead; died; note†; key†; daughter‡
DA	District Attorney (American lawyer); dagger*
DAM	barrier; restrain
DD	doctor of divinity (doctor, theologian)
DE	of French
DEE	river
DEN	study; retreat
DES	some French
DI	Diana (princess); 501

DIS	Pluto; hell; underworld etc.
DO	act; cheat; cook; ditto (*the same*); note; party; work
DON	fellow; nobleman; put on; university teacher
DR	doctor [also clued by MB, MO]
DU	of the French

E	East; Eastern; bridge player; Spain*; energy*; English; note†; key‡
EA	each; river*
EAR	listener; organ; spike*
EC	London district
ED	editor (*journalist*); Edward
EER	always
EG	for example, for instance
EGG	bomb; cocktail; encourage
EL	the Spanish
ELI	priest
ELL	measure; length
ELY	see
EM	printer's measure (*measure*); them
EN	printer's measure (*measure*)
EON	age
EP	extended play (*disc, record*); epistle (*letter* or *short letter*, short denoting abbreviation)
ER	hesitation; (the) Queen
ERA	time, age
ERE	before
ERR	blunder; sin; wander
ET	and French
ETA	Greek character
EX	former; one-time
EXE	river

F	female; feminine; foot; forte (*loud*); note†; key†
FA	note
FE	iron
FF	fortissimo (*very loud*)
FO	Foreign Office
FR	Father; French
FT	feet; foot

G	gramme; note†; key†; good‡
GAL	girl
GEL	jelly
GEN	low-down (*information*)
GG	Gee-gee [i.e. a horse]
GI	American soldier (*soldier, doughboy* etc.)
GO	bargain; energy; in good condition; ready; success; work
GR	King George

H	hard; hospital; hot; hydrogen
HA	laugh
HAM	(poor) actor

HAS	bears
HE	His Excellency (*ambassador*); (high) explosive; the man
HER	the woman ('s)
HI	hello
HM	His or Her Majesty
HO	house
HP	hire purchase (*never-never*)
HR	hour
HT	high tension
I	one; Italy
IC	in charge
ICE	diamonds
ID	fish; I had; I would
IDE	fish
IE	that is (that's)
IF	provided; poem (Kipling)
II	eleven
IL	the Italian
ILL	badly; unwell etc. [these words are also used as anagram indicators]
IM	I am
IMP	little devil (*mischievous child* etc.)
IN	at home; batting; in fashion; not out; wearing
IO	ten
IRA	terrorists
IRE	anger; rage etc.
IS	exists; island
ISM	theory
IT	Italian; sex-appeal (*SA*); the thing
IV	four
IX	nine
JE	In Paris, I (*I, being French* etc.)
JO	little woman
K	constant; thousand; King
KA	double*; genius*
KM	kilometre
KO	kick off; knock out (*decisive blow*)
L	50 (*many†*); lake; Liberal; learner (*inexperienced driver, novice* etc.); left; pound (*sovereign*)
LA	the French; Los Angeles; note; look*
LAB	Labour
LAM	beat; pound
LB	pound
LE	the French
LEG	limb; member
LEI	wreath*
LES	the French
LET	allow(ed); hindrance; permit(ted)
LI	51

LIT	drunk; loaded; settled
LO	look; see
LOG	record
LOT	large amount
LP	long playing (*record*)
LT	Lieutenant

M	1000 (*many*†); married; make; masculine; maiden over (*maiden*)
MA	Master of Arts (*master, scholar, graduate* etc.); mother
MB	doctor
MC	master of ceremonies
MD	1500; doctor
MI	motorway; note
MO	doctor; short time (*second* etc.)
MP	member of parliament (*member, politician, representative* etc.); mounted police (*mountie(s)*); military police
MR	mister
MS	manuscript (*handwriting, writing*)
MU	Greek character
MUM	mother; quiet
MY	gracious me etc.

N	nitrogen; North; Northern; bridge player; pole; new*; knight‡
NB	nota bene (*note*)
NE	north-east
NET	capture etc.; fabric etc.
NI	Northern Ireland (*Ulster*)
NIL	love; nothing
NO	refusal; number
NT	New Testament (*part of Bible, new books* etc.)
NU	Greek character
NW	north-west
NY	New York

O	zero (*duck, love, nil, ring, round* etc.); old; oxygen
OC	Officer Commanding (*commander*)
OK	okay (*all right*)
ON	about; being broadcast; leg [cricket side]; on the menu etc.
OP	opus (*work*), operation
OR	alternatively; before*; gold; yellow
OS	Ordinary Seaman (*sailor*); outsize (*very large*)
OT	Old Testament (*part of Bible, old books* etc.)
OX	bull
OZ	ounce; wizard place

P	page; parking; penny; piano (*softly*); power; president
PA	father, etc.
PAR	standard
PAS	dance; step
PC	policeman (*copper*)
PE	physical education, gym
PEN	author, writer; enclosure, prison

PER	by, for each, a*
PET	favourite; cherished
PHI	Greek character
PI	confusion*; Greek character; religious
PM	Prime Minister; in the afternoon
PO	Post Office; river (*Italian flower*)
PP	pianissimo (*very softly*)
PR	prince; price; public relations
PRO	for; public relations officer
PS	postscript (*second thoughts* etc.)
PT	physical training (*gym*)
Q	Queen
R	King; Queen; right; river; take*
RA	Royal Academy; Royal Academician (*artist*); Royal Artillery (*gunner(s)*); sun (god)
RAB	Butler [R. A. Butler]
RAG	(cheap) newspaper
RAM	butter; sheep
RAT	desert(er); scab
RC	Roman Catholic
RD	road
RE	about (concerning, touching etc.); Royal Engineer(s) (*engineer(s)*, *sapper(s)*); religious education; note etc.
RED	bloody; cent*; communist; revolutionary
REP	agent; traveller
RET	soak
REV	vicar etc.
RM	Royal Marine(s) (*jolly*)
RN	(Royal) Navy
ROT	corruption; decay; rubbish etc.
RR	Right Reverend (*bishop*); Rolls Royce
RT	right
RU	rugby
RUN	manage
RY	railway (*rail, line(s)*)
S	South; Southern; bridge player; pole; Saint; son‡
SA	South Africa; South America; sex appeal (*it*)
SE	south-east
SEA	main
SET	put; group etc.
SH	quiet [interjection]
SHE	the woman; novel [Rider Haggard]
SIN	err; evil; wrong etc.
SO	therefore; well; note
SOL	sun
SON	boy; disciple
SP	starting price (*odds*)
SPA	spring
SPY	agent

SS	steamship (*ship*) [*on board* or *on board ship* denotes that something is to be placed inside the letters SS]; saints; Sunday School
ST	saint (*good man* etc.); street (*thoroughfare* etc.); stone
STY	filthy place
SUB	substitute; stand-in etc.
SUN	newspaper (*tabloid*)
SW	south-west
T	time*; model† [old Ford car]
TA	Territorial Army (*army, terriers, volunteers*); thank you; thanks
TAN	beat; brown
TAR	sailor
TE	Lawrence; note
TED	Edward; (Edward) Heath
TEE	peg
THE	article
TI	note
TIC	spasm; twitching etc.
TIN	money; cash; vessel
TIT	bird
TOM	big bell; cat
TON	hundred; weight; large amount
TOR	hill
TRY	attempt; essay etc.
TT	teetotal; teetotaller (*abstaining, dry, on the wagon* etc.); race [bikes on Isle of Man]
U	Universal (film certificate) (*for all to see, on view to all, suitable for children* etc.); upper-class (*uppish, socially acceptable, posh, superior* etc.)
UK	United Kingdom
UN	United Nations
UP	in court; excited; at university
UR	old city [from whence came Abraham]
US	America; American; you and me
USE	application; custom; employ(ment); practice; practise
V	five; verse; versus (*against, opposing* etc.)
VI	six
VOL	volume
W	West; Western; bridge player
WE	you and I
WI	West Indies
X	cross (*kiss, sign of love, times* etc.); ten
XI	eleven (*team* etc.)
Y	yard; year
YE	you [old]
YR	year; your
ZO	cross*
ZZ	(sound of) snoring

Appendix 2: Bibliography

Further reading and further solving

Other Books on Crossword Theory

Afrit's book (*Armchair Crosswords*, Warne, 1949) has long been out of print (and it is not held by either the Bodleian Library or the British Library). The preface is short and the most significant section is reproduced in this book on p.59. Other books out of print are:

Anatomy of the Crossword by D. St. P. Barnard (Bell, 1963)
Ximenes on the Art of the Crossword by D. S. Macnutt (Methuen, 1966)
Crosswords by Alec Robins (Teach Yourself Books, Hodder and Stoughton, 1975): subsequently revised as *The ABC of Crosswords* (Corgi, 1981).
How to do Crosswords Better by May Abbott (Collins, 1975): an entertaining book by the *Daily Telegraph* crossword editor with many illustrations on how to clue the word TRAIN, also a glossary. Sadly it is non-Ximenean.
Crossword Solving by Don Putnam (EP Publishing, Know the Game Series, 1975): crisp and to the point, by the former crossword editor of *Games and Puzzles*.

Books on Crossword History

The books by Barnard, Macnutt and Robins have interesting historical components, as do these two other books (again sadly out of print):
The Strange World of the Crossword by Roger Millington (Hobbs/Joseph, 1974; Coronet, 1976)
A History of the Crossword Puzzle by Michelle Arnot (Random House, 1981; Macmillan Papermac (1982)).
Both are strong on early US history and contain many interesting puzzles including the 'leadergram' or 'double-crostic', a close relation to the crossword.

Reference Books

Chambers English Dictionary is a must for all solvers and is particularly useful for obscure words, as used in advanced cryptic puzzles. The crossword setter will also need the *Concise Oxford Dictionary* to check on whether a word *is* obscure (basically if it's in it, it isn't). The *Oxford Encyclopedic Dictionary* is also particularly useful with its inclusion of proper nouns. In the same category are *Collins English Dictionary* and the *Reader's Digest Universal Dictionary*. *Longmans English Dictionary* is recommended by *The Guardian*. For American words and spellings *Webster's Third International Dictionary* can be useful. It may be helpful to have a one-volume encyclopedia, and I would recommend *The Cambridge Encyclopedia*. To complete the crossworder's lexical database I recommend a good atlas such as *The Times Concise Atlas*; *Brewer's Dictionary of Phrase and Fable* (published by Cassell); and *Everyman's Dictionary of Fictional Characters* (published by Dent).

The above books should contain all the words you're ever likely to come across, but of course you will meet the words in various contexts. Quotations are popular with crossword setters, not just in quotation clues but in special quotation puzzles. You will therefore need *The Oxford Dictionary of Quotations*. If you want to access words according to category use *Chambers Word File*, *Chambers Word List*, *The Newnes Crossword Dictionary* (first published by C. Arthur Pearson in 1932), Bloomsbury *Crossword Lists/Crossword Solver* or *The Complete Crossword Companion* by Jeremy Howard-Williams (published by Granada). For synonyms you will want a *Roget's Thesaurus* (I prefer the Harper and Row edition, though one must make allowance for American spelling). Also recommended is Anne Bradford's *Longman Crossword Solver's Dictionary*.

The next category of books may be deemed 'crossword cribs'. They list words according to length in some way and can help the solver with the incomplete answer. (Needless to say, they are also very helpful to crossword setters.) Chambers leads the field here with *Chambers Words*, *Chambers Back-Words*, *Chambers Anagrams*, *Chambers Crossword Completer* (listing by alternate letters), and *Official Scrabble® Words*. Also very useful is the *Longman Crossword Key* (listing e.g. all 9-letter words with the third letter 'u' in alphabetical order). (*Walker's Rhyming Dictionary* published by RKP is an old classic, but has been eclipsed by *Back-Words*.) For setters the Franklin Spellmaster (on a Collins database) is most useful. Put in _L___E_S into this pocket-size computer and up come ALBUMENS, ALMONERS and over a hundred other possibilities. For phrases according to length *The Modern Crossword Dictionary* is very useful as is *The Crossword Phrase Dictionary* by R. J. Edwards (published by Stanley Paul as one of a number of crossword books which also includes the *Crossword Completion Dictionary*). It is small wonder that branches of W. H. Smith have a shelf called Crossword Reference books—and you may find *Chambers Crossword Manual* near many of these other books.

You may also of course find the *Manual* among the crossword puzzle books. There are far too many of these to list them all, but I would single out the Azed books (among others published by Chambers), the *Independent* books published by Penguin, and *More Jumbo Puzzles from The Times* from Times Books (which includes an extra-large jumbo for the Diamond Jubilee of *The Times* puzzle).

And so I could go on. If you're setting for the *Church Times*, *Cruden's Concordance* will be useful, and doubtless the *Oxford Companion to Literature* would be useful if you were setting for the 'Bognor Book Club Review'. If you can't afford all the books you need or you're solving a puzzle about telephone directories, then of course you will have to visit the library. If you live near a large library you can look up the *Encyclopedia Britannica* and the complete *Oxford English Dictionary*—but also look out for a set of three old American books under the title *The New Century Encyclopedia of Names*. For proper names it is magnificent.

Crossword Clubs

If you want to solve hard puzzles and get involved in correspondence about crosswords, I would recommend the Crossword Club. For details you should write to The Editor, Coombe Farm, Coombe Lane, Awbridge, Romsey, Hants SO51 0HF. Also in the UK you can join *One Across*, which has mainly 15×15 specials and some articles. For details write to Christine Jones, The Old Chapel, Middleton Tyas, Richmond, North Yorkshire DL10 6QX.

In America a bimonthly publication with cryptic crosswords is offered by The American Crossword Federation, 113 Kings Walk, Massapequa Park, NY 11762.

In Australia the Crossworders Club runs from 58 Galston Road, Hornsby Heights, NSW 2077, and the Secretary is Carole Noble.

By now you have more than enough to get started—but don't get on the train without a pencil!